CM0092477S

Lieutenant Colonel Valentine Blacker.

WAR WITHOUT PITY IN THE SOUTH INDIAN PENINSULA 1798–1813

War and Military Culture in South Asia, 1757–1947

www.helion.co.uk/warandmilitarycultureinsouthasia

Series Editors

Professor Emeritus Raymond Callahan, University of Delaware
Alan Jeffreys, Imperial War Museum
Professor Daniel Marston, Australian National University

Editorial Advisory Board

Squadron Leader (Retired) Rana Chhina, Centre of Armed Forces Historical
 Research, United Service Institution of India
Dr Anirudh Deshpande, University of Delhi
Professor Ashley Jackson, King's College London
Dr Robert Johnson, Oxford University
Lieutenant Commander Dr Kalesh Mohanan, Naval History Division, Ministry of
 Defence, India
Dr Tim Moreman
George Morton-Jack
Dr David Omissi, University of Hull
Professor Peter Stanley, University of New South Wales, Canberra
Dr Erica Wald, Goldsmiths, University of London

Submissions

The publishers would be pleased to receive submissions for this series. Please contact
us via email (info@helion.co.uk), or in writing to Helion & Company Limited, Unit
8 Amherst Business Centre, Budbrooke Road, Warwick, CV34 5WE

Titles

War without Pity in the South Indian Peninsula 1798–1813

The Letter Book of Lieutenant-Colonel Valentine Blacker

War and Military Culture in South Asia, 1757–1947 No. 7

Edited and with introductory notes by David Howell

Helion & Company

Helion & Company Limited
Unit 8 Amherst Business Centre
Budbrooke Road
Warwick
CV34 5WE
England
Tel. 01926 499 619
Fax 0121 711 4075
Email: info@helion.co.uk
Website: www.helion.co.uk
Twitter: @helionbooks
Visit our blog http://blog.helion.co.uk/

Published by Helion & Company 2018
Designed and typeset by Mach 3 Solutions Ltd (www.mach3solutions.co.uk)
Cover designed by Paul Hewitt, Battlefield Design (www.battlefield-design.co.uk)
Printed by Lightning Source Limited, Milton Keynes, Buckinghamshire

Letter Book open source
Introductory text and annotations © David Howell 2018
Images open source unless otherwise individually credited
Maps drawn by George Anderson © Helion & Company Limited 2018

Every reasonable effort has been made to trace copyright holders and to obtain their
permission for the use of copyright material. The author and publisher apologvize for any
errors or omissions in this work, and would be grateful if notified of any corrections that
should be incorporated in future reprints or editions of this book.

ISBN 978-1-912390-86-1

British Library Cataloguing-in-Publication Data.
A catalogue record for this book is available from the British Library.

All rights reserved. No part of this publication may be reproduced, stored in a retrieval
system, or transmitted, in any form, or by any means, electronic, mechanical, photocopying,
recording or otherwise, without the express written consent of Helion & Company Limited.

For details of other military history titles published by Helion & Company Limited contact
the above address, or visit our website: http://www.helion.co.uk.

We always welcome receiving book proposals from prospective authors.

Contents

List of Illustrations

List of Maps

War and Military Culture in South Asia, 1757–1947
Series Editor's Preface

The aim of this academic historical series is to produce well-researched monographs on the wars and armed forces of South Asia, concentrating mainly on the East India Company and the Indian armed forces from 1757 until 1947. Books in the series will examine the military history of the period as well as social, cultural, political and economic factors, although inevitably the armies of the East India Company and the Indian Army will dominate the series. In addition, edited volumes of conference papers, memoirs and campaign histories will also be published. It is hoped this series will be of interest to both serious historians and the general military history reader.

The resurgence of interest in the history of warfare in South Asia has been very apparent in the growing historiography of the colonial period, particularly in the era of the World Wars. For example in the field of Second World War studies and the period until Partition, Daniel Marston and Tim Moreman have spearheaded this historical research with their volumes: the prize-winning *Phoenix from the Ashes: The Indian Army in the Burma Campaign* (2003), *The Indian Army and the End of the Raj* (2014) and *The Jungle, the Japanese and the Commonwealth Armies at War* (2005) respectively. These are complemented by Raymond Callahan's *Churchill and His Generals* (2007), a seminal work published in the United States that deserves better attention in the United Kingdom, and Steven Wilkinson's *Army and Nation: The Military and Indian Democracy since Independence* (2015). In addition, are the important wider studies of Christopher Bayly and Tim Harper, *Forgotten Armies: The Fall of British Asia, 1941-1945* (2004) and Ashley Jackson on *The British Empire and the Second World War* (2006). The most recent publications include *Approach to Battle: Training the Indian Army during the Second World War* (2017) published in this series, as well as Tarak Barkawi's *Soldiers of Empire: Indian and British Armies in World War II* (2017) and Raymond Callahan's *Triumph at Imphal-Kohima: How the Indian Army Finally Stopped the Japanese Juggernaut* (2017). Furthermore the Indian home front has been covered in Yasmin Khan's social history of the period entitled *The Raj at War: A People's History of India's Second World War* (2015).

The aforementioned rise in interest has been mirrored in India as eight volumes of the official histories of the Indian Armed Forces during the Second World War were reprinted in India in 2012 and another four in 2014 (they were originally published between 1954 and 1960). As Squadron Leader Rana Chhina stated at the launch of the reprints: 'As a resurgent India seeks to be a major player on the world stage, it behoves it to discard its narrow post-colonial world view to step up to reclaim the role that its armed forces played out on a global scale' during the Second World War. This resurgence is amply demonstrated by the publication of Srinath Raghavan's excellent overview *India's Wars : The Making of Modern South Asia* (2016), alongside the Kaushik Roy's *India and World II: War, Armed Forces, and Society, 1939-45* (2016) snd Anirudh Deshpande's *Hope and Despair: Mutiny, Rebellion and Death in India, 1946* (2016). However, even in this crowded arena, there is still much research and work to be published on both war and military culture in South Asia during the Second World War.

The series editors, members of the editorial advisory board and our publisher, Duncan Rogers of Helion, are all delighted to be involved in this series, most of the volumes of which are also being published in India under the Primus imprint. We hope it will be of interest in the UK, India but also globally.

Alan Jeffreys

Acknowledgements and Notes on Editing

The Letter Book of Lieutenant Colonel Valentine Blacker is a sequence of letters written by the Madras Army Cavalry Officer from 1798–1813 to his father, a clerk in Holy Orders in Armagh, Ireland. Each letter was then copied into a book with a date and location usually preceding the text. Valentine's early letters to his father were recorded without the usual formal greeting or closing endearment, however their inclusion does commence after 1801. Whether the letters were not faithfully copied or the familial expressions just omitted by Valentine is unknown but seems unlikely. The use of deferential, formal language between father and son is archaic but behind the stilted courtesies there remains a strong current of affection.

Politically incorrect and inappropriate comments have not been omitted as there is little justification in attempting to censor the comments of long dead generations according to the more liberal consensus of the 21st century. (Indian place names and titles have been anglicised but it has not been possible to identify every location using a contemporary gazetteer.[1] Identified locations are given footnotes where appropriate.)

There are amusing episodes with an occasional witty or sardonic comment which provides another dimension to the supposedly serious character of the army officer. The punctuation in the Letter Book is either non-existent or appears as a series of dashes. In order to assist the structure of sentences punctuation has been inserted.

A copy of the original handwritten 186 manuscript pages was used to transcribe it into text using a voice recognition system and then compared with a later typed copy.[2] Occasional passages have been omitted where, in the editor's judgement, the content failed to justify inclusion. The Letters here are presented chronologically which is not necessarily the order they were received by the Rev'd Dr St. John Blacker.

All the letters unless otherwise stated are from Valentine Blacker.

The additional letters were written to Valentine or his Father by their relative, the Adjutant General of the Madras Army Lieutenant Colonel Barry Close, providing further evidence of a close knit family unit albeit separated by considerable distance.

---

1   E. Thornton, *A Gazetteer of the Territories under the Government of the East India Company.* 4 volumes. (London: W. Allen 1854).
2   Ruth Johnson Cunningham, a thesis towards a Master of Arts degree, Duke University, North Carolina, United States of America, 1966.

A background and relevant passages have been provided to assist with context. Appropriate footnotes have been included for clarification or further detail such as an officers' promotion and career record. Abbreviations and acronyms have been used for rank and titles in footnotes.

Where errors exist the fault is entirely mine.

My acknowledgement and grateful thanks to Bharat Sanghani, Douglas Johnson, Sonia Deadman, David Swift, and David Vanstone, for their time, assistance, and comments. To Roger and Sue Davies, Camden for possessing a 'Djinn'. Julian Smith, Clarendon Bookshop for sourcing much relevant material. Ruth Johnson Cunningham, M.A. USA who wrote an unpublished thesis on Valentine Blacker's Letters. The Staff of the Rubenstein Library at Duke University, North Carolina, USA and the staff at the British Library, Africa and Asia Reading Room, for their good humoured patience with my endless questions.

Finally to Catharine who badgered me into making the effort.

Preface

In 1603 English sailors employed by an Elizabethan trading company walked ashore at Pulo Run, a two mile wide sliver of land on the eastern archipelago of Indonesia; they were looking to find spices, specifically nutmeg trees, which grew abundantly on the island but were a scarce commodity in the West. Found in enormous quantities, the nutmegs were bought cheaply, later making handsome profits when sold in Britain and Europe. These were the first tentative steps of The Honourable East India Company, (HEIC) granted a Royal Charter in 1600 for the purposes of trade but through its military power gradually established what became the 'jewel in the crown' of The British Empire.[1]

Within 60 years the presence of the British Company in India as merchants and traders began to change. William III authorised the formation of a new East India Company in 1698 in competition with the original, but the two companies were merged in 1708. That year the Company's original charter was confirmed and enhanced by Queen Anne. Madras and Calcutta were becoming major trading stations, built, established and fortified by The HEIC. Bombay, a Crown colony through marriage, had been sold to the Company in 1668 as 'surplus to Charles II's requirements.'[2] Trade may have been the founding principle of the HEIC yet by 1686 a martial bias was slowly emerging among its senior servants to defend and preserve property and interests.[3]

Britain was one of four European maritime nations who had significant ambitions in India: Portugal and Holland had already reaped considerable benefits and France had signalled her intentions as early as 1503 when two ships had sailed from Le Havre to trade in the East but were never heard of again. In 1604 the French had formed a

---

1   H. Yule & A.C. Burnell *Hobson Jobson, A Glossary of Colloquial Anglo Indian Words and Phrases.* (London: John Murray, 1903) p. 462. The HEIC became known as 'John Company' a personification of its title and used to secure a form of reverence from the native population.
2   J. Keay, *The Honourable Company. A History of the English East India Company* (London; HarperCollins, 1993) p. 131.
3   J. Wilson, *India Conquered.* (London: Simon and Schuster London, 2016) p. 29. The English presence in India was 'small and anxious' using violence as the solution to most difficulties when not accommodated.

trading company which came to naught; it was not until 1664 that La Compagnie des Indies Orientale was founded by Jean Colbert and granted a fifty year monopoly. The first French presence in India was established in 1667 at Surat; Pondicherry followed in 1693 but by 1714 lack of money, investment and Royal inertia caused trade and commerce to languish. The death of Louis XIV in 1725 galvanised French banks and traders to re-establish their ambitions in India this time supported by military force.

There were four stages to the eventual British securing of India: The fortifying of Madras, Calcutta and Bombay. The conquest of both south eastern and south western India including the coastal areas of Malabar and Coromandel. Aggressive legislative structures were imposed which dispossessed the native rulers of states, particularly in Mysore, and the imposition of 'Resident Agents,' backed by military force reducing local potentates to vassal governors.[4]

Nominal control of the Company's affairs was vested in two governing bodies, The Board of Control appointed by Parliament who directly supervised the government of The Company's possessions including the appointment of Governor Generals and a Court of Directors. The Directors had responsibility for the 'day to day' administration of affairs in India including the Army. In truth the Governor General had wide powers which he could use without fear of interference from the Board or the Court. London was at least three months away in terms of communication; there was no alternative than to trust the man on the spot.

Later it was argued that a 'Golden Age' began in India in 1798.[5] The rationale for such a statement were the merits of secure rule, a fairer system of revenue collection, reduction in banditry, a bona fide administration, less corruption and a progressive system of government. The annexation of territory[6] was also indisputable; a country the size of Spain, Germany and France combined had been subdued. This 'Golden Age' however was short lived terminating catastrophically in 1858.[7]

The native Indian view was quite different. From 1739, when 150,000 residents of Delhi were purportedly slaughtered by the Persian invader Nadir Shah, to the recapture of Delhi by the British in 1857 and the 3,000 executions in reprisals, the period was known as 'The Twilight.'[8]

---

4   H. Yule & A.C. Burnell, *Hobson Jobson, A Glossary of Colloquial Anglo Indian Words and Phrases,* The Resident Agent, a senior British official posted in a diplomatic role to a Native State to liaise and advise the ruler and his Ministers. A form of indirect rule to ensure subsidiary alliances were maintained.
5   P. Mason, *The Men who Ruled India.* Part III. (London: Jonathan Cape, 1987).
6   G.B. Malleson, *The Native States of India.* (London: Longman Green, 1875). Over 500 Princely or Native States were not part of British India but were subject to subsidiary alliances. Over 40 Princely or Native States were annexed by the British between 1800–1948.
7   The Indian Mutiny 1857–59 or First Indian War of Independence. All aspects of Government were ceded to the Crown in 1860.
8   W. Dalrymple, *The City of Djinns.* (London: HarperCollins, 1993) pp. 95–99.

The beginnings of the 'Golden Age' coincided with the arrival in the Sub-Continent of Valentine Blacker a young Irishman, appointed as a Cadet to the HEIC Madras Army, he arrived in Madras on 30 September 1798. He wrote home frequently to his father and family members; his letters being a valuable source of the military and social attitudes of the day. His particular 'bete noire' was the disparity between the service regulations of the King's Regiments set against those of the Company Army. All his correspondence features what must have been the 'officers mess' view on the wars, caste system, religion, local culture and inadequacies of Company rule. They provide an insight into the social and political outlook of an insular, separated society holding firm to its culture, deprecatory about the customs of those whom it governs but reluctant to interfere.

The influence of the French in India declined from the mid 18th century but those intervening years had seriously tested the East India Company commercially and militarily: it was to be another 58 years before the The HEIC was removed entirely from the government and political affairs of the Indian sub-continent.

Young men from Britain, attracted by the search for adventure and fortune in India, continued to arrive principally to join the Company's Army or as one of the 'heaven born' civil service.[9]

9   'Heaven born' The term was first used in the late 18th C. in relation to 'Heaven born Generals' but became a sobriquet applied to the relatively small number, usually less than 1000, of British born Civil Servants in India.

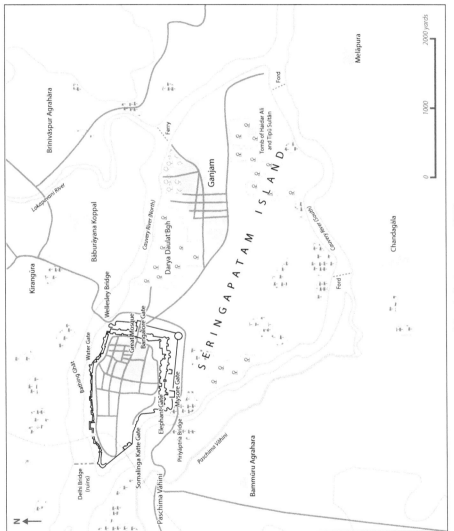

Map 1 Seringapatam 1799.

xvii

Map 2 Mysore 1810.

Background

India was formed during the Cretaceous period, lying north of the equator it has been likened to a giant net into which the races and people of Asia fell and became caught. Separation from Asia by the Himalayas and the rest of the world by sea has not impeded invaders or migrants. Settled by Homo Sapiens 30,000 years ago, the earliest recorded invaders were the Aryans around 1,500 BC. Over the centuries, India suffered many more incursions, notably the Persians, Alexander the Great, Tamerlane, Genghis Khan, the Scythians and the Huns. For many centuries it was a patchwork of hetereogenous states rather than one country. During the 8th century Muslim invaders arrived and continued until the establishment of The Mughal Empire in the 16th century. Later Europeans, Portuguese, Dutch, Danish and French all established trading posts on Indian coastal districts. The British East India Company in 1639 purchased a foothold on the East Indian coast in a marshy swamp that later became Madras: Bombay and Calcutta were trading successfully by 1697. The British Company had come to trade but gradually became the controlling agent for a succession of native princely states. When these alliances, treaties or simply trade were threatened, the Company utilised the British Navy and force to defend its interests. Indeed a Company official writing in 1680 complained that 'the native rulers have the knack of trampling upon us and exacting what they please.'[1]

Two events, the capture of Madras in 1746 by a French force and the seizure of Calcutta by an Indian Prince, Nawab Siraj-ud-Dowlah in 1756 accelerated and cemented British determination to uphold and safeguard its interests. The Company, whether it wanted to or not, was inexorably dragged into military alliances and the mire of Indian politics. Furthermore, the future was set for political and violent conflict.

In 1748 twelve companies of infantry were recruited into the Company's service. From that year on the size and recruitment of the army grew exponentially. The establishment of a Company army and the ready support of Crown forces altered the balance

---

1   J. Bowle, *Imperial Achievement* (London: Secker and Warburg, 1974) p. 92. In 1662 400 soldiers employed by The Company arrived in India. By 1665 300 of these men were dead from disease. Within 150 years the Company Army in the three Presidencies was over 200,000 strong. p. 92.

of power within the sub-continent and the British population. It was not long before the military outnumbered the merchants. This however was still not government but rather an armed monopoly on trade. French aggression proved to be of relatively short duration as by 1761 their military authority in India was virtually finished.[2]

Robert Clive's[3] victory at Plassey against Siraj-ud-Dowlah in 1757 and the defeat of the Dutch in their ill advised attempt to gain power in 1759 had confirmed the British as the paramount power in India. Not that the Honourable Company seemed exactly happy with the situation when they wrote to Clive, 'you seem so thoroughly possessed of military ideas, that you forget your employers are merchants.'[4]

Despite the absence of any other European opposition in India, for the next 100 years the cost of such paramountcy was to be imprinted onto the Company's balance sheet.

In some respects the British had begun to rule a civilisation wedded to long standing and enshrined tradition, having imposed themselves on an older, larger and in certain respects, more sophisticated civilisation than their own.

A treaty signed by Clive in 1765 was to gradually transform the Company's principal ethos from trade and commerce to the function of 'Diwani rights' or collection of revenue and provision of security.[5] The constitutional and political implications of this treaty may have been lost on the Princely Mughuls who agreed it but was to gradually lead to the aberrant Government of India by a British commercial enterprise.[6] In future the native rulers of India would be compelled to pay the Company for its services.

British India was divided into three Presidencies, Bengal, Madras and Bombay. Although each had its own army, civil service and set of governing codes administered by a Governor General, Bengal being the largest took precedence with Calcutta as the Capital of British India.

2   G.B. Malleson, *History of the French in India* (London: Longman & Co. 1868) p. 492–569 Defeated at the Battle of Wandiwash 1760, the French retreated to Pondicherry where they surrendered in January 1761. The Nizam of Hyderabad, Scindiah of Gwalior and Ranjit Singh in the Punjab all still employed French commanders in their Native State forces.

3   C.E. Buckland, *Dictionary of Indian Biography* (London: Swan Sonneschein 1906). Robert Clive, 'Clive of India' 1725–74 regarded as a 'resourceful and courageous' soldier of fortune who profited immensely from his time in India as both Commander in Chief and Governor General. His greatest victory was at Plassey in June 1757 when 3000 Company troops defeated an army estimated at 30,000. C. Barnett, *Britain and Her Army 1509–1970*. (London: Allen Lane 1970) p. 201 'Plassey was not much of a battle, numbers were meaningless in Indian warfare.'

4   J. Bowle,. *Imperial Achievement* p. 90.

5   H. Yule & A.C. Burnell, *Hobson Jobson, A Glossary of Colloquial Anglo Indian Words and Phrases,* Dewani Rights settled by The Treaty of Allahabad 16 August 1765.

6   'The Princely Mughals' were Shah Alamm II and Shuja-ud-Daula <http://www.cambridge.org/gb/academic/subjects/history/south-asian-history/princes-mughal> (accessed August 2017).

Towards the end of the 18th century, the British grip on India was tightening in the North East, Southern India and the Eastern coast of the Bay of Bengal. Princes who still 'independently' ruled territories or states had their petty insecurities and jealousies levered to the advantage of the Company. Any sign of disaffection such as correspondence with the French or gross mismanagement of their affairs (including sexual deviancy and financial profligacy), invariably resulted in the imposition of a 'Resident Agent' reinforced by the presence of Company troops or even their deposition from power in favour of a more compliant functionary.

The earlier respect and admiration for Indian life, culture and society had begun to wane by the end of the 18th century being replaced with criticism and even distaste. New moralities were rising which frowned upon the 'gorgeous East' and led to the more 'shallow existence of western provincialism.'[7]

In February 1797 Arthur Wellesley, an Anglo-Irish Colonel, arrived at Calcutta in command of the 33rd Regiment of Foot.[8] His principal task was to mount an expedition against Spanish Manila in the Philippines but he was recalled to Calcutta by November. He remained in India for the next seven years, studying previous conflicts against native rulers and the topography of the south of India. Wellesley's 33rd Regiment was already part of the Madras Army,[9] when in December 1798 he accepted the command of an army forming at Arcot,[10] but quickly relinquished it in favour of General George Harris on 29 January 1799.[11]

In May 1798 the Colonel's older brother Richard Wellesley, 2nd Earl of Mornington,[12] arrived in India as the new Governor General. (Although titled 1st Marquess Wellesley, for conveniece he is referred to in the text as Mornington to

---

7   J. Bowle, *Imperial Achievement*, p. 208.
8   *His Majesty's Regiments of the British Army* (London: Metro Provincial Publications, 1949) p. 64. Formed in 1702 became 33rd Regiment of Foot in 1751. Underwent many name changes but incorporated 'Duke of Wellington's' in title in 1853. Fought in India during the 4th Anglo Mysore War 1799 under Colonel Arthur Wellesley. Now part of The Yorkshire Regiment.
9   P. Stanley, *White Mutiny, British Military Culture in India* (New York: University Press. 1998) pp. 71–79 provides a mid 19th C., view but which is relevant to this earlier period. Conditions of Service including pay and pensions were different between the armies of the King and the Company. It was a matter of continual resentment within the Company's Army at the sneering attitude adopted by Kings Regiments. Officers of Kings Regiment's found the Company's Army discipline 'unacceptably lax' not recognising the key racial and religious 'mix' of the troops.
10   In preparation for the forthcoming war against Tippoo Sultan.
11   C.E. Buckland, *Dictionary of Indian Biographyy*. George Harris 1746–1829, fought in American War of Independence and wounded at Bunkers Hill. Major General C-in-C. Madras Army 1796. Retired 1800. Created 1st Baron of Seringapatam and Mysore 1815. Described by the Governor General Mornington as a 'good old twodler, but a mere man of straw.'
12   Ibid, Richard Colley Wellesley 1760–1842, 2nd Earl of Mornington 1781, created 1st Marquess Wellesley in 1799.

avoid confusion.) Mornington was almost at once confronted with a crisis involving the native state of Mysore in Southern India which had been ruled by Hyder Ali from 1761 until his death in 1782.[13] His son Sultan Fateh Ali Khan Shahab, known as Tippoo Sultan had inherited the throne together with his father's implacable hatred towards the British as embodied in The HEIC. Hyder Ali had demonstrated his military prowess in 1768 by forcing the Company to the negotiating table during the 1st Anglo Mysore War 1767–69. Tippoo Sultan, Hyder's son and Commander in Chief had also achieved significant success against the British in the 2nd Anglo Mysore War 1780–84 when his troops invaded The Carnatic and Tanjore.[14] British and Company forces were defeated in a number of engagements, forced to negotiate and sign The Treaty of Mangalore, the last occasion that a native ruler dictated the terms.

The 3rd Anglo Mysore War 1790–92

Tippoo breached the terms of the Mangalore Treaty by invading the Kingdom of Travancore an ally of the British.[15] This time the British, although unsuccessful during campaigns in 1790 and 1792, had a better measure of their foe eventually succeeding in besieging Tippoo's capital at Seringapatam[16] where he surrendered. Defeat was a humiliation for Tippoo, his sons were taken hostage for security against the payment of war indemnities and he was forced to cede territory to his enemies.[17]

The 4th Anglo Mysore War 1799

Tippoo's defeat did little to reduce his contempt for the British or his desire for the recovery of his ceded territories, reputation and power.[18] In May 1798 a proclamation issued in the Isle de France by the French announced the design of Tippoo was

---

13   E. Thornton, *A Gazetteer of the Territories under the Government of the East India Company* 1854 A Muslim principality in Southern India. In 1749 Hyder Ali appeared in the Mysorean Army and by 1760 had become virtual ruler with the French General Lally as his C-in-C.
14   Ibid. The Carnatic and Tanjore form part of the States of Tamil Nadu and Andhra Pradesh.
15   Ibid. A native state 4500 sq miles in Southern India, within the Madras Presidency, ruled by a Rajah.
16   Ibid. Seringapatam, fortress and capital of Mysore on an island 3 miles long in the Cauvery River.
17   H. Dodwell, *The Nabobs of Madras* (London: Norgate and Williams, 1926) p. 76 The estimates for the prize money were £5,000,000 which included £2,000,000 in jewellery and gold.
18   V&A Museum London, Tippoo had a mechanical toy made depicting a Tiger devouring an European East India Company Soldier. It is now in the V&A.

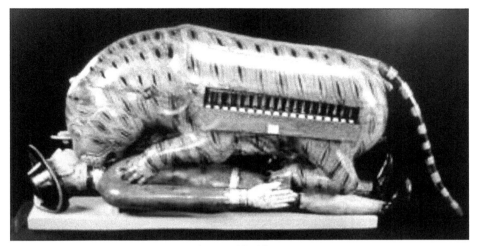

Tippoo's Toy Tiger.

to rid his country of the British, inviting French citizens to join his standard.[19] He entered into correspondence with Napoleon who having recently invaded Egypt re-assured Tippoo that he would assist him to throw off 'the iron yoke of England.'[20] Napoleon's optimism was misplaced as his naval forces were defeated at the Battle of the Nile in August 1798 crushing any realistic opportunity of further French military intervention in British India. Mornington increased the security of Southern India by removing the French trained forces and officers of the Nizam of Hyderabad.[21] The military establishment at Madras was also reformed under the acting Governor, General George Harris. Lieutenant Colonel Arthur Wellesley was appointed the new commander of the Nizam's force which now included his 33rd Regiment.[22] The Company's relationship with the Nizam had been re-defined but other native rulers, particularly the Marathas were less accommodating, continuing to secretly maintain

19   Mauritius in 1715 was colonised by the French and named Isle de France. Surrendered to the British in December 1810 who then governed until Independence in 1968.

20   D.A. Bingham, *A Selection of the Letters and Despatches of the First Napoleon.* (London: Chapman and Hall 1884) Vol.I p. 362 'he more than once returned to the idea of … seating himself upon the throne of Delhi.'

21   C.E. Buckland, *A Dictionary of Indian Biography,* Nizam of Hyderabad, dynasty founded in 1713 and originally the title of the native who ruled the state on behalf of the Mughal Emperor.

22   J. Weller, *Wellington in India* (London: Frontline Books 2013) pp. 61–66 Arthur Wellesley, suffered a military setback at Sultanpetah Tope, southwest of Seringapatam when his command failed to achieve their objective sustaining 25 casualties incl. 8 men captured. Wellesley apparently 'much agitated' blamed his setback on the lack of a daylight reconnaisance.

a 'treacherous correspondence' with the ruler of Mysore. Negotiations were attempted with Tippoo but he declined such offers 'with studied evasion.' The British prepared for war. General Harris was placed in command of an army of over 21,000 troops including 4,500 Europeans.

In 18th century India, officers went to war with formidable amounts of equipment and baggage requiring equally large numbers of natives to work and carry for just one. Those who did not wish to ride were carried in palanquins.[23] The number of troops was far exceeded by non-combatant camp followers, bearers, cooks, syces (grooms), grass cutters, khitmugars (waiters), khansamas (chief providers or Butlers) all of whose duties were further constrained by the caste system.[24] The movement of such forces was ponderous but astonishing considering how effectively they traversed huge distances and fought battles.

Hostilities commenced on 6 March 1799 when Tippoo's forces attacked the British line under General Stuart near Periapatam;[25] this however proved to be Tippoo's last rebellious throw of the dice. In this initial encounter Tippoo was defeated with 1500 casualties. When he attacked General Harris at Mallevelly he was defeated a second time with 700 casualties. Having retreated to his capital, the island fortress of Seringapatam, Tippoo sent a suggestion to Harris that they should meet in mortal combat, 'to save further bloodshed,' unsurprisingly this was declined.

Lieutenant General George Harris, C-in-C Madras 1796– 1800, circa 1800.

Major General Arthur Wellesley, India 1804. (Courtesy Government Art Collection)

23   H. Yule, & A.C. Burnell, *A Glossary of Colloquial Anglo Indian Words and Phrases.* A box type litter with extending poles for an individual to be carried in by 4 – 6 men.
24   J.H. Hutton, *Caste in India.* (London: Oxford University Press, 1961) Caste, originally a Portugese term 'casta' for race or breed. The artificial division of society in India into high or low status.
25   Now Piriypatna a small town of 20000 pop. 70 km from Mysore.

The Siege at Seringapatam May 1799, a contemporary print. (Courtesy of Library of NSW Australia)

During his fighting withdrawal Tippoo also deployed 'a harassing fire with rockets' which were manufactured at Toorkhunhooly.[26]

Siege operations began against Seringapatam on 3 April during which Wellesley carried all Tippoo's defences on 27 April west of the city which was stormed on 4 May 1799. In the street fighting that followed Tippoo was killed and buried with full military honours.[27] The success of the operations against Tippoo were ascribed to Valentine Blacker's uncle the Madras Army Adjutant General, Barry Close. His 'ability, zeal and energy' and 'having the assistance of so excellent an officer as Colonel Close to execute so skilfully what had been planned in the closet' was remarked upon by William Hickey, a gossipy diarist who formed one of the establishment in Calcutta.[28] Mysore was returned to the princely Hindu Wodeyar family,[29] previously ousted by Hyder Ali in 1760 but a large proportion of the state was annexed and incorporated into British India with smaller parcels given to the Nizam of Hyderabad. After Tippoo's defeat Wellesley was appointed military governor of the city instead

26 E. Moor, *A Narrative of the Operations of Captain Little's Detachment Against Tippoo Sultan.* (London: George Woodfall 1794) p. 169. Rockets had previously been deployed against the British by Tippoo Sultan during the 3rd Anglo-Mysore War in 1792.

27 J.W. Stempel,.ed. *Autobiography of the British Soldier. Anonymous Officer* (London: Headline Publishing 2007) pp. 105–7.

28 W. Hickey, *Memoirs of William Hickey 1790–1809*, ed. Alfred Spencer (London: Hurst and Blackett. 1925,) Vol. IV, pp. 227–9.

29 L.K.A.Iyer, *The Mysore Castes and Tribes.* (Bangalore: Mysore Govt. Press 1935) 5 vols. Vol.I p. 106. Wodeyar family, Maharajahs of Mysore ruled the State from 16th C to 1947, bar the period 1760–1799.

of Lieutenant Colonel David Baird who had led the storm.[30] On 11 May Arthur Wellesley was appointed temporarily to govern Mysore.

The administration of Mysore was changed dramatically. The new Maharajah Krishnarajah III was a 5 year old minor and the powers of government were to be vested in the new Resident Agent of the Governor General, Lieutenant Colonel Barry Close.[31] His nephew Valentine Blacker was to serve as Commanding Officer of the Resident's Cavalry escort. The young native ruler was also required to retain and pay for a military force for defence and security at a cost of 7 lakhs of Rupees a year. The Governor General, Mornington was an imperialist who believed that British rule over the sub-continent was right and proper.[32] He encouraged the formal annexation of native states when necessary, desirable or merely possible. Surat formerly possessed by France, Tanjore and parts of Oude were taken into British possession, these gains in territory adding to the Company's military and administrative costs. He was also a pragmatist who recognised that either the Company had to disengage from India with the threat of bankruptcy or continue the enlargement of its territories. There was little by way of an alternative strategy that the Honourable Company's Court of Directors could adopt. The Company had already borrowed over £1,000,000 from the British Government in 1771, so whether right or wrong, Mornington took the view the expansion of territory and improvement in administration had to continue.[33]

The Poligar Wars 1799–1804

The removal of Tippoo Sultan however only contributed marginally towards peace and security in Southern India. Huge districts were beset and controlled by Poligars who varied in style from feudal chiefs to marauding outlaws and frequently both.[34]

30   C.E. Buckland, *A Dictionary of Indian Biography*, Lt. Colonel David Baird 1757–1829. Went to India 1779 with the 73rd Regiment of Foot. Wounded and captured during 1st Mysore War by Tippoo Sultan and remained a prisoner for 4 years. After his release by 1798 he was a Major General and led the storm of Seringapatam when Tippoo was killed. Fought in the Egypt Campaign 1801 and the Peninsular War where his left arm was shattered. In a letter on 24 January 1831 Wellesley described him as, 'gallant, hard headed, lion hearted but he had no talent, no tact.'

31   E. Ingram, (Ed). *Two Views of British India; The Private Correspondence of Mr Dundas and Lord Wellesley* (London: Adams & Dart 1970). Mornington had been more than impressed by Close describing him in fulsome terms. He had been much less impressed by General Harris. See previous fn.

32   W. Donigher, *The Hindus, An Alternative History* (London: Oxford University Press. 2010) p. 580. 'They knew who they were; Englishmen with a God given right to rule.'

33   The loan was converted to an annuity in 1833 charged on the revenues accrued from India. The Company's monopoly on trade was eventually curtailed and then abolished. India was opened for the free market.

34   H. Yule & A.C. Burnell, *Hobson Jobson, A Glossary of Colloquial Anglo-Indian Words and Phrases,* Poligar, the term is peculiar to the Madras Presidency.

They maintained sizable 'armies' of ill-disciplined, brutal retainers who plundered the countryside but when pressed by regular troops retreated to forts within dense jungle. The East India Company viewed them occasionally as 'petty princes' providing them with arms in order to carry out 'dirty work' likely to be refused by soldiers. In 1802 the Court of Directors issued instructions for their oversight:

> It is our positive utmost injunction that force never be resorted to against any of the Poligars ... unless in case of actual rebellion, until every lenient and concil-iatory measure has been tried without effect. It is our anxious wish to owe the obedience of the Poligars and of all others of our tributaries to their confidence in our justice rather than dread of our power.[35]

Despite this intermittent policy of appease-ment the Poligars remained an obstacle to civil order. Two wars were fought against them between 1799–1804 which were vividly commented upon by another Madras Army Officer, James Welsh, in his journal.[36] During the 2nd Poligar War in 1801 Welsh witnessed Valentine Blacker being twice wounded and losing 'a favourite charger.' The Southern Poligar's character was defined by simple treachery combined with an anxiety to sell their fidelity at a price: there appears to have been one ruthless exception, a Pathan adven-turer named Dhoondia Waugh who domi-nated the Bednore district of Mysore incurring the anger of Tippoo by his constant depreda-tions. He had been incarcerated in irons at Seringapatam but set at liberty in 1799 by 'the humanity of the conquerers.'[37] Needless to say he abused his freedom, recruited followers

General James Welsh, Madras Army.
(Courtesy of www.geni.com)

35   T.H.Beaglehole, *The Development of Administration Policy in Madras,* 1792–1818. (Cambridge: University Press, 1966) p. 65.
36   J. Welsh, *Military Reminiscences extracted from A Journal of nearly Forty Years Active Service in the East Indies.* (London: Smith Elder & Co. 1830). 2 Vols. Vol. 1.pp. 76–84. E. Dodswell & J. Miles, *Alphabetical List of the Officers of the Indian Army 1760–1834* (London: Longman Browne Orme & Co 1838,) Cadet 1789, Lieut, 1792, Captain, 1800 Major, 1807 Lieut. Col. 1813, Commandant 1824, Colonel 1829, Maj. General 1837. Died 1861.
37   E. Thornton, *History of the British Empire in India.* (London: W. Allen, 1841) Vol. III p. 93–95.

from the remnants of Tippoo's cavalry and led a force not particularly troubled with any acute sense of conscience. He persuaded local chiefs hitherto peaceful and law abiding to betray their trust and join him in a turmoil of 'unrelenting cruelty, rapine and murder.'[38] In an unsuccessful demonstration of psychological warfare Wellesley offered 30,000 rupees for Dhoondia Waugh 'Dead or Alive.'

Separating his forces Wellesley sent Lieutenant Colonel Simon Dalrymple[39] with a light cavalry column from Chittledroog[40] to destroy a 250 strong Poligar force and seize two of their forts.[41] Colonel James Stevenson advanced into Bednore and on 17 August defeated Dhoondia's army at Shirkapoor.[42] However, Dhoondia escaped with 5,000 troops until fallen upon by Wellesley with 1,400 troops at Conaghulland on 10 September 1800. Wellesley formed his troops into one line and attacked 'The King of Two Worlds' who again allegedly fled the field into Maratha territory where no British force was at liberty to follow.[43] Accounts differ about Dhoondia's ultimate fate, whether he was 'plundered' by the Marathas or in fact 'destroyed' during the battle of 10 September. Two other Poligar leaders Kattambomman and Subramani Pillai were executed after capture, their forts razed and their land returned for cultivation.

The 1st and 2nd Anglo Maratha Wars 1775–1781, 1803–1805

Before the arrival of Valentine Blacker the 1st Anglo Maratha War had ended in 1781: with neither side gaining victory the British agreed a peace treaty signed at Salbai with the Maratha leader Mahadjie Scindiah in May 1782.

The defeat of Dhoondia Waugh in 1800 was followed by significant discord among the Marathas. Mistakenly described as an Empire, but in essence a confederacy formed in the early 17th century, it existed solely for the objectives of its constituent members who frequently quarrelled amongst themselves. A warlike society, the Marathas fought and defeated the Moghuls who had attempted to subjugate them in

---

38 Dhoondiah's 'cruelty and rapacity' was matched by British ruthlessness when Poligar garrisons were 'put to the sword.' See letter 1 August 1800.

39 J. Weller, *Wellington in India* (London: Frontline Books, 2013) p. 88–89. Dodswell & Miles. *Alphabetical List of the Officers of the Indian Army 1760–1834*. Lieut. Colonel Simon Dalrymple, Madras Army, Ensign 1778, Lieutenant 1782, Captain 1793, Major 1794, Lt. Colonel 1799, d.1804 India.

40 Chittledroog, see letter 29 August 1799.

41 L.K.A. Iyer, *The Mysore Tribes and Castes*. Vol. II p. 142 A group of Banjaras in Dalrymples force endeavoured to join the enemy. Seven of their ringleaders were summarily hanged; as Dalrymple explained to the remainder, 'our vengeance was not less to be dreaded than our liberality to be desired.'

42 J. Weller, *Wellington in India*. Colonel James Stevenson, Captain 1784, Major 1788 Lt. Colonel 1796, Colonel 1799. Commanded 1st Brigade Floyds Cavalry against the Poligars. Left India sick 1804. d. St Helena 1805. Wellesley regarded Stevenson "a subordinate whom he could trust so completely and so safely.' p. 252.

43 'Ubhaya-Lokaheeshwara,' The King of Two Worlds, a self-styled title.

the Deccan.[44] From these victories the Marathas gained experience and a measure of cohesion. During the ensuing years the authority of individual Maratha rulers had dwindled and devolved to one individual, the Peishwa who in 1795 was the duplicitous Baji Rao II.[45] His power had now waned to the extent that 'civilian dissentions monotonous in repetition and appalling in brutality'[46] was rife. The discord had led to the Battle of Poonah in 1802 between two Maratha rival factions, Scindiah and Holkar.[47] Victory was gained by Holkar, causing Scindiah, terrified for his life, to appeal for help through the Agent at Poonah to the Governor General.

The Resident at Poonah, Lieutenant Colonel Barry Close, although relatively new in post, viewed this crisis jointly with Mornington as an ideal opportunity to establish 'the interests of British power in the Maratha Empire.' A treaty was negotiated by the British which included an interesting change in phrase. Hitherto the British had always referred to the 'British Empire in India' but the treaty referred to the 'British Empire of India.' The Peishwa Baji Rao II's nominal authority was upheld, albeit by six battalions of sepoys provided by the Company, his position secure from threats but with only limited control of the 'Maratha Empire'. Mornington claimed that the Marathas had been 'given boundaries and pent within them.' Unfortunately the boundaries proved to be a chimera. The main Maratha protagonists were unhappy and dissatisfied after the treaty was signed. The Peishwa found it too restrictive, Scindiah did not believe it applied to him and Holkar maintained an indifference. The heated arguments over the treaty turned towards further conflict. Mornington, thoroughly annoyed by the latest intransigence from Maratha leaders regarded it as a 'just cause' for war.

The list of resources available to Holkar alone is contained in a letter from Lieutenant Colonel Barry Close, Adjutant General to Major General Arthur Wellesley. Close advised Wellesley that a spy had brought the information from Holkars camp at Poona that day but Close felt the numbers would require 'some abatement.'[48]

44   E. Thornton *A Gazetteer of the Territories under the Government of the East India Company,* The Deccan, a large plateau extending over most of the 'triangle' of S.India rising from 100m in the North to 1000m in the south.
45   H. Yule & A.C. Burnell, *A Glossary of Colloquial Anglo-Indian Words and Phrases,* Peishwa, Peshwa. From the Persian for 'leader,' a chief minister of the Marathas. The last Peishwa Baji Rao died in exile 1851 at Cawnpore.
46   E. Thornton, *History of the British Empire in India.* Vol IV pp. 390–404.
47   C.E. Buckland, *Dictionary of Indian Biography,* Scindiah Dowlut Rao 1770–1827 Maharajah of Gwalior, succeeded his adoptive father 1794 and began to organise an army under French officers. A defiant ruler who frequently breached treaties, he and his successors fought the British until 1844. Yeswant Rao Holker 1775–1811, a one eyed Maratha adventurer and freebooter who after a defeat by General Lake in 1805 made peace and ceded territory. He became Maharajah of Indore the same year but was insane by 1806.
48   Bennel, A.S. Ed. *The Maratha War Papers of Arthur Wellesley January to December 1803* (Stroud: Army Records Society, 1998) p. 26.

Statement of the Forces of Jaswant Rao Holkar 7 February 1803

	Cavalry	Infantry	Guns
Nagu Rao Jevali	5,000		
Shah Ahmed Khan	6,000	800	
Mir Khan	5,000	4,000	40
Fateh Singh Mane	10,000		
Dukkeries[1]	20,000		
Hindustani	10,000		
Holkars		3,000	46
Vickers Brigade		2,500	35
Dodds Brigade[2]		1,500	20
Heavy Park of Artillery			22
Aligoles[3]		2,100	
Total	56,000	15,900	157

Notes
1   H. Yule & A.C. Burnell, *Hobson Jobson. A Glossary of Colloquial Anglo-Indian Terms and Phrases*, Dukkeries is not present. Probably a phonetic interpretation of 'Deccanies,' Mahommedan inhabitants of the Deccan.
2   J. Weller, Wellington in India. Lieutenant William Dodd. A deserter from the Madras Army wanted for murder. Dodd served in Holkars European Officered Battalions. He escaped after the War. p. 122. I can find no reference to Vickers but presumably he too was a European Officer with Holkar.
3   H. Yule & A.C. Burnell, *Hobson Jobson. A Glossary of Colloquial Anglo-Indian Terms and Phrases*. 'Aligoles,' Irregular Troops used in this case as Artillery Park Guards or for 'desperate service.'

The 2nd Anglo–Maratha war commenced in early 1803 bringing the British army considerable success at Ahmadnagar in August 1803 and victory at the Battle of Assaye in September 1803 where the British force was commanded by the newly promoted Major General Arthur Wellesley.[49] He had split his force for tactical and geographical reasons intending that Colonel James Stevenson with his smaller force would prevent the enemy moving south by one route whilst Wellesley was travelling north by another. On 23 September Wellesley found himself on the plains of the River Kaitna facing a 12,000 Maratha strong infantry force led by the Rajah of Berar together with 20,000 horsemen commanded by Scindiah. He had discovered the enemy sooner than anticipated but decided to join battle. Although suffering heavy casualties, four out of every ten men, his daring attack against superior odds proved

49   B. Horrocks, & D. Boyd, *Famous Regiments, The Royal Engineers* (London: Leo Cooper. 1975) p. 145. When asked in old age what was the 'best thing he had ever done in the fighting line,' Wellington answered, 'Assaye.'

successful. By a Treaty in December 1803 with Scindiah 'Hindustan was closed to French influence and intrigue for ever.'[50]

The Governor General believed that this would be an end of the conflict but had reckoned without the supposedly indifferent Holkar. Yeswant Rao Holkar viewed the British and the Company with disdain, basing his indifference on the premise that the British feared him. Prompted by Holkar's impossible demands which kept the Company's army committed in the field at huge expense, Mornington reacted swiftly and with fury: The 2nd Anglo Maratha War re-ignited in April 1804.

Having applied to leave India Wellesley, the 'Sepoy General,'[51] took no part in the second phase of hostilities: he left India forever in 1805 with £42,000 in prize money.[52]

This time the British were less successful militarily than previously. Colonel William Monson[53] suffered a defeat in Rajputana and General Gerard Lake,[54] a talented soldier, although victorious against Holkar at Furruckabad and Delhi, suffered ignominy at the siege of Bharatpur between January and February 1805 when four assaults on the fort failed with over 2,334 casualties. Holkar eventually surrendered at Amritsar on 24 December 1805.

The Court of Directors in London, already alarmed at Mornington's policy of annexations and the increasing costs of the war, recalled the Governor General with a view to his dismissal but Mornington pre-empted them by resigning. He had forseen this; in a letter to his friend Addington in October 1801 he wrote: 'It is evident that I do not possess that degree of confidence in the opinion of The Court of Directors which is necessary to inspire confidence in the discharge of my duties.'[55]

In his role as Governor General his indifference to 'orders' from home had revealed the fatuity of a system which attempted to govern India from England.[56] Mornington in certain respects had been very successful. He had added vast territories to British

50   H. Compton, *Military Adventurers of Hindustan* (London: T. Fisher Unwin, 1893) p. 325.
51   'Sepoy General' a term of derision used by Napoleon.
52   H. Maxwell, *The Life of Wellington* (London: Sampson, Low & Co., 1900) 2 vols. p. 65, vol.1 'he felt dissatisfied with the degree of recognition' but he had received, 'even for those days, singularly rapid promotion ... and opportunities of distinguishing himself.' H. Dodwell, *The Nabobs of Madras.* p. 65, Maj. Gen. Arthur Wellesley described prize money in basic terms of plunder. 'What you could lay your bloody hands and keep.'
53   C.E. Buckland *A Dictionary of Indian Biography* Col. William Monson 1760–1807 went to India with 52nd Regt.in 1780. Fought against Tippoo and Marathas. Brig. General 1804 but suffered a heavy defeat by Holkar that year. MP for Lincoln 1806.
54   Ibid. *A Dictionary of Indian Biography*, Gen. Gerard Lake 1st Viscount Lake 1744–1808. Commander in Chief India and Member of Council 1801–1805, successful in 2nd Maratha War but after the casualty toll at Bharatpur he was forced to retire.
55   E. *Two Views of British India, The Correspondence of Dundas and Wellesley.* Letter to Addington. p. 14.
56   I. Butler, I. *The British in India – A Miscellany 1971.* Mornington had even appointed his younger brother Henry, not an employee or nominee of the HEIC, to various posts provoking outrage from the Court of Directors.

India, Muslim power in Mysore was neutralised, the forces of the Nizam of Hyderabad purged of French troops and influence, the Poligar chiefs subdued, the Peishwa tied down in treaties, Scindiah reduced to a mere vassal and Holkar an ally now that he was The Maharajah of Indore.

The 3rd Maratha and Pindari War 1817–19

Richard Wellesley, 2nd Earl of Mornington.

The 3rd Maratha war ignited for similar reasons as its predecessors with the added dimension of Pindaris.[57] The dissatisfaction of the Peishwa Baji Rao with his status, he was possessed of the basest attributes, characterised by 'the grossest sensuality and destitute of all honourable principle'[58] and nursed a specific antipathy against the British. The five great Maratha chiefs and leaders, Scindiah of Gwalior, Holkar of Indore,[59] Bhonsal of Nagpur, the Maharajah Gwaekwad of Baroda and the Puar of Dhar had not only continued their depredations across Southern India but supported and fostered the military system of the Pindaris led by a Karim Khan. The Pindari marauders were all well mounted, armed with spears, to a lesser extent with matchlocks and enjoyed the reputation as the 'most desperate and profligate of mankind,' trusting much to the chance of plunder for supplying their wants. They carried no baggage, travelled 30 to 40 miles a day with great rapidity, using torture and amputation for the extraction of information on where treasure was hoarded. During the period 1814–16 their raids into the Madras Presidency persisted in creating terror and alarm despite an attack led by Major Lushington.[60] On Christmas Day 1816 he led the

57   H. Yule & A.C. Burnell A.C. *Hobson Jobson. Glossary of Anglo-Indian Terms and Phrases,* Pindari, Pindarry, Pindarree, the origin is obscure but first noted in 1706. A member of a band of plunderers with 'dissolute habits.' R. Orme, *A History of the Transactions of the British Nation in Indostan from the year 1745* (Madras: Pharoah & Co. reprinted 1863), 3 vols. p. 572 (1759) refers to 'Pandarums' as foot plunderers. L.K.A. Iyer, *The Mysore Tribes and Castes,* p. 395 Vol. IV. 'The Pindaris were plunderers and freebooters, villains, while they robbed and murdered defenceless women, they prayed five times a day.'

58   E. Thornton, *The History of the British Empire in India.* vol. IV, pp. 556–7.

59   G.B. Malleson, *The Native States of India.* pp. 186–190. Jeswant Rao Holkar had become insane and an adopted boy, Malhar Rao Holkar, a minor b.1806, was chosen to rule as Maharajah. During his minority his adoptive mother Tulsa Bai reigned as Regent. Described as 'handsome but perverted by vicious habits.' Maratha and Pathan rebels committed to destroying British influence seized and beheaded her in December 1817.

60   E. Dodswell, & J. Miles, *Alphabetical list of the Officers of the Indian Army 1760–1834.* James Law Lushington K.C.B., entered HEIC as a Cornet 1797 4th Native Cavalry. Lieutenant, 1799, Captain 1804, Major 1812, Lieutenant Colonel 1819, Colonel 1829, Major General 1837. M.I.D 1817 for meritorious service at Cowan.

4th Madras Native Cavalry in a successful attack routing an estimated 3,000 Pindaris at Cowan, southwest of Poonah, killing and wounding 800.[61] The British attempted to persuade the Maratha chiefs to join them in suppressing the Pindaris, to which they ostensibly agreed but failed to act; unsurprisingly it was discovered they were still secretly in collusion with the pillagers from whom they received their 'chouth,' a quarter share of the plunder. In 1817 the Pindaris led by their leaders Cheetoo, Karim (Khureem) Khan, Namdar Khan and Wasil Mahomed[62] finally overstepped the mark. Three bands numbering 10,000 had separated and ridden into the territories of the Nizam and the Company at Ganjam. In the course of twelve days they plundered 339 villages, murdered 182 people, severely wounded 505, and maimed over 3603; property was plundered to the value of £250,000.[63]

The Governor General, the Marquis of Hastings[64] authorised the assemblage of two armies advancing from the North and the South to encircle the Pindaris. At the same time a watchful eye was being kept on the Marathas by Colonel Sir John Malcolm, then with the Army of the Deccan.[65] The tension was heightened by the assassination of a Minister of a native state whilst on a visit to the Peishwa Baji Rao. The main assassin, Trimbuckjee,[66] was shielded by the Peishwa until pressure from Mountstuart Elphinstone,[67] the Resident at Poonah, forced his imprisonment. Trimbuckjee's subsequent fortuitous escape convinced the British that Baji Rao was implicit in the murder and had even encouraged Trimbuckjee, once free, to raise arms against them. Balanced on the precipice of war the Peishwa's resolve temporarily failed whereupon

61   E. Thornton, *The History of the British Empire in India.* vol. IV p. 423, Captain Thomas Darke 4th Native Cavalry was killed in the encounter.
62   P.F. McEldowney, *Pindari Society and the Establishment of British Paramountcy in India* (University of Wisconsin 1966) After the Pindaris were defeated Cheetoo evaded capture but had the misfortune to be killed by a tiger. Khureem Khan surrendered to the British and was granted lands at Goruckpore to retain his support. Namdar Khan also surrendered and Wasil Mahomed took poison after his capture.
63   J. Baillie Fraser, J. *Military Memoirs of Lieutenant Colonel James Skinner, C.B.* (London: Smith Elder & Co. 1851) 2 Vols. (Ambala: The Civil & Military Press, Ambala. Reprint 1955) pp. 122–23.
64   C.E. Buckland, *Dictionary of Indian Biography*, Francis Rawdon, Marquis of Hastings 1754–1826. Entered Army 1771, Adjutant General in America 1778, succeeded as Earl of Moira 1793, General 1803. Governor General and C-in-C India 1813–1823. Created Marquess of Hastings 1816.
65   E. Dodswell, & J. Miles, *Alphabetical list of the Officers of the Indian Army 1760–1834.* Sir John Malcolm b.1769 joined HEIC at what seems an impossibly young age and gazetted as a Cadet 1782 in Madras, Ensign 1783, Lieutenant 1788, Captain 1798, Major 1802, Lt.-Colonel 1804, Colonel 1813, Major-General 1819. Resident, Mysore 1802–12; On furlough 1813–16. Governor at Bombay 1827–30. Died 1833. Undertook several diplomatic missions to Persia. Author of works on the history of India and Persia.
66   C.E. Buckland, *A Dictionary of Indian Biography.* Trimabakji Danglia captured by Lieutenant, Swanston in June 1818, he remained a prisoner for life.
67   Ibid. Mountstuart Elphinstone 1779–1859, British administrator, Resident at Poonah 1811 and Lieutenant, Governor of Bombay 1819. Author of 'History of India' 1841.

he conducted negotiations with the British resulting in a new treaty on 13 June 1817.[68] Herein lay the mischief which would lead to war. The treaty of nineteen articles determined that the Peishwa: could not negotiate with any other power, had to renounce his title of Peishwa and all connection with other Marathas, the Maratha confederacy was to be dissolved and its territory was to be transferred to the Company.

In a contemporary understatement, a description of The Peishwa's position, 'was dissatisfied, and though unreasonably not unnaturally. It was impossible he could forbear contrasting his present humiliated state with his former lofty pretension.'[69]

Some Maratha chiefs encouraged the Peishwa's 'dissatisfaction,' by conscripting troops and horsemen 'unremittingly.' By the 1 October 1817 they had opted for war but rather than acting cohesively each chose to fight independently thus costing them any hope of victory and the loss of autonomy over their native states. Hostilities commenced on 5 November 1817 when the British Residency building at Poonah was attacked and razed.

Captain Valentine Blacker Assistant Quartermaster General estimated the Rebel Native and British forces as follows:

Army	Cavalry	Infantry	Artillery Guns
Scindiah	14,250	16,250	140
Holkar	20,000	7,940	37
Peishwa	28,000	13,800	85
Rajah of Nagpore	15,766	17,826	85
The Nizam	25,000	10,000	
Ameer Khan[1]	12,000	10,000	200
Pindaris	27,000	15,000	20
sub-Total	142,016	90,816	567
Total	**233,399**		
Hastings: The Grand Army & British Kings Regiments.	43,687		
Hislop: The Army of the Deccan & Irregulars.	74,487		
Total	**114,174**		

Note
1 J. Baillie Fraser, Military Memoir. Ameer Khan, a Pathan originally from Afghanistan and another freebooting leader of the Pindaris, allied with Holkar. He had raided the Holy City of Gokul in Mathura as early as 1805. After his and Holkars defeat he retired to a residence at Tonk with a pension from the British. pp. viii, 64–77.

68   The Treaty of Poonah.
69   E. Thornton, *History of the British Empire in India.* Vol. III p. 439.

The Army of the Deccan under Hislop moved northwest from Madras and the Grand Army under the Commander in Chief Lord Hastings moved southwest from Cawnpore having incorporated the Central Division of the Bengal Army. Some 300,000 camp followers travelled with the Armies.[70] On 10 November 1817 cholera broke out amongst troops in the Division and forced a move to Erich a comparatively elevated country but the disease continued to ravage the troops. On 20 November the C-in-C Lord Hastings received intimation that Scindiah, believing the British cause was lost due to the disease, was prepared to break the treaty of June 1817.

The Grand Army eventually recovered and the Pindaris suffered early defeats but were not finally suppressed until March 1819. Defeat followed too for the Maratha chiefs[71] who were not only forced to concede territory but had the indignity of being replaced with those of a more favourable disposition to the British[72] or had Resident Agents imposed upon them.

Blacker himself led two attacks; the first at Nagpore resulted in his men suffering 58 killed, 243 wounded and 6 men missing before the attack was abandoned, 'the abandonment of the attack whether it be; or be not called premature, proceeded from a cause which will always affect the best troops. They saw no advantage to be obtained ...[73] The second at Mehidpoor, 'Colonel Blacker's attempt could not prudently have been made in front of the batteries of the enemy.' There were also queries about the conduct and use of Silladar cavalry who later plundered a Pindari camp and seized a 'quantity of booty.[74]

The British had suffered a major reverse in July 1818 when Captain Sparkes 10th Bengal Infantry with a detachment of 107 sepoys was attacked by Gonds and Arab mercenaries in Betul district.[75] Only a Naik (Corporal) and 8 men survived.[76]

The last triangular Maratha fort at Dhamaunee[77] was subjected to six hours of artillery battery and surrendered on the 23 February 1818.[78] British casualties were 19

70 H.C. Wylly, *Neills 'Blue Caps' The Madras European Regt.* (Ballydehob, Cork: Schull Books Reprint 1996) Vol.1 1639–1826.
71 V. Blacker, *A Memoir of the Operations of the British Army in India 1817, 1818, 1819* (Black, Kingsbury, Parbury and Allen, London 1821) pp. 86–90. Holkar suffered a defeat in a sharp encounter on 21 December 1817 with Colonel John Malcolm at Mehidpoor.
72 R. Reynolds, *The White Sahibs in India.* (London: Secker and Warburg, 1937) Not everyone agreed with what had been done, 'the case of the Marathas offers an unhappy and unique combination of everything that can embitter subjection.' p. 63.
73 W. Wilson, *History of the Madras Army.* 1882 Vol. IV 1746–1826 p. 52.
74 Ibid.
75 R.V. Russell, *The Tribes and Castes of the Central Provinces of India* (London: Macmillan & Co 1916) p. 39 Gonds, a large group of tribal people in the Deccan plain.
76 R.G. Burton, *The Maratha and Pindari War 1817.* Compiled for The General Staff India 1910. (Uckfield: Naval & Military Press, reprint 2004) p. 104.
77 Dhamoni, now a heritage site.
78 *Cobbets Political Register,* May, 1806 p. 702. Artillerymen in Native regiments were known collectively as 'the Golandaze or Golundaz.'

British Camp, Third Anglo–Maratha War 1817–19, by Capt. J. Barton.

officers and 308 troops killed or wounded mainly from small arms fire. The enemy suffered less with 43 killed and 95 wounded.

Hostilities ceased with the fall of the huge fortress at Asseerghur[79] in April 1819 and the two British armies gradually dispersed.

The prosecution of the War by Hastings had been entirely successful but at a cost of 750 killed, 2,500 wounded and 16 British or Native troops missing. At the siege of the Fort of Talneir, an unfortunate incident occurred which cost the lives of the enemy garrison. The British Commanders besieging Talneir sought the surrender of the garrison and fort. Whether or not there was a misunderstanding is a moot point but a party of officers and troops entered the fort through a series of unmanned wicket gates. On arrival at the final gate they were granted access but immediately attacked and Major Gordon and Captain McGregor were killed. Lt.Colonel McGregor Murray and others were severely wounded. The survivors were saved by the presence of mind of a Guardsman who prevented the wicket being closed thus allowing a rescue party to enter. The British, believing the mainly Arab garrison had behaved treacherously,

---

79   E. Thornton, *A Gazetteer of the Territories under the Government of the East India Company* Asseerghur in the Bombay Presidency. E. Lake *Journals of the Sieges of the Madras Army* (London: Kingsbury, Parbury and Allen, 1825) pp. 151–180. The fort was 1100 yards x 600 yards and accessible by only two routes, the remainder being protected by precipices 80–120 feet in height. Its capture was later commemorated in 1851 by a presentation medal issued to surviving officers and men.

Massacre of officers at Talneir from a contemporary print, 1821. (Courtesy Brown University Rhode Island USA)

put all 300 to the sword and the Killadar was summarily hanged.[80] At the time, these events were reviewed by the Court of Directors but no further action taken. Accounts however vary as to the precise circumstances and a later history denounced the British retribution as 'acts contrary to the usages of war.'[81, 82]

The Blacker and Close families

The first traceable Blacker was an earlier Valentine born in 1597 from Poppleton in Yorkshire. Both the Blacker and Close families were from Yorkshire farming stock. The Blacker family had arrived in Ireland as part of the 17th Century 'plantation of Ulster' by English and Scottish Protestants who were granted land in the Province to ensure support for the Crown and established religion. Valentine settled at the manor of Carrobrack in 1660 and re-named it Carrickblacker, county Armagh. By 1684 a

---

80   H. Yule, & A.C. Burnell, *Hobson Jobson. Glossary of Anglo-Indian Terms and Phrases.* 'Killadar' first used in 1341 the custodian of a fort or palace. Latterly the Commandant of a fort.

81   V. Blacker, *Memoir of the Operations of the British Army in India.* (London: Black, Kingsbury, Parbury & Allen, 1821) pp 228–232.

82   E. Thornton, *History of the British Empire in India*, Vol. III pp. 507–532.

descendant George Blacker was a Lieutenant Colonel and High Sheriff of Armagh who supported the Stuart cause but his son William fought at the Battle of the Boyne in 1689 for William III. His grandson, born 1743 became the Reverend Dr St. John Blacker.

The Close family first owned significant estates in county Monaghan around 1640 with later properties in Down and Armagh.The two families were united by the marriage of St. John Blacker and Grace Close of Elm Park in 1767. Thirty years later their son Valentine joined his maternal uncle, the Adjutant General of the Madras Army in India.

Lieutenant Colonel Barry Close was born in 1756, joining the HEIC Madras Army in 1771 as an Infantry cadet in the 20th Madras Native Infantry. Commissioned Ensign in 1773 he was promoted Lieutenant and appointed Adjutant in 1777. A Captain by 1783 in 1790 he was appointed Deputy Adjutant General of the Madras Army. Promoted to Major in 1796 this was quickly followed by promotion to Lieutenant Colonel in 1797. By the time of his nephew Valentine's arrival, Close was the Adjutant General of the Army, a fluent Persian speaker and acting Chief of Staff to General Harris. His skill and 'extraordinary talents' during the 4th Anglo–Mysore War resulting in the victory over Tippoo Sultan in 1799 gained him a presentation sword from the Directors of the Honourable Company. His was the first appointment as the Resident Agent to the Mysore Court. Remaining a 'Political Officer'[83] he was posted to Poona in

Major General Sir Barry Close (1756–1813), Adjutant General Madras.

1801 where he was instrumental in assisting the Governor General to ascertain the full extent of problems within the Maratha confederacy.[84] A full Colonel in 1803 Close remained at Poonah until July 1806 when he took charge of troops, unnecessarily as it turned out, to suppress the mutiny at Vellore.[85] He was later sent to Hyderabad to deal with the serious disturbance and indiscipline over allowances and pay amongst officers

83   Political Officer: Indian Political Service formed in 1783. HEIC and Kings Regiment Officers were assigned to 'political' duties with native Indian rulers and tribes. Officers retained their ranks and salaries and were promoted within the service <https://en.wikipedia.org/wiki/Indian_Political_Department> (accessed August 2017).
84   Poonah, a city South East of Madras which was the Maratha capital for two hundred years. From 1800 a Resident Agent was present but the City was seized and governed by the British after the 3rd Anglo Maratha War. Now Pune.
85   'The Mutiny' had been suppressed. See letter 18 October 1806.

of The Madras Army in 1809 taking his nephew Valentine with him.[86] Retiring as a Major General in 1812 and awarded a Baronetcy he returned to the UK where he died unmarried in 1813. A monument, originally destined for St Paul's Cathedral, was eventually erected to his memory at St. Mary's Church, Madras in 1819. Close was a major factor in determining Valentine's career in India together with that of his other nephews and relatives. His had been a key role in welcoming and 'mentoring' Valentine, marking his progress in the Madras Army. Arthur Wellesley not known for hyperbole, said of Close, 'he is by far the ablest man in the Company's Army.'

The Life of Valentine Blacker

Valentine Blacker was born on 19 October 1778 in Armagh, probably at Elm Park, a large country residence owned by his maternal grandparents.[87] He was baptised on 26 October the same year. His father the Rev. Dr St. John Blacker, a clerk in Holy Orders, rector of Moira, and afterwards prebendary of Inver was born 28 September 1743 and had married Grace, daughter of Maxwell Close Esq in October 1767. Her family resided at Elm Park, county Armagh and she was the sister of the Army officer in India, Lieutenant Colonel Barry Close. Valentine Blacker was the second youngest of five brothers, one of whom, St. John joined him in the Company's military service in India. There were four sisters of whom Grace and Charlotte, his younger sisters also travelled to India. His cousin Robert Close went to India with St. John where they were assisted and mentored by Valentine. Little is known of Valentine's childhood or adolescence although there is reference in his letters to being a member of the Yeomanry: which regiment of Yeomanry is not established, the County Armagh Yeomanry founded in 1796 or the Cheshire Yeomany founded in 1797 are the most likely considerations.[88] 1798 was clearly a momentous year for the Blackers. The Rev Dr St. J. Blacker aged 55 years had moved to Chester where his wife Grace died and Valentine left home to join the Honourable East India Company's Army.

Valentine's application record is comprised of a one line entry. His baptism confirmation[89] signed by his father and his Madras Army Service number 889. It also shows his sponsor as Thomas Fitzhugh, a Director of the East India Company.[90]

---

86 See letter 4 September 1809.
87 S. Barden, *Elm Park 1626–1954.* (Belfast: Ulster Historical Foundation, 2004) A 17th Century mansion owned by the Close family near Killylea 5 m. west of Armagh Northern Ireland. In 1922 became a school which closed in 1954.
88 See letter 6th October 1798.
89 Africa & Asian Collection IOR/L/MIL/9/108/356 dated 8th March 1798. His baptism was dated 26/10/1778.
90 <http://www.academia.edu> Thomas Fitzhugh 1728–1800. Director of the HEIC for various periods from 1785 to 1799. His final period in office 1797–1799 co-incides with Valentine Blackers application. Fitzhugh owned property in Denbighshire and London. It has not been possible to establish the exact relationship with the Blacker family.

Doubtless as he gathered together what he considered the necessities of his future life he was 'gulled' like most 'Griffins' by shopkeepers and outfitters into purchasing an excess of equipment;[91] 'just so much plunder' for tradesmen was how an Officer Cadet of the Bombay Army expressed it.[92] Valentine makes reference to 'his desk' on board the ship taking him to India presumably in the belief that such an article was impossible to find in the sub-continent. A later booklet published in 1820 indicates how essential letters of introduction are for a Cadet arriving in India and provided guidance on a range of equipment and clothing necessary for travel to the sub-continent including three large 3' trunks for clothing, one 2' 6" trunk of books plus a hat box and bedding.[93]

Valentine left the United Kingdom from Portsmouth on board '*The Berrington*' built at London in 1783 with three decks, 144 ft in length and owned by Donald Cameron but used in the service of the HEIC until 1798. It was later sold to a Thomas Newte but continued in service with the HEIC until 1799. The Captain of *The Berrington* during Valentine's voyage 1798–99 was a George Robertson and the fare cost £95.

The young recruit recorded incidents which occurred during the 16 week journey in letters home to his father providing a picture of the tedium suffered by travellers on those lengthy sea voyages, not to mention sea sickness and having to endure the same company day after day.[94] The ceremony of 'the crossing of the equator' passed off with him being shaved, followed by his expressions of disappointment at lack of progress and then excitement at the arrival of an Albatross and a butterfly.

On 29 September at 0500hrs he recorded: 'Land. Land. We are at last gratified with this long wished for prospect.'

At a time when status, influence and patronage counted for everything Valentine was thus triply blessed ; after his boat successfully negotiated the dangerous Madras surf and in receipt of a letter welcoming him to India, he stepped ashore and a waiting palanquin promptly conveyed him to the stately residence of his uncle, Lieutenant Colonel Barry Close, the Adjutant General of the Madras Army.[95]

Valentine's arrival had coincided with a troublesome recurrence of French intrigue resulting in the the outbreak of the final war with the Kingdom of Mysore. The

---

91   C. D'oyley, *Tom Raw, The Griffin* (London: R. Ackermann, 1824) a term seemingly first used in 17th century and popular at Madras, denoting a person, usually a military cadet, new to India and unfamiliar with the life and culture.

92   F. Hitchman, *Richard Francis Burton KCMG, His early Public and Private Life* (London: Sampson Low, 1887) Vol. I p. 111–112. Sir Richard Francis Burton, Soldier, Traveller and Author. 1821–1890. An officer in the Bombay Army 1842–53.

93   *A Cadets Guide to India.* By A Lieutenant of the Bengal Establishment (London: Black, Kingsbury, Parbury & Allen. London, 1820).

94   F. Hitchman. *Burton*, 'all begin by talking together and end up talking to themselves' Vol. I p. 113. Valentine after a few weeks describes himself as extremely busy!

95   British Library Africa and Asia Collection ref. WD 856. The Garden House, the residence of Barry Close. It may have still been in existence in 1817 when The Garden House, Madras was resided in by a Colonel Mackenzie.

first hint of which in the Letters occurs in one from Lieutenant Colonel Close to Valentine's father. He refers to: 'our neighbour Tippoo is in close correspondence with them' (the French) ... 'In case of war we shall be strong in men, but our finances are in an exhausted state.'

Valentine did not enter into military life immediately but spent time acclimatising himself and studying Hindi and Urdu, the most common and phonetically similar languages. Initially he accepted his uncle's advice to enter the Infantry and having been promoted Ensign on 27 August 1798 was posted to the 2nd Battalion 12th Regiment of Native Foot on 6 October 1798.[96] During that month however he met a group of senior army officers at his uncle's house and General George Harris told him that he 'should have the first vacancy in the Horse.'[97] A Madras Cavalry Regiment would probably have been his first choice but he was posted in January 1799 as a Cornet to 1st Regiment of Native Horse in the Nizam of Hyderabad's Service. The Regiment was commanded by Lt. Colonel K. Macallister:[98] Valentine was promoted Lieutenant on 4 September 1799.

In 1799 the establishment of The 1st Regiment of Native Horse comprised of:

1 Lieutenant Colonel	24 Havildars
1 Major	24 Naiks
2 Captains	6 Trumpeters
1 Captain Lieutenant.	420 Troopers/Sowars
6 Cornets	6 Puckallies[1]
2 Sergeants	1 Surgeon
6 Subadars	1 Assistant Surgeon
12 Jemadars	

Note
1   H. Yule, & A.C. Burnell, *Glossary of Colloquial Anglo-Indian Terms and Phrases*. Puckauly, a man who fills the 20 gallon water skins and delivers them on a bullock, 'a water carrier.' In Madras there were 10 Puckallies per Cavalry Regiment.

96   W. Wilson, *History of the Madras Army*. 29th November 1782 'orders were given for the completion of the establishment of the 12th Battalion' then fixed at 35 Battns. each of nine companys. Vol. II pp. 125 & 173.
97   See letter 1st October 1798.
98   E. Dodswell, & J. Miles, *An Alphabetical List of the Officers of the Indian Army 1760–1834*. Joined HEIC 1777, Lieutenant, 1778, Captain1796, Lieutenant Colonel 1799, Major General 1809, Lieutenant Gen 1812. Died 1820 England.

During 1798 Arthur Wellesley and his brother, Richard the Governor General, had determined that the forces of the Nizam posed an unwarrantable risk by virtue of it being staffed by French officers. The pair contrived, by artifice and threat, to purge the officers from the Nizam's army and by October 1798 the French Officers had left and a 'subsidiary force' established. This was quickly replaced by The Nizam of Hyderabads Contingent with British Officers. Valentine participated in the 4th Anglo Mysore War later becoming Adjutant and second in command of the 1st Regiment Native Horse. He records these early days of service, forbearing to mention as to whether he was aware of any shortcomings in the troops performance which was indicated later in September 1803 when Arthur Wellesley described the Contingent as 'worse than useless.'[99] (By 1809 matters may have improved. A report described the 1st Regiment of Native Horse as 'well composed. The men are small but connected together and of good description and caste'.)

Promotion within the Madras Army, to which the Contingent was attached, was within each regiment until the rank of Major was reached when it reverted to the whole Corps. There was also a battery of Horse Artillery with each regiment but this attachment was abolished in 1819.

India was to be Valentine's life and home for the next 27 years: achieving high rank in the Madras Army, author of a major published military work, appointed Surveyor General of The Survey of India and recipient of a significant honour from his King and the British Government.

Valentine's letters commence in 1798 when he was first in the Infantry to 1813 by which time he was the Quartermaster General of the Madras Army. Writing of his posting to the 12th Regiment of Foot in 1799, a brief mention of a subsequent transfer to the Madras Cavalry and then writing with clear excitement describing his new uniform as a Cornet in The Nizam's Contingent. He participated in the early stages of 4th Anglo–Mysore War becoming Adjutant and second in command of the Contingent and witnessed the 19th Dragoons[100] 'pistolling' wounded men left on the battlefield.[101] Unfortunately, due to illness, he missed the siege and storming of Seringapatam resulting in the death of Tippoo Sultan.

In December 1799 Lt. Colonel Barry Close was appointed the Resident Agent at Mysore and Valentine became the commander of his uncle's cavalry escort.[102] In 1800 during operations at Wynaad against Varma Pazhassi, Rajah of Kottayam.[103] he was

99   R.G. Burton,. *A History of the Hyderabad Contingent* (Calcutta: Office of the Superintendent of Government Printing, 1905). pp. 8–17.
100 19th Light Dragoons, founded in 1781 and initially numbered the 23rd for service in India. Renumbered to 19th 1786. Fought at Seringapatam, Assaye and Vellore, remained in India until 1806. Disbanded 1821 <https://wiki.fibis.org/w/19th_Lancers> (accessed August 2017).
101 See letter 27th March 1799.
102 See letter 20th December 1799.
103 Pazhassi, the Rajah, under the influence of the former Ruler of Mysore had waged a guerilla war against the British post Tippoo's death. He was finally killed and the district

appointed Aide de Camp to Colonel Stevenson. Whilst fighting in the 2nd Poligar War of 1801 Valentine sustained a leg wound, had his horse killed and was mentioned in despatches. He was appointed Military Secretary to Brigadier Pater[104] in 1802 who commanded the Southern Division. Before joining General David Baird's army in the 2nd Maratha War he was appointed Captain of Guides and Assistant Quartermaster General of the Madras Army.[105] Between July 1804 and April 1805 he was temporarily in charge of the Quartermaster General's Dept., and led an attack against Droog forts at Neural and Moogral.[106]

The Quartermaster General at Fort St George, Alexander Orr,[107] in August 1806 wrote a glowing testimonial of Valentine to Lt. General Sir J.F. Cradock,[108] K.C.B. C-in-C Madras,

> I consider it no less an act of justice than a duty incumbent on me, before I quit the station of Quartermaster General to state to your excellency my opinion of the merits of Captain Blacker, who for a period of nearly four years, has been my assistant in office, and Captain of Guides. In carrying on the duties of my department, I have ever found the utmost readiness in Captain B to afford me his assistance: which from his active zeal, his general and local knowledge, and his professional talents, could not fail to be attended with beneficial consequences. His skill in regulating the marches of troops, in pointing out the most proper ground for encampments, and in providing the supplies of an army is well known to those officers who served with the army in the field under General Stuart in 1803. Captain Blacker has been indefatigable in instructing the native guides in the principles of geometry and surveying and he has brought that corps to a degree of perfection in their duties which was never before equalled.[109]

of Wynaad now Wayanad, Kerala was annexed <en.wikipedia.org> (accessed August 2017).
104 E. Dodswell & J. Miles, *Alphabetical List of the Officers of the Indian Army 1760–1834.* Captain 1782, Major 1790, Lt. Colonel 1796, Colonel 1798, Major General 1805. Retired 1812, d.1817. Commanded 2nd Brigade Cavalry at Seringapatam 1799.
105 K. Phythian Adams, *The Madras Soldier 1746–1946* (Madras: The Government Press 1948) p. 158. The Madras Corps of Guides formed in 1787 but their role was changed to surveying 4 years later (not to be confused with Queen Victoria's Own Corps of Guides).
106 J. Bell, 'A System of Geography' (Glasgow: A, Fullerton & Co.1832) 6 vols. Droogs: Isolated rock forts usually commanding narrow passes.
107 E. Dodswell & J. Miles, *Alphabetical List of the Officers of the Indian Army 1760–1834.* Orr appointed Cadet Madras Army in 1781, Lieutenant, 1788, Captain 1798, Major 1803 Lt. Colonel 1805, retired 1809.
108 Cambridge Alumni Database, Major General John Francis Cradock, 1st Baron Howden 1759–1839. He replaced General, James Stuart as C-inC from 1804–1807, his only tour of duty in India <http://venn.lib.cam.ac.uk< (accessed August 2017).
109 *The East India Military Calendar, 1823* (Uckfield: Naval and Military Press Reprint 2007) Vol. I p. 322.

The appointment to the Company's Army of his brother St. John and his arrival in India together with his cousin Robert Close caused Valentine much pleasure as well as considerable fretting over their health and future prospects.

In 1806 he was appointed Deputy Quartermaster General and later joined the military operations commanded by Colonel J. Chalmers at Quilon.[110]

His two spinster sisters, Grace and Charlotte travelled to India in 1808 and rapidly made 'good marriages'. Valentine does not mention either of these forthcoming events until after they had taken place. This is not surprising given the delay of the mail and that courtships and marriages were conducted with a speed which would have been regarded as 'with undue haste' in the UK. The Indian climate frequently proved lethal and disease could strike from nowhere, 'rendering a healthy man at breakfast, dead by midnight.'[111]

Charlotte married on 8 December 1808, Colonel John Munro a former Quartermaster General of the Madras Army and a 'political officer'. During 1809 Valentine and Munro were involved in countering the open rebellion of the Madras Army Officers over 'Tent Contracts'.[112]

Charlottes sister Grace was married on 6 May 1809 to Robert Alexander a civil servant.[113]

In July 1809 Valentine returned to St. Thomas Mount, Madras, to take charge of the Quartermaster General Dept. and marched with Colonel Close to Seronge on military operations. From there in April 1810 he was recalled to HQ and whilst still holding a Captains' rank appointed Quartermaster General, an appointment he retained until 1823. Captain Blacker's status was a focus for comment in an extract from a secret minute of 27 August 1810 by General Hewitt,

> The evil of appointing officers deficient in rank, however eminently qualified by talent for these appointments I have already noticed: but I hope it will not be supposed that I am casting the slightest reflection on the deserving officers now holding the appointments of Adj. General and Quart. Mast. General, who, though but permanent Captains are yet, in zeal and talent every way qualified

110 E. Dodswell, & J. Miles, *Alphabetical List of the Officers of the Indian Army 1760–1834*, Col,. Sir John Chalmers K.C.B. b.1755.joined HEIC 1775, Ensign 1776, Lieutenant, 1780, Captain 1792, Major 1796, Lt. Colonel 1799, Colonel 1809, Major General 1812. Commanded 17th Madras Native Infantry during rebellion at Cochin and Travancore. Died at sea 1818 en route to UK.

111 A. De Courcy, *The Fishing Fleet, Husband Hunting in the Raj*. (London: Weidenfield and Nicholson, 2012) p. 241.

112 F. Mount, *The Tears of the Rajahs, India 1805–1905*. (London: Simon & Schuster, 2016) Referred to as a 'scam to be tidied up' p. 82, the contract was established in 1802 whereby CO's were responsible for the contracts necessary for logistics when mobilised. See letter 4 September 1809 and footnote.

113 Robert Alexander is listed as a member of the Governor in Council at the Supreme Court of Madras 1814.

to discharge the duties entrusted to them with credit to themselves and benefit to the service.'[114]

On the 6 July 1812 Lieutenant General Sir Samuel Auchmuty, Commander in Chief wrote:

> Nor can I conclude this paragraph without recording my entire approbation of the zeal, ability and general information which prove the judicious selection of Lieutenant Colonel Blacker for the office of quart. mast.-gen of the army, which he fills to my entire satisfaction and with every advantage to the public services.[115]

During Valentine's later correspondence it is noticeable that the subject matters on military affairs diminish and focus more on family and property.

On 22 December 1813 Valentine married Emma Johnson at St. Mary's Church, Fort St George, Madras[116] and they resided in Valentine's nine acre garden residence known as Blackers Gardens in Mount Road, Teynampett, Madras. There were four children from the union, Samuel Valentine Barry, Maxwell, Murray McGregor,[117] Emma Louise Rosa.

The final copy letter in the letter book was written on 5 August 1813 to his Father and was received by him on 22 December 1813 the date of Valentine's marriage to Emma Johnson. There is no mention in his last letter of any forthcoming nuptials.

During the years 1813 and 1814 we have little written information about Valentine, his life or activity. In his role as Quartermaster General on 4 February 1814 he had 'signed off' the Madras Army accounts for the years 1811–1813 together with The Commissary General William Cowper both reporting on savings and reductions of 3,666,324 Pagodas.[118]

114 *East India Military Calendar, 1823* (Uckfield: Naval and Military Press, Reprint 2007) Vol. 1. pp. 323–324. Lieutenant General George Hewitt. C-in-C Madras 10 April 1810–27 Sept. 1810.

115 Valentine Blacker was still a substantive Captain (see Service record). It is difficult to believe that Hislop made a mistake. Whether Blacker was a Lieut-Colonel by Brevet at this time is not recorded. He was not promoted into the rank until 1823.

116 The National Archive Bengal Marriages.1693–1948 N-2-5-55.

117 Samuel Valentine Barry Blacker took Holy Orders and became a Vicar in Norfolk, Maxwell Julius followed a similar path taking Holy Orders. Murray McGregor became a lawyer.

118 Africa and Asia Collection. IOR/D/156/ff 90–95.
    H. Yule, & A.C. Burnell, *Hobson Jobson, Glossary of Colloquial Anglo-Indian Terms and Phrases*, 1903. Pagoda, a gold coin peculiar to Southern India. In 1818 the Rupee became standard currency. At that time a Pagoda was worth 31/2 Rupees.

He was on active service in 1815 when attached to the 'Army of Reserve' commanded by Sir Thomas Hislop on the frontier.[119]

Hislop also considered Valentine Blacker in positive terms once he was Commander of the 'Coast Army' in November 1814, 'I have the greatest reason to think myself fortunate in having such able and zealous assistants at the head of the military departments as Lieutenant Colonels Conway, Blacker and Morison.'

During March 1816 Captain Blacker received a translation of a letter written by a Shaik Kypauly that contains the phrase, 'Pindaris were gathering with design for the greatest ravages.'[120]

He receives further evidence regarding the Pindaris from Colonel Marriot writing from his camp at Kurnaul 30 March 1816, 'as these predatory horse are present and pointing at my position I do not intend to make any movement of consequence until I can determine properly the route they will take …'

In April 1816 Captain Blacker as Quarter Master General wrote to the Chief Secretary of the Madras Government advising that Pindaris are 'plundering the Nizam's territory, the Nizam is preparing his defences and that the information is based on a native letter.'[121] Blacker then proposes to send out 'disguised sepoys and guides' to report on the situation and orders are issued for Major Knowles[122] to return to camp with 800 Silladar Horse.[123]

In 1817 Valentine was appointed Quartermaster General of the Army of the Deccan, again under the command of General Thomas Hislop during the Maratha and Pindari Wars 1817–19.[124]

Captain Valentine Blacker was sent to levy conscription in Scindiah's dominions as the Maharajah had shown little energy in producing the 5,000 cavalry which the treaty demanded. On 11 February 1818 Captain Valentine Blacker commanding 'Scindiahs' contingent of 3,000 horse joined Major General Dyson Marshall[125] at Beirseah then

119 *The East India Military Calendar* (Uckfield: Naval & Military Press 2007). p. 322. Denominated the 'Army of Reserve' due to the (operations of the Bengal Army in Nepal.
120 African & Asian Collection, IOR/H/602 Secret Despatches and Correspondence 1816.
121 African & Asian Collection, IOR/H/602 Secret Despatches and Correspondence 1816.
122 E. Dodswell,& J. Miles, J. *Alphabetical List of the Indian Army 1760–1834.* Major Joseph Knowles CB.Ensign 1796, Lieutenant 1797, Captain 1804, Major 1812, Lieutenant Colonel 1818. Died Bombay 1824.
123 H. Yule, & A.C. Burnell, *Hobson Jobson, Glossary of Colloquial Anglo-Indian Terms and Phrases.* Silladar, a system whereby a Trooper provides his own horse and arms in a unit of irregular cavalry.
     A. Macleod, *On India* (London: Longmans, 1872) pp. 112–80.
124 C.E. Buckland, *A Dictionary of Indian Biography*, General, Sir Thomas Hislop. 1st Baronet. b.1764, attended R.M.A. Woolwich. Joined 39th Regt.1778. Appointed C-in-C Bombay Army 1812. C-in-C Madras 1812. Defeated the Marathas 1817 but much criticised for severity at Talneir. Died 1843.
125 *The East India Military Calendar.* Appointed to the Bengal Army 1771, Ensign 1773, Lieutenant, 1778, Captain 1781, Major 1794, Lieutenant Colonel 1796, Colonel 1808,

marching against Saughur where the majority of the forts of the Pindaris eventually capitulated.[126, 127]

Valentine had been promoted to Major on 1 September 1818 when a Maratha chief called Ghokal Sing with a force of 3000 mainly Rajpoots troops was challenging the Government over the terms of a disputed inheritance. They should have been confronted by a Company force south of Ragooghur but by a midnight march managed to avoid battle.[128] On 22 November Sing was discovered by Major Valentine Blacker who attacked him on a confined plain. Blacker's Scindiah Contingent suffered fifty casualties. Sing was wounded three times but escaped the field which was the signal for his followers to do likewise. Ghokal Sing was later captured, released early and granted possession of the fort of Ragooghur in Malwa district.

Blacker, still commanding the Scindiah Contingent, was present at the siege and fall of Asseerghur ending the 3rd Maratha War in April 1819. His troops had enjoyed the mixed pleasure of witnessing the destruction of one of their master Scindiah's virtually impregnable and rebellious forts. Blacker describes it 'as the last effort of the Maratha struggle.'

On 14 October Major Valentine Blacker had been appointed a Companion of the Bath.[129]

After the war in addition to his military duties he was occupied for the next two years writing his *Memoir of the Operations of the British Army in India during the Maratha War 1817, 1818 and 1819.* A 494 page comprehensive account of the conflict against the Marathas and Pindaris with over 40 maps and plans. Published in 1821 the dedication is to 'The Officers of the British Army in India' simply addressed as his 'Fellow Soldiers.'

Military Surveying was a key to successful campaigns against native armies fully familiar with their own territories. Letters from Sir George Hislop between 1806–09, whilst Valentine Blacker was Deputy Quarter Master General insist that the Quartermaster General, Madras 'will be a repository for all Geographical and Topographical Surveys of Territories dependent on Fort St. George … and all maps must be transferred to the Quartermaster General.' Towards the end of the Maratha and Pindari War Blacker commented 'I likewise have in my possession material for preparing maps of the seat of the war explanatory of the movements

---

Major General 1811, Lieutenant, Gen, 1821.appointed K.C.B., died India 1823. Vol. 1 p. 395.
126 E. Thornton, *A Gazetteer of the Territories under the Government of the East India Company.* Beirseah, a town of 3000 homes in the Province of Malwah twenty miles north of Bhopal.
127 Ibid. Saughur, principal town in a district of the same name containing a large military cantonment and fort.
128 R.S. Chaurasia, *History of the Marathas* (New Delhi, Atlantic Publishing 2004) p. 152.
129 J. Perkins, *The Most Honourable Order of the Bath.* (London: The Faith Press, 1920) CB, Companion of the Order of the Bath, founded 1725. Military Officers were given a separate classification in 1815.

of several corps and topographical plans ... these may contribute to the benefit of the service.'[130]

On 14 April 1818 an officer had written from Madras, 'Blacker and Morrison are coming overland from Poonah by way of Beerapore – the former intends to complete from routes a map of the theatre of the war.'

Blacker sailed with the C-in-C Sir George Hislop and returned to Calcutta on 30 April 1820 which he spent working on the 'prize committee'[131] until 8 July.

A note by the Military Secretary to the Commander in Chief dated 31 July 1821 states that Valentine Blacker was 'permitted to resign the position of Quartermaster General of the Army to return to Europe on sick certificate' and expressed the 'high sense of the eminent and scientific services of Lt. Colonel Blacker as Quartermaster General during a period of ten years.'[132] It is also fair to say that he came back to the UK to finalise the publication of his book.

Blacker had written his will in 1817 but in codicils dated 27 January 1821 there were reversions to his children in the event of Emma's re-marriage.

It may be that the effects of his campaigning in the Deccan had a deleterious effect on his health as by 9 January 1822 he was in Europe, 'medical advisers having strongly urged me to pass the present winter in the mild climate of the south.'

Whilst in Florence in December 1822 he was informed by the Directors of The East India Company that he was to be the Surveyor General of India and that they hoped he could proceed to that appointment in Spring 1823.[133] Valentine applied for an extension of leave on medical grounds which was granted but a further application for an extension to September 1823 was refused. His colleague George Everest wrote in an undated letter 'Blacker is very ill in France and not expected before the end of the year.' His health must have improved as Valentine left England in June 1823 and returned to Calcutta to his new appointment in command of the Trigonometrical Survey of India as Surveyor General and promoted Lieutenant Colonel to be based in Calcutta.[134] He had enjoyed a previous brief experience in the survey role around Mysore in 1800 during which he had nurtured hopes of an early appointment and had prematurely purchased survey instruments.[135] His captaincy and leadership of

130 African and Asian Collection IOR/MIL/8/381, pp 161–163.
131 See letter dated 28 February 1808.
132 HEIC Army Officers returning to the UK on furlough had to relinquish their regimental post or staff appointment and seek a new military appointment on return.
133 B. Crosbie, *Irish Imperial Networks* (Cambridge: University Press, 2012). A clear suggestion made by the Author that, unsurprisingly, the appointment was 'helped by strong family connections and influential patrons.'
134 The Trigonometrical Survey of India known as the Great Survey was commenced in 1802 and conducted by HEIC Army Officers. Its purpose was to scientifically measure the sub-Continent of India but was independent of the Topographical and Revenue Surveys until 1875 when all three were amalgamated. <www.surveyofindia.gov.in> (accessed August 2017).
135 See letter 26 August 1800.

the Madras Guides had stood him in good stead too as he took charge of the Survey Department from the tenure of Major General John Anthony Hodgson.[136]

Immediately elected to The Asiatic Society of Bengal he produced and read two papers on Barometers and Atmospheric Hygrometers.[137]

Accurate maps were of strategic importance to the Army and Valentine's was a key appointment co-inciding with the East India Company's further territorial expansion which required a 'single coherent scientific institution to make sense' of the accumulated geographical records and papers. The Great Trigonometrical Survey was established in Calcutta, the capital of British India in order that the 'disparate Presidencies' could be monitored and a controlling influence exerted over the acquisition of scientific knowledge, essential for the single cartographic image of India.

In his new role he took a strong line on the importance of the Great Trigonometrical Survey as the only foundation for surveys and maps. In a letter on 11 August 1824 he states that: 'the case is beyond challenge' and maintained an insistence for a uniform system of maps and surveys, especially the new four miles to the inch atlas later adapted from France. He raised the levels of awareness on the importance of Trigonometrical Surveying and persuaded the Directors of The Company on the imperative of an Ordnance Survey similar to that commenced in his native country of Ireland in 1824.[138]

Although Lieutenant Colonel Blacker may have written a pamphlet entitled 'Construction of a graticule for a General Atlas of India' this bore little resemblance to the first published sheets which were not published until 1827.[139]

His health however showed signs of weakening, on 24 January 1824 he wrote,' I am severely afflicted with rheumatism and obliged to use the pen of another' and again in June 'I am positively prohibited from stirring out while the sun is up.'[140]

Valentine's early military experiences had been blighted by 'fever' but the incidence of illness seems to have abated later in his career or at least do not feature largely in his letters. His letters do not reveal a lifestyle that would provide an indicator for his later ill health. No record of extravagant meals followed by drinking bouts indeed the opposite is true. There is no indication of him having smoked nor is it likely that he would write to his father, a clergyman, about any soldierly exploits with prostitutes,

136 E. Dodswell & J. Miles *Alphabetical List of the Officers of the Indian Army 1760–1834*, J.A. Hodgson 1777–1848, entered 10th Native Infantry HEIC 1798, Lieutenant 1800, Captain 1814, Major 1824, Lieutenant Colonel 1828. Surveyor General of India 1821–23, 1826–29.
137 National Archive of India. Blacker, V. *Register of Meteorological Observations*, Surveyors General's Office, Calcutta 1825.
138 B. Crosbie, *Irish Imperial Network*, 2012.
139 C. Markham, *A Memoir of the Indian Surveys*. (London: W. Allen & Co.1872) p. 437.
140 R.H. Phillimore, *Biographical Records of The Survey of India. 1815–1830* Vol. 3 (Calcutta, The Surveyor General, 1945).

a major source of illness within the HEIC military.[141] Casual mistresses, 'sleeping dictionaries' were the general pattern for officers but the arrival of his brother and sisters in Madras would have terminated any such relationship. Generally speaking he appears to have led a healthy life and determining any factor accounting for his later 'rheumatism' is nigh impossible. Clinically the symptoms would have been recognisable but any treatment relatively ineffective.

Illness was a recurring problem for all Europeans and during the earlier years his sickness absence must have been substantial but unremarkable for the time.

Other than family Valentine's major preoccupation was with money and how military positions were remunerated. Men were judged mainly on their status which directly linked to their income or at least their prospects. His moral stance on 'profiteering' from lucrative roles is commendable in an age when it was seen as a perquisite and he maintains a strong sense of integrity towards how his income is earned and refuses to 'milk the system' contrary to many of his colleagues. The fact that nepotism, merely a different form of corruption, was virtually endemic would have been lost on him as that is how society at his level operated. By the standards of his day he was 'the pea green incorruptible.'

Somewhat surprisingly the Letters contain very little of a religious dimension which so frequently plagues the diaries and letters of military men whose proselytizing makes for tedious reading.[142] He does display the racial attitudes of the day both towards the native population generally and their beliefs. Religion, however does not appear to be a factor in his life as there is no reference to worship, regimental church parades or attendance at Sunday church services.

Valentine Blacker died on 4 February 1826 as a result of 'a fever.' His colleague Everest wrote 'Colonel Blacker fell a victim to fever contracted, it is supposed, from the noisome vapours generated by the cleaning of an old tank in the grounds of the Surveyor General's Office.'[143] He was buried in South Park St. Cemetery Calcutta.[144] His estate was valued at 60000 Rs.[145]

---

141 E. Wald, *Vice in the Barracks 1780–1868.* (London, Palgrave 2014) p. 48. A 24 percent average sickness rate from venereal infections 1802–35 among the ranks. It is unlikely that officers differed to any greater extent.

142 1) H.T.B St. John, *All is Well, Letters and Journals* (London: J. Jackson, 1847). St John was a Lieutenant, in the 1st Regiment Madras Native Infantry, 2) H. Eyrl, *Diary of Private 3905 Henry Eyrl, 19th regiment of Foot, The Green Howards, 1855–62,* unpublished (Leicestershire and Rutland Record Office. Ref. DE1633).

143 R.H. Phillimore, *Biographical Records of The Survey of India. 1815–1830,* Vol. 3. Medical Boards recorded incidents of sickness in Regiments at an average of 5 percent for 'Fever, flux, hepatitis and other disease'. Blacker's death is unlikely to have had any significant relationship with his rheumatism and probably stemmed from a bacterial source.

144 The National Archive, Bengal Deaths and Burials N-1-16-105. South Park St. Cemetery opened in 1767 and used until 1830 for Christian burials. Contains approx. 1600 tombs and is now a heritage site. The road has been re-named.

145 *The Daily Telegraph* 17 January 2017 carried an obituary of David Blacker. During his life he had maintained that his ancestor 'Colonel Valentine Blacker, was Surveyor General of

A later Surveyor General described Valentine Blacker: 'with the exception of Colonel George Everest [he] was the ablest and most scientific man that ever presided over this expensive department.'[146]

Service: Valentine Blacker, Madras Army[1]

2nd Battn 12th Regiment of Native Foot	Oct 1798	Ensign
1st Regiment The Nizam of Hyderabad's Horse	Jan 1799	Cornet, 2nd Lieutenant and Adjutant
Bodyguard Escort to The Resident of Mysore	Dec 1799	1st Lieutenant
2nd Regiment of Madras Native Cavalry	Apr 1800	
Resumed as o/i/c Bodyguard Escort	Apr 1800	
1st Regiment The Nizam of Hyderabad's Horse	1801	
Military Secretary to C/O Southern Div.	1802	Lieutenant and Brigade Major
Captain Commandant of Guides, QMG Dept.	1803	Captain/Lieutenant[2]
Assistant Quartermaster General Dept Madras Army		
Assistant Quartermaster General Dept	1804	Captain
Deputy Quartermaster General	1806	
Quartermaster General	1810	
	1814	Brevet Major
	1818	Major
Surveyor General, India	1823	Lieutenant Colonel

Notes
1   E. Dodswell, & J. Miles, J. Alphabetical List of the *Officers of the Indian Army, Madras Army pp.12–13. The East Indies Military Calendar, pp. 321–5.*
2   Captain Lieutenant; with the rank of Captain but receiving Lieutenants pay.

India and died in a duel over a woman (in which his opponent also died) in Calcutta in 1823.' Such family stories abound but there is no evidence to support this.
146   C.E. Buckland, *A Dictionary of Indian Biography*, Major General Andrew Waugh, Surveyor General India, 1843–61. Waugh identified and named Mount Everest.

The Letters

Letter Books first appeared in the late 17th century and became increasingly popular in literate families where close relatives were abroad and provided a chronological account of events for the wider family to enjoy.

Mail to and from India took at least three months depending on sailing times and the weather. Ships were frequently lost or captured during hostilities, with post on captured British vessels opened by the French for obvious reasons, then usually forwarded on much later to the addressee.

The Letter Book of Valentine Blacker is a manuscript copy of letters addressed to his father St. John Blacker. The originals are presumably lost but someone, most likely his father, faithfully wrote out a copy of each letter in the order they were received into a bound single volume. The dates of receipt are not recorded until March 1802. The handwriting appears to be the same over the fifteen years that Valentine sent his letters and we rely on the 18th century clergyman for the accuracy of the copying: an opportunity to compare the original with a copy actually occured on 2 August 1804 when Valentine's father copied out the original letter and then reproduced a second copy with his own corrections and amendments but the substance of the letter is unchanged. Although Valentine had no pretensions regarding the publication of his letters he encouraged his father to produce and edit the Letter Book which provides an excellent record and example of the life of a young Army Cavalry Officer in India. Given that Valentine was often writing from tented camps, with limited materials and suffering 'from bile' or the after effects of fever they are a remarkable record of the routine of 18th – 19th century military life. His participation in three 'colonial' wars, battle wounds, struggles with sickness, deaths of friends, colleagues and his horses, the excitement at the receipt of letters, disappointment when they fail to arrive and the continual yearning for news of home. The majority of the letters were written early during his time in India doubtless indicating a degree of homesickness. Additionally, the letters offer an occasional glimpse of an officer's social life with the hierarchical conventions that were so rigidly observed.

The Letter Book is a leather bound quarto volume with ruled pages and the name 'Valentine' stamped in gold on the spine. The 183 pages are closely written with approximately 500 words to the page and cover the period from July 1798 to August 1813.

It is not clear why the letters cease in 1813. That Valentine had ceased to write home seems unlikely, alternatively perhaps his father just ceased to copy them. The Rev. Dr St. John Blacker would have been aged 70 in 1813 and although there is no available record of the date of his death he must have died at some time between 1813 and probate being granted for his will on 16 August 1815.[1]

In 1962 The Letter Book was purchased by The Rubenstein Library of Duke University, North Carolina, USA from Winifred Myers, an antiquarian bookseller in London. It remains in the USA and has never been published.[2]

1   National Archive reference Prob.11/1571/282.
2   Some authorities have given that the letter book was published in 1798. Given that this was the first year of the letters commencing and did not finish until 1813 clearly this was not possible.

THE LETTER BOOK OF VALENTINE BLACKER 1798–1813

1798

Valentine Blacker to his Father Rev Dr St John Blacker

13 July 1798

After my last despatch by the *Calcutta*,[3] which probably may not arrive with you as soon as this as they are to lie at Saint Helena for the homeward bound, I found nothing to engross a sheet of paper as the novelty of the objects at sea began to wear off and seeing and conversing with the same company still afforded no new occurrences to expatiate upon. This joined to a weeks seasickness and an unwillingness to persuade myself there was any urgent necessity to begin today what I thought may as well be done tomorrow prevented my continuing anything in the form of a journal. From this I hope you will not conclude that I was inattentive to everything as I happened to be for short time in writing to England: on the contrary I have been extremely busy. A worthy descendant of Sir William Temple is my chief companion, we have our alloted hours for walking and reading, his only fault is he is rather too generous, for not content with allowing me the use of his library he has made me a present of about two dozen of the most valuable books. If possible we shall all be in the same Regiment, he was to have gone into the church but the Bishop of Derry an intimate of his father forgot his promise: and my friend changed his design of entry into the church to that of going to India in quality of cadet. I hope it won't tire you to give you a further attempt of Colonel Carlisle's goodness to me.[4] When I was indisposed he insisted on my keeping possession of his cabin and takes all opportunities of giving me information concerning the country I am going to and describing my uncle to me. "When you go to Madras you will inquire for the Adjutant General's office and there you'll see a little black bearded, yellow complexion man with dark penetrating eyes. You'll deliver your letters and as such is his manner that he'll never probably offer to shake your hands with you but say perhaps to some of his intimates, 'I shan't open my self to this lad till I see what he is made of.' That will be your time to be on your guard and show yourself worthy of his patronage."

In advancing towards the line we had a continuation of our good weather till we got into a latitude where we met a calm and made little progress for some days, at length a breeze sprung up and a wafted us to our shaving ground.

3   W. Hickey, *Memoirs of William Hickey*. (London: Hurst and Blackett, 1925) Vol. IV p. 421. *The Calcutta*. An East Indiaman built in 1788 and served with HEIC until 1795 when taken into service by the Royal Navy. Captured in 1807 by the French.

4   E. Dodswell, & J. Miles, *Alphabetical List of the Officers of the Indian Army 1760–1834*. pp. 30–31 There are two Charles Carlisle's listed joining the Madras Army in 1778. In 3 out of 5 promotions the dates are identical and the year of death for both is 1804.

My opinion of my own ability is not so very great that I should attempt to describe this highly tragicomical stunt after so many able men/see Sir G. Stauntons Embassy to China/(sic) had I not been desired so to do by my dear friends at Chester, whose orders I shall ever obey.

A lengthy description of the ancient mariners ceremony of crossing the equator involving shaving and dousings with water has been omitted.

After being shaved we were becalmed for a few days, when a south east trade wind blew but not having enough of the eastern we were obliged to run towards the American Coast and from thence we ran in a direction and straight for Rio De Janeiro. Anxious were our hopes that we might put in there which increased as we have advanced to it, till arriving at within two day sail of it, the North East Trade blew and carried us off in an Easterly direction.

All our hopes of seeing the land were blasted for some time and we began to comfort ourselves with the expectation of touching at the Cape. We had hoped to have got some vegetables at Rio De Janeiro as we have been living on animal food and musty biscuit with stinking water ever since we crossed the Tropic of Capricorn. The wind in this latitude at this season of the year in general blows very strong but fair so that we proceed nearly 200 miles a day on average and that we may not be at loss for employment the Captain exercises the great guns and has fixed on me among the other active young men to handle one of the sponges. Exercising the small arms is often an evening amusement where I have been promoted to my old post of fugal man.[5]

A calm which still continues to impede our progress sometimes affords us amusement of being able to catch sharks and watch the whales which come in great numbers about the ship even by times within the ships length of us. I had formed a very different opinion on the sharks size having heard the many accounts heard and seen frequently of the swallowing a man's body sometimes but this, none of the sharks I have seen, could do by any means. Their means of hauling the animal into the ship requires a good deal of dexterity and is rewarded with an extraordinary share when he is cut up. As soon as the shark is hooked a man goes down by a rope onto the water and slips a loop over the fishes head and tail. Should the man not be expert or the shark break off the sailor's life is in all probability gone, but being nicely slipped over they are both hauled up. The last one we caught was so ravenous as to lay hold in its teeth of the cat's head, a large piece of wood that is near the head of the ship and it held it so hard that five of its teeth were left sunk in the wood in forcing it away.

Two thousand words on life at sea on The Berrington has been omitted until the ship is close to the Indian coast and approaching Madras.

I have got everything ready to land at the minutes warning and by Colonel Carlisle's advice I have a note written to my uncle, informing him that I am arrived per the *Berrington* after a prosperous voyage of 16 weeks and that I shall wait on him with

---

5   *Concise Oxford Dictionary* (Oxford: Clarendon Press, 1954). A Fugal man: 'A soldier placed in front of a regiment whilst drilling to show the motions and time.'

letters from England by the first boat, this I am ready to dispatch by the first boat that comes to see who we are.

28th September 1798

It now approaches 12 and everyone is impatient to know where we are as no land has been seen yet and several false alarms given. There is one circumstance that has stopped every one which is that there was scarcely three days intervention between the time considered our landing, as a distant object or rather endeavored not to think about it at all, and the time when we began to suppose ourselves on the point of getting ashore.

The beautiful skies we have every evening at sunset would baffle the pencil of Gilpin himself. They are interspersed with tints that I as an inhabitant of England has no idea of. The most beautiful blues quite unlike what it is generally termed the sky blue with orange, yellow even sometimes of verdigrease green. Whilst we were admiring one of these fine evening prospects some days ago we were surprised with the appearance of breakers near us and were accordingly on the lookout however we did not run on any rocks.

29 September 1798

5 o'clock in the morning. Land. Land. We are at last gratified with the long wished for prospect and a most delightful one it is. A flat country thickly planted but here and there diversified with dark blue mountains. The Nabob of Arcot's palace and magnificent buildings are the most striking objects as you advance towards Madras on which is lavished every endeavor that luxury can suggest.[6]

We anchored about 12 in the roads and Colonel Carlisle took the challenge of sending my note to my uncle and in about 2 hours I received the following answer which banished all the apprehension I entertained of the cool reception I had painted to myself.

From Lt, Colonel B Close 30 September 1798

My dear nephew,
I send a boat *illegible* for you and a person on my part waits your landing with a palanquin to convey you to me, I hope to take you by the hand in an hour or two. I should have sent the boat for you yesterday evening but the surf was too high. Yours very affectionately, B: Close.

---

6   Umdat_ul-Umara, Nawab of the Carnatic. A Nawabi established by the Mughal Emperor in 1692. In 1798 Umdat-ul-Umra ruled from Arcot until his death in 1801 when government affairs were taken over by the HEIC <en.wikipedia.org/wiki/>(accessed August 2017).

30 September 1798

I proceeded immediately by the boat and experienced a curious sort of scene. In putting off we experienced a curious sort of song, rowing in time to a sort of song they have for the occasion and answered at different intervals by the man at the helm, but when we came into the surf they quickened their time according to the urgency calling out as fast as they could repeat it, Yell Yell, luckily I was not wet and on landing I was conveyed in no small style to his country seat about 2 miles from the shore. I should rather term it a palace but as I have neither learned its name or seen all yet I shall forbear attempting a description for some days.

Here I was received with all the affection possible and introduced to Mr Webb his companion.

I forgot to mention that as the ship came to an anchor we were surrounded with a boatfuls of debashes[7] wishing to know if we wanted money, also some of the inhabitants brought letters to different persons on board, they carried them in a cap on the top of the head, these people are excellent swimmers for one of them was knocked off his, I forget how it is called, it is but composed of three pieces of timber fastened together on which he sits like a tailor and paddles away, by a wave and his piece of timber carried away but I soon after discovered him rise again and take his place.

Next morning after breakfast I delivered my letters and had about an hours conversation with him. He retired then until dinner time.

Every morning he gallops onto The Mount about 9 miles off and back again to breakfast at 8:30.[8] When breakfast is over he drives his Phaeton[9] to the fort where he remains in his office till 4:00 o'clock then back to the garden again. We have a tolerable long interval between breakfast and dinner everyday 10½ hours as we never dine until after seven and retire to bed after getting up from table.

1 October 1798

Close took me to breakfast with Henry Montgomery,[10] here were assembled all the horse officers I believe on the establishment and after a sumptuous repast, consisting of niceties of every sort, there was an exhibition of horsemanship between the natives and other Europeans. I thought the former excelled in management of their studs but the latter had the advantage in the sword exercise. And there were rather cruel

---

7   H. Yule, & A.C. Burnell, *Hobson Jobson. A Glossary of Anglo Indian Colloquial Terms and Phrases,* Debash or Dubash, originally in 17th C. Madras an interpreter, later a 'dressing boy' for a European. Also an interpeter or business broker in Guzerat.

8   St. Thomas' Mount a local hill with houses of Portuguese construction.

9   Phaeton a type of four wheeled horse drawn carriage with one or two seats facing forward.

10   *History of Parliamentonline.org* 1790–1820. Henry Conyngham Montgomery 1765–1830, joined HEIC Army 1782, Cornet 1783, Lieutenant, 1792, Captain 1800, Major 1804. Served with Cavalry at Seringapatam. Whilst on furlough in UK was struck from the Army Roll in 1806 on becoming an MP. Later a Lieutenant Colonel in Donegal Militia and Inspector of Yeomanry (accessed, April 2016).

experiments used, for two bulls were let loose, each of which had their backbones cut in two at a single blow. I was introduced to about five times as many as I recollect the names of among others Colonel Aston the famous pugilist the Prince of Wales kept too much company with.[11] Thence we drove to the fort. On the way the Colonel told me he spoke to Montgomery, who was going across India to purchase of horses, to choose one for me. He asked me which I preferred to enter infantry or cavalry. I answered and said cavalry. My reasons – that in general they were esteemed a more gentleman like set of men and almost all men of rank, the service more agreeable and the pay better. He said 'twas all true but that the infantry opened a greater field and they rose in rank quicker.'

I was introduced to General Harris, the Commanding officer, who told me I should have the first vacancy in the Horse with some time to consider. Close talked a good deal during the day to me of the difficulty of making a choice, he set forth the several advantages of each. In the evening I dined with a large party of the military and General Braithwaite.[12] There is a vast difference between the quantity drank after dinner in Ireland and here. Our dinner and all the time we remained at table did not exceed 2½ hours and when the General rose everyone was up in a moment.

4 October 1798

We have settled nothing yet. These few days past I have passed in driving to the fort in the morning and reading the rest of the day when I return. The rest of my companions are surprised in no small degree at my style.

My friend Temple is greatly depressed about the situation he finds affairs here and says if he does not get into the Horse he will return to England by the '*Berrington*.'

6 October 1798

I am assigned to an Infantry Corps, 2nd battalion 12th Regiment but will have it in my power to go to the Cavalry if I don't like the Foot. The Colonel seems inclined to the infantry but says occurrences might happen which would render of the other preferable and for that reason chose out the aforementioned Corps from its situation at Vellore in the heart of the country. I am studying Dundas at present which is the standard of all military manoeuvres here as well as in England and is the same I practiced with the Yeomanry.[13] I have been unfortunate as some of the rest of the passengers who had lost their writing desks with all their letters, hat cases and I

---

11   176 *The Lady's Monthly Museum, Or Polite Repository of Amusement and Instruction* (London: Dean & Mundy, 1816) Vol IV, p. 52. Colonel Henry Harvey Aston b.1762, a well known sportsman and pugilist, commissioned in 12th Regiment 1794, killed in a duel, India 1799. See letters 29 November & 27 December 1798.

12   E. Dodswell, & J. Miles, *Alphabetical List of the Officers of the Indian Army 1760–1834*, General John Braithwaite, joined HEIC Madras Army 1762, Major 1770, Lieutenant Colonel 1772 Colonel 1779, Major Gen 1793. Died London 1803.

13   D. Dundas, '*Principles of Military Movements*' (London: T. Cadell, 1788).

my case of saddlery. The Captain shamefully will make no compensation, he says his Sailors are great rascals. I was fortunate enough not losing more, all my things being stowed with the Sailors on the same deck. *The Thetis* sprang a leak and all the male passengers were obliged to work at the pumps 12 hours each day and to throw overboard guns, muskets, passengers chests and even the Captain's instruments.[14] The ladies were transferred to the *'Asterley.'*

Colonel Massey now preparing for England says he will take charge of my letters.[15] I will now describe my uncle's house … A large square, has two storeys, and with three doors in each front and two on each side. The doors are all furnished with Venetian blinds to make it as airy as possible. The whole lower part of the house is one large hall through the centre of which runs a colonnade of pillars except the staircase on one side and my uncle's bedchamber on the other. Breakfast and dining in the hall which is 58 by 36 feet. The pillars are of a white composition scarce possible to be known from marble. On the upper story are two sitting rooms joined by three doors with Venetian blinds and occupy the same space as the Hall does. On one side a bedroom over my uncles, on the other is the head of the stairs and a small room I occupy. Mr Webb has his rooms in a distinct building. Mr Webb is Secretary and high in office. As to the number of servants I know not nor do they themselves. About 12 attend at dinner the same number in the stable, 24 Palanquinn bearers, cooks, scullions and the lamp lighters etc I can have no notion of. Some of these have lived with him since he was an Ensign and many since he was a Lieutenant.

The Garden House is 3 miles from Madras, surrounded with cocoa and bamboo trees. I am busy at the drill to prepare myself for the campaign which is expected immediately after the rains. The troops are encamped and the forts are repairing. I commence this day the Hindoostan language. My uncle's generosity seems to have no bounds, he is fitting me out in the most liberal manner, he has presented me with the same camp equipment he himself had when he bore the same rank he does now, with furniture, Regimentals and the best charger the country produces, to an enormous sum. I see no way at present to show myself worthy of his goodness than by paying particular attention to all his advice which is constantly delivered in the most delicate matter. The Corps to which I am appointed is commanded by Major McDonald, my uncle's intimate friend and he told me he would take the command of a Corps himself and would have me under himself.[16] For some time after my arrival I was

---

14   William Howard Hooker Collection. *Logbook of the Thetis.* Vol. 1 1984. East Indiaman owned by HEIC and built 1786. Made seven journeys to India and Far East. Broken up 1806.

15   E. Dodswell, & J. Miles, *Alphabetical List of the Officers of the Indian Army 1760–1834,* Colonel Cromwell Massey, 1742–1845. Entered HEIC Madras Army and commissioned Ensign, 1770, Lieutenant, 1776, Captain 1783, Major 1794, Lieutenant Colonel 1796, Colonel 1800, retired 1800. Died at Ramsgate aged 103.

16   Ibid, *Alphabetical List of the Officers of the Indian Army 1760–1834.* Possibly Major Donald Mcdonald who joined HEIC 1770, Major 1797, died 1799.

left unmolested by the mosquitos, but for these some days I have been attacked by them and it is with difficulty I can refrain from using a currie combe upon myself. If Mosquitos do not attack you, you are supposed not to be in a good state of health. I have delivered my grandmother's present of the hunting whip. The expression of my uncles portrait is stronger than in the miniature. Accounts are just received of the French expedition against Egypt, a supposed intermediate step to India to join Tippoo against us. My uncle tells me he expects in one month more I shall be a Lieutenant. How much more fortunate than he was he having been 7½ years. My pay will be £240 per annum but you must keep servants and an upper one costs £12 per annum.

The chart will be delivered to you by Colonel Massey and any attention that can be paid to him is due on being intimate friend of my uncle.

From Lieutenant Colonel B Close 14 October 1798 to Rev Dr St John Blacker

I have just finished a letter to my brother Samuel as I was apprehensive I might not have time to write to you by the present conveyance and I charged him to deliver a message to you all of the kind I am sure would contribute to your happiness.

Valentine joined us here on the 29th ult. after having had a short and agreeable passage and were it not for the melancholy event of which he brought the intelligence and which has been so distressing to us all I should have felt the occasion of his arrival as one of the happiest occurrences that I have experienced in life.[17]

He enjoys a good share of health and as he is well informed and appears to possess a sound sober understanding it is scarcely possible that he cannot fail in his present work to which he seems much attached. He left England well fitted and as he will soon be supplied with the few articles he can want him, he will ere long proceed to join his Corps at Vellore which is commanded by an excellent officer and a friend of mine to whom I shall not fail to recommend him. You will be delighted to hear all his good fortune in being high in the general list of ensigns and that in the due course of things a few months must make him a Lieutenant. I have put him in the way of studying the most useful of the country's languages and if he can once attain a proficiency in them the days to his success will be direct and open. He writes to you no doubt and I dare say will give you a reason to suppose that he is not likely to be displeased with India. We have been extremely uneasy about Ireland but as we now understand that the Marquis Cornwallis is gone over with extra powers we trust that by this time the principle insurgents have been seized and punished and the country in general restored to tranquility.[18]

---

17   Death of Close's sister, Grace.
18   A Rebellion in Ireland against British rule from May to September 1798. It was led primarily by The United Irishmen, a revolutionary group and with atrocities committed by both sides.

The North I perceive from different accounts has of late been less disturbed than that of the South so should trust the family will be enabled without suffering much apprehension to hold their ground at Elm Park.

We have long been tranquil in this country and indeed we are likely to continue so if the French do not find their way to India, we have just received intelligence of them having invaded Egypt and got possession of Cairo without the meeting any serious resistance. Our neighbour Tippoo is in close correspondence with them and we must not be surprised to hear of a party of them having joined him on the Malabar coast. In case of war we shall be strong in men but our finances are in sordid state.

In respect of your present intentions of sending out your youngest son I can only say that I shall be happy to see and to render him all the assistance in my power.

I remain etc B Close

19 October 1798
I was attacked in the night with all the appearance of fever but it turned out to be bile, my uncle sent Physicians to me who in curing reduced me to a skeleton. I was ran away this morning by an Arabian racer for a mile, it was surprising to see the buffalo drivers clear the road of these animals and had John Gilpin being of the party he would have soon been left behind.

Mr Webb gave a breakfast today and had a General and Colonels and ladies, and the ladies we had though a Sunday, cards and billiards in the morning. One party chose tea and when brought would not have it. Then she chose coffee which she treated in the same way but the ham it was delicious and to which she did ample justice.

I am studying hard the Hindoostan. My friend Temple is appointed in the same battalion with me and we are to set out tomorrow. Our suite consists of 60 men I bring a debash and cook and shall get my servant at Vellore, the palanquin boys and the cooleys, bearers of our trunks augment the number.

We set out at nine in the evening and at five had been carried 25 miles, the motion of the Palanquin is most agreeable and the bearers can let you down and take it up without awakening you.

The Gentoos who are the cooleys are a weak set of men but carry great weight by tying the trunk to a branch of the bamboo which they place upon the shoulders and the elasticity of the bamboo breaks the *illegible*.[19] Every person carries upon his shoulder a Brass pot to cook his rice and when they rest they get faggots, one tends the fire, one makes plates from the leaves and others cutting the meat to make their curry. It is only the lower order that eat meat, the higher will not. When the palanquin boys set down they run to the next tank to wash themselves and their clothes as they study coolness very much. Tanks are pools of water situated at small distances from

19   H. Yule, & A.C. Burnell, *A Glossary of Colloquial Anglo-Indian Terms and Phrases*, Gentoos, a Portuguese term for a 'heathen,' a Hindu as opposed to Muslim.

each other. The turban is the only exception to coolness it consists of 15 or 16 yards of cotton or linen rolled around their head.

Having sent off our servants we found everything ready at the Choultry for breakfast. Choultry's are houses built for the accommodation of travellers by bequests of rich inhabitants. We sent off our servants resolved to remain for the day as we go much quicker than our baggage and walked to a large sheet of water where some were employed fishing with a bait and others with a frog as a fly. On one side a Brahmin sat under a banyan tree of a free and communicative disposition who was much surprised at a watch. I explained the motion of the wheels to his attendants and would have held it to his ear which he would not suffer but held out a string lest I should touch him. We sat in our palanquins in the heat of the day and read. As we were going to set out we heard many instruments at a distance which was the procession of one of the guards. We immediately went to the pagoda distant about three miles. The pagoda is a square building diminishing to a point at the top the sides are covered with different figures of men and beasts. The residence of the idol is surrounded by a high wall, after waiting a long time the idol at length appeared upon the throne richly gilt and borne by about 20 men. His appearance resembled a doll. The Brahmins followed chanting their prayers in the Sanskrit a language intelligible only to themselves.[20] Dancing girls went before hand in hand and dancing at particular places ornamented with silver rings on their arms and legs and pendants from their ears and nose. The dance not adapted to show a fine figure being quite a repetition of one motion of the feet and arms. The procession went round the tank and then the idol after having been presented with offerings of different kinds entered the pagoda. A great number of Pilgrims attended.

The inhabitants are uncommonly superstitious. The man who accompanied us from the Choultry would not return without a second and then not without a light least he might tread upon a snake. He staid so long to get the lantern that we thought he had left us entirely. Our situation was very unpleasant, three miles from the Choultry, very dark, none of the inhabitants to be seen in the midst of a wood and without the smallest idea of the way. At length he returned with light and gave us our accounts of the 'deviltram' forming himself into various shapes which he himself had seen.[21]

The next morning we arrived at the Rajah's Choultry 12 miles west of the last stage. It has an immense tank in a beautiful situation. Upon our next stage we had a view of many fine pagodas.

2 November 1798

We arrived at Arcot. We dispatched our luggage and ascended a high hill where we met an old man with a long gray beard. In his company we view the place of worship, our conductor was a devotee who lived a life secluded from the world. The river at

---

20   Ibid. The classical language of the Brahmins. Sanskrit was first recorded in the 6th C.
21   Deviltram, not in Hobson Jobson. An apparition presumably.

Arcot though very broad is yet affordable except in floods which time it is very rapid and has swept away pagodas. The Nabob has a fort here commanded by European officers 'picked from the dregs of our Army.'[22]

After sleeping in about 6 hours we set out for a Choultry about halfway between that and Vellore. We ascended a high mountain very difficult of access but from it had an extensive prospect of the seat of the war and was the boundary until then of the British dominions.

We attempted to descend a short way but after getting halfway down we were quite at a stand and obliged to deviate from a water course which we had pursued. This brought us to the cave or den of some wild beast which we departed from as soon as possible least the courtesy of the owner should insist upon our entrance into it.

These mountain's are much infested with tigers and until lately were unsafe to be travelled. About a fortnight since they carried away a bullock from a river near to this. Returning from this not a little alarmed we saw at a distance an animal bounding with great activity towards us which we immediately concluded to be a tiger but it proved to be an overgrown monkey who ran up a tree and began to chatter at a great rate showing his teeth. The next stage brought us to Vellore where we waited upon Major Mcdonald who commands the battalion and on introducing my uncle's letters was received very friendly. His hospitality we concluded from his old black butler who hearing us give directions to a servant to have dinner stepped forward and said 'his Master had not risen. No, no you dine with my master.' The Major gave us his house in the fort, he living 2 miles from the town.

14 November 1798
We have fixed upon a house, very good one having a grove of Cocoa trees to the right and on the left a plantation of oranges, my own property richly laden with fruit. A kitchen garden also a great recommendation here but until a certainty of war will not do anything to it. This house is famous for snakes, two or three have made their way into the house and been killed. The musk rat is also troublesome by taking the pomatum from the hair when you are asleep.

The ditch that surrounds in the fort is full of 'alligators' so that were you by missing a foot to fall into it you would be destroyed immediately.[23] I am kept very busy the whole day drilling in which I make great progress from the lessons I had in the Yeomanry and the adjutant says he will report me capable of falling in in a few days.

---

22 D. Chandler, and I. Beckett, *The Oxford History of the British Army* (London: Oxford University Press, 1996).
Barnett, *C. Britain and Her Army 1509–1970*. (London: Allen Lane, 1970) Terms such as 'Arch Knaves' 'Dregs of Society' 'Scum of the Earth' were widely used from the 17th C into the 20th C.
23 Alligators are non existent in India. There are at least three primary species of Crocodile.

29 November 1798

Mounted guard this day for the first time and went through all the manoeuvres without mistake. The duty is very strict, not anything but necessity must call you from your men and what sleep can be had must be in your Regimental's even the black stock must not be dispensed with.

The troops are all marching with their cannon towards the Mysore country and in eight weeks we expect to be near Seringapatam.

We are under the command of Colonel Aston an active officer so that you may and expect to hear of something brilliant from the 2nd battalion.

Scarce a week but I received a letter from my uncle.

Appearances on war seem to some to subside but not so entirely as to admit our dismissing our attendants for carrying our luggage. I am very sorry for it. The taking of Seringapatam would be of consequence to a subaltern and the expense of keeping 10 men at six shillings per day is expensive. We are under a hot sun for 5 hours every day manoeuvering and every Sunday must stand 2 hours having the articles of a war during which time should you attempt to remove a mosquito from the nose you would incur a reprimand. Our changing linen 3 times a day is of great use.

No two people can live more happily than Temple and I do. We breakfast at nine, dine at four, have tea at eight and by this we avoid the custom of eating and drinking in the middle of the day which is the cause of half the disorders Europeans are subject to.

I had a fine excursion a few days since to the summit of the highest mountain in the Carnatic. It commands a most extensive prospect that the top covered with craggy rocks the valley is planted and some sewed with rice.Vellore is a port of great importance commanding the passage into Mysore. There are three other forts and built it is said by the Marathas 200 years since.

The alligators in the ditch are from 20 to 30 feet long and of great use to prevent soldiers wishing to desert from swimming the ditch.

There is little difference in the heat between summer and winter after the sun is risen for some time. In the latter part for that time we keep two or three hankerchiefs between our waistcoats and shirts.

The horse my uncle gave me is very large, a great perfection here so docile that I can make him describe in gallop the figure of eight in 50 by 30 feet. The Maratha horses are so trained that they can turn at right angles by rearing on the hinder legs and from this expertness in the management the use of their cavalry depends as they will never act as a close body. To make their horses fat they feed them upon sheep's heads, a common food is cut grass and grain they call gram.

War seems determined on. Lord Mornington and the Commander in Chief are on their way from Bengal. The gun roads are repairing and our battalion is to form a part of the detachment which is to accompany their lordships and the staff by which means I will be with my uncle.

I wish we were in camp as we are at field expenses without being on field pay. Our senior officers say Tippoo will be no more in two months, I hope it will be true having a great desire to mount the ghauts[24] and visit Seringapatam.

27 December 1798
Colonel Henry Hervey Aston has been killed in a duel by Major Allen and the command of the battalion is given to Colonel Wellesley.[25] We are now ordered to a cantonment near Arcot and from thence to march in a body to Chitterbure.

1799

1 January 1799
After two days march we arrived at Wallajanagha where I read over my dear Father your affectionate letter as you desired. I have been promoted a few days to a lieutenancy which came apropos as ensign's pay was rather scanty.

4 January 1799
We were reviewed this day by Colonel Wellesley and our battalion attained much approbation. A camp life is unpleasant at first but use reconciles all things. We are out twice a week about 6000 and march through woods, rivers and everything that comes in a way in order to be perfect.

My uncle is made Persian interpreter to the Army, very contrary to the inclination of the Commander in Chief but no person in the Carnatic was especially qualified for that purpose and it might be apprehended he would give up his Adjutant Generalship. It will be worth £1900 per annum.

So great a difference has now arisen by regimental rank that my uncle wishes me now to go into the cavalry, which I am well disposed to do. My pay will be in the field £500 but will be obliged to keep three horses. This sum however is diminished from the expense of European articles, wages of servants and the different way of living as here every officer has his own horses and there is no mess.

I am appointed to the 1st Regiment of Native Horse and have joined.[26] We are obliged to ride without stirrups. In the last war this Regiment was obliged to retreat and two of the younger officers from not knowing how to ride well were cut in pieces.

Our uniform is very brilliant, the scabbard of the sword is nearly all silver. Our epaulettes are a collection of strong silver chains wove together and cover the shoulders before and behind. The helmet is adorned with a high silver crest from which

24   H. Yule, & A.C. Burnell, *Hobson Jobson A Glossary of Colloquial Anglo-Indian Terms and Phrases,* Ghauts or Ghats. Ranges of mountains that run parallel to the western and eastern coasts of southern India. Can also mean a set of steps leading down to a river.
25   J. Weller, *Wellington in India.* p. 35.
26   The Nizam of Hyderabads Contingent.

hangs a large mane of a red horse hair. The silver alone is worth £20. I apprehend I shall soon be changed into the infantry again as my uncle who has now re-joined the Army tells me he has another post in view for me in the infantry and to remain with the Nizam where there is double pay.[27]

This depends upon my progress in the Hindoostan language which I can now speak tolerably well, I expect to begin the Persian language in two months.

Our encampment extends 6 miles, 20,000 men all belonging to the 'Coast' and are to be joined by 10,000 cavalry of the Nizam.

7 February 1799

We have been moving these some days and are near Vellore. The old officers think we shall not have war as an account is received that Bonaparte has been killed.

No one knows anything as the few are sworn to secrecy.

8 February 1799

The ships are expected to sail immediately if there should be a delay you shall hear more if not by the next fleet from Valentine Blacker.

5 March 1799

Riaccotta Grand guards, pickets, Regimental duties and all those pretty amusing things have employed my time so much as scarcely to give me time to address myself to Chester.

We are now within 9 miles of Tippoo's country, in full force and excellent condition with such an Army as England never produced before in India. Six Regiments of cavalry supported by 35,000 well disciplined infantry and about 7000 of the Nizam's Horse.

6 March 1799

With this force which entered the enemy's country and encamped under the hill fort of in Neildroog,[28] taken the day before by a battalion under Major Cuppage.[29]

---

27   Valentine remains with the Nizam of Hyderabads Contingent in the 1st Regiment of Native Horse and there is no suggestion of a post elsewhere for the time being. W.Y. Carman, *Indian Army Uniforms* (London: L. Hill Books, 1962) does not describe any early uniform of the Hyderabad Contingent but it must have been 'variegated as was most native costume' p. 106–8. There is no record of a special uniform. No detailed standard seems to been applied until reforms of 1826 led to general order in May 1827. p. 106. On p. 108 there is a print of an officer in uniform in the Nizam 3rd Cavalry 1845. R.G. Burton, *A History of the Hyderabad Contingent*, provides a description of the 1827 uniform. p. 285.
28   Neildroog, a hill fort nr Berar.
29   E. Dodswell, & J. Miles, *Alphabetical List of the Officers of the Indian Army 1760–1834*. Lt. Colonel John Cuppage, joined HEIC Army 1777, Ensign 1778, Lieutenant 1782, Captain 1794, Major 1798, Lieutenant Colonel 1800, Colonel 1810, Major General 1813, Lieutenant General 1825. Died England 1828. There are two John Cuppages and

Just going to breakfast after the fatigues of the morning, the trumpet sounded to boot, saddle and mount immediately as the enemy were in sight. We were ready in a moment and left the ground being rather in a confined situation. Upon showing ourselves the party went off immediately and we took a position 5 miles in advance of our former one.

7 March 1799
The horseman in front were busy all day burning off the forage and laying waste the country, Tippoo's barbarous and weak policy. About 11:00 pm when all were asleep private orders arrived to mount immediately and two battalions to parade immediately; we marched not knowing what this search expedition was for, we halted at about 9 miles distance, laid down at our horses heads about 4 hours and were then remanded to our lines. As Brunswick's Duke with 30,000 men marched into France and then marched out again, we learned afterwards we were to have stormed the Kummer-ud-Deen Khan camp of horse 10 miles distance,[30] but the guides lost their way in a jungle and our General wandered about in the dark the whole night. Further intelligence said they were not of sufficient force to be of consequence.

8 March 1799
We changed ground and at the distance of 6 miles encamped when a report prevailed the baggage of our Regiment was attacked. I had a strong desire to make a dash at them and bring myself into some notice and told our major the report who said he would go out with me. Taking six troopers from the picket we found about 20 whom we pursued for miles when an orderly came galloping after us to return.

Those horsemen are generally well mounted and unaccustomed to gallop through the jungle and when at a little distance flourish of their swords but then take to their heels with great precipitation. We retired in good time as we perceived eighty of them after us. Some time after the following a gentle a reprimand appeared in orders. 'It is with pleasure Major-General Floyd perceives the ardour of his officers to give chase to the enemy's horse but as it is more military to remain in their lines on such occasions, he requests they will not give any more such proofs of their alacrity.'[31]

one Alexander Cuppage listed between 1770 and 1778. Anon, *A Postscript to the Origin, Progress and Consequences of the Discontents of the Madras Army* (J. Ridgeway London 1810). Vide General Order pub 1st May 1809 p. 267, Lieutenant Colonel John Cuppage was removed from a Staff Appointment in 1809 and ordered to join the corps to which he stood attached arising from the insurrection of Officers at Vellore.
30 Tippoo Sultan's Cavalry Commander.
31 *The East India Military Calendar,* Vol. 1. pp 436–8. Sir John Floyd, b.1748. Commissioned 1760 in Elliotts Light Horse later Kings Royal Hussars. Gazetteed as Lieutenant Colonel in 23rd later 19th Dragoons for duty in India. Arrived Madras 1782. Wounded at Bangalore 1791, Second in command to General Harris at Seringapatam and Chairman of prize committee for Tippoos seized treasure. Returned to UK 1800. Lieutenant, General 1801. Died 1818.

9 March 1799
We halted and I had the pleasure to see myself appointed with a Captain Walker[32] to join his Highness the Nizam's Contingent for the purpose of forming an additional Regiment of cavalry from the Nizam's troops. We joined immediately.

10 March 1799
Made a long march and were much harassed. Our party forms the advance which is the post of honour and fatigue too. We scoured the country during the march to protect the baggage from the enemy's horse, a small march is a pleasant enough but to be on horseback from 5:00 am to 5:00 pm is not agreeable. In the morning we had but small parties to vie with but about noon two large bodies of cavalry appeared amounting to 5,000 men. As the Grand Army is seperated from the Nizam's detachment we formed in order of battle twice. The detachment is commanded by Colonel Wellesley, Lord Mornington's brother and there is annexed to it an European Regiment and six battalions of Coast Sepoys.[33] They did not attack us but sent down parties to annoy our baggage. We opened our guns upon them but did not kill many and they dispersed. The rear guard of the baggage owing to the inexperience of the subalterns who commanded it were cut to pieces. We got of our baggage with little loss and killed a number of the enemy's horse. During the conflict Barry was riding out on one of the flanks with the Quartermaster General when two pikemen dashed out from behind a village, my uncle was foremost and could not turn back as the other did to gain the Nizam's Lines to which they were near, by which Barry became their only object and seeing him in the staff uniform it increased their eagerness in the pursuit, they were well mounted but he was upon an Arab which had won two races and though they were within two pikes length of him in short time he completely left them behind.

11 March 1799
Halted.

12 March 1799
Marched 12 miles, the baggage well covered and nothing lost but Captain Walker and I were much harassed keeping small parties off. My horse is completely knocked up, we were 12 hours without dismounting. Twice or thrice we attempted to dismount and sit under a tree but were no sooner dismounted than they came galloping up

---

32   E. Dodswell, & J. Miles, *Alphabetical List of Officers of the Indian Army 1760–1834*, Possibly Patrick Walker who had joined the Madras Cavalry in 1780. Promoted to Lieut. in 1792 and substantive Captain 1799. Died 1817.

33   Coast Sepoys formed from Independent Company's and raised in 1759 to defend Fort St. George from the French threat. Originally of 5 battalions with 10 companys each they were separated in 1769 into The Carnatic and Circar Battalions covering the North and South of the Madras Presidency.

endeavoring to surprise us. So far, we had been on the defensive on account of their numbers, but a party of them burning a village we made a dash to save the forage. There were some 500 of them and 200 of us. Many trees prevented their seeing our strength and they made off, our intent being only to seize the forage we halted and drew up in front of a hedge that we might not be attacked in the rear. Our party except a few lately in the French Service were not under command the rest were soldiers of fortune from Constantinople or the borders of Russia.

To describe this manner of fighting I must refer you to Homer's Battles except that some have matchlock guns which they can present and load in the most dexterous manner at full speed. The enemy seeing our numbers so few came galloping back ashamed of their flight and we found our situation disagreeable, there being but us two to command, the party being but three days under our command paid but little attention to us. We skirmished about 12 minutes when we heard some guns open, the enemy fell in some places and fled. It happened to be the Head of the Grand Army which arriving at the top of the hill seeing our situation fired a few 6 Pounders among them. We exchanged a few shots with them after that but no lives lost.

13 March 1799
I have now got my rank and allowances settled: Cornet in the 1st Regiment, Lieutenant and Adjutant with the Nizam's.[34] My additional allowances will be about £400 per annum.

14 March 1799
Marched 12 miles and arrived within 3 miles of of Bangalore, seven or eight days march from Seringapatam.

The rearguard had a little business today but we saw nothing except one party too small to give us disturbance.

25 March 1799
From the 14th to the 18th was so constantly employed when not marching as scarce to give time to take the necessary refreshments. This is very different from an European campaign where the country is well known. We, the detachment belonging to the Nizam are left to look out for passes through the jungle and over precipices which all oblige us to go sometimes miles out of our way. All the villagers receive us very kindly and even fire at their own horse owing to the inhuman policy of Tippoo who burns all the villages hay and wastes the country to prevent any forage falling into our hands. I have not been able to mention the names of a halting ground but may perhaps get a map to send with this, the general proceedings I cannot give as several expeditions were undertaken which I did not know for two or three days afterwards and I

---

34   Lieutenant was his temporary rank whilst serving in the additional regiment under Capt. Walker.

confine myself to my particular proceedings. On the 18th we were sent in pursuit of a party who attacked our baggage for about 2 miles. Our horses were bad and could not overtake them. Captain Walker and his party went one way and I with a few troopers another, when we met he had dismounted one fellow himself and brought his horse off. We resolved not to follow any more as our troop was completely knocked up when we perceived a small party close to us that had come nearer than they expected and were making their escape as fast as possible. We left the troops behind under the native Commandant and pursued them with 3 well mounted troopers. After a short time we came to the bed of a small river the banks of which were high but there was no alternative and they precipitated themselves in. We followed and I had the luck to pistol one fellow in the shoulder who threw himself off and ran under the close jungle on the banks of the river. We pursued them thus until we had taken five horses and four men and finding we had gone far enough we returned with our prizes.

Had the rascals not been so overcome with their fear they must have been more than enough for us but they did not know how many there were of us and we met with little resistance when we got up with them.

But all this extraordinary fagging for eight days, exposed to the sun from morning till evening, was a little too much for me, not being hardened yet to the climate and I was taken severely ill immediately after the march and have been unable to accompany the troop for these six days but came in a palanquin.[35]

26 March 1799

I am now however tolerably recovered and shall take up my post tomorrow, I have been in readiness some days if anything that was to happen. Tippoo has been receding from us these two days. He sent a few days ago a challenge to General Harris to meet him singly pace an effusion of blood but as this is not the Generals mode of fighting it was declined.

We have been several times in much distress for water it is a most affecting sight to see the followers who cannot carry any with them lying down and crying out for water. In order to distress us more he has drained several tanks equally detrimental to his own subjects as to us and not only that but he has poured a poisonous herb called Mithledge into some of them.[36] Its strength is such that if it touches you it will blister and if it touches a beast both skin and hair pulled off and when it incorporates well with the water to drink is death. Some officers who drank of it the date it was put in are extremely ill. Certain news is just arrived that General Stewart,[37] commanding

---

35   Valentine was sick and off duty from 19–25 March when he again takes up his pen.
36   Probably 'Milk Hedge' an irritant purgative, but also used homeopathically.
37   *Oxford Dictionary of National Biography*, General, James Stuart 1741–1815. Commanding the Bombay Army. General James Stuart 1741–1815.Commanded the Bombay Army 1797–1800. An Edinburgh Graduate who joined the 78th Foot a Highland Regiment. Went to India in 1782 as a Lt. Colonel, Major General 1795, Commander in Chief Madras 1801, Lieutenant General 1802. Fought in American War of Independence

the Bombay detachment, coming to meet us has had an action with Tippoo and has given a compleat drubbing. We are pushing on to meet Stewart at Mysore 10 miles south of Seringapatam. From the accounts brought in today we expect an engagement tomorrow and everything is regulated accordingly. All the Nizams Horse are to charge if possible as it is so different from their usual mode of fighting and their chiefs have promised to do all they can. The body is to be lead on by Captain Walker so if anything happens to him I am to supply his place and I must be due a good night in order to prepare for the labours of the day by a sound sleep.

26 March 1799

We saw the enemy's lines at a great distance but they did not seem inclined to wait for us though we knew they consisted of 12,000 foot 15,000 horse we made a short march but cannot remain in our present situation for want of water.

27 March 1799

After a march of 9 miles we discovered the enemy drawn up in line of battle on a fine commanding ground to dispute the possession of some fine water with us. They fired some shot at us who were in the advance but seeing the line advancing they opened a hot cannonade and we were ordered to fall in the rear until further orders, these orders were obeyed with alacrity as nothing annoys troops more than to be cannonaded without any use. The Grand Army was not at this time arrived but Colonel Wellesley formed his line though not a third of the enemy's force returned the cannonade. As of the cavalry forming in the Rear it was put under my command and Captain Walker attended Colonel Wellesley. The guns were kept in constant fire for about one and a half hours and three Regiments of cavalry and six of infantry belonging to the Grand Army had formed on our right. The enemy has greatly the advantage of us in situation and the Colonel finding our guns had not sufficient effect sent to inform General Floyd he was going to advance, expected his assistance, which he did to within musket shot and the 33rd and 74th and some of our battalions of Bengal and Coast Sepoys kept up a close fire for some time. Tippoo's cavalry from a dash they had been obliged to take charged and some forced their way through the Scotch Brigade and 74th Regiment, of the latter they butchered some men lying in the rear sick. As I had some latitude in my orders and thinking we would now be called upon I brought up the cavalry then under my command consisting of two troops of regulars and about 1000 irregulars, whose orders were to do just as we did, when I luckily met an orderly who informed me we were wanted immediately and I soon after to relinquish my command to Captain Walker.

The cavalry of the Grand Army had now begun the charge and we formed a second line to cut off any who escaped them. Of those who had charged our line scarce any

and campaigns in Southern India his last being 2nd Anglo-Maratha War 1803–05. He returned to the UK in poor health in 1805.

had escaped and we pursued the task about 3 miles whilst their infantry were charged off the field by the bayonet. It was well enough advancing in the heat of the action but returning over the field of battle was a melancholy site. The 19th Dragoons who have many years been in the country and signalized themselves on every occasion did not seem to have compassion as they pistolled every man who had any life in revenge for the many cruelties exercised on them by Tippoo. We encamped and halted the next upon the ground we had won. Our loss is not worth mentioning not having lost an European officer, though the enemy suffered much, by their not annoying us as much as they did before

29 March 1799
Marched 14 miles in order to join General Stewart. In this march we completely deceived Tippoo who had retreated to within a few miles of Seringapatam where he took up the same advantageous position he had done in the last war during a bloody battle. By this march we have seized upon quantities of horses and ammunition laid up in a small park.

The cavalry were employed in sweeping the country for cattle, however it had a number of miserable animals we willingly relinquished upon the appearance of a superior body of cavalry and waited so long for the parties we had sent out we were scarce able to make a good retreat and to make the matter more absurd the line supposed that we were enemies and prepared four six pounders to open upon us when they discovered of their mistake.

30 March 1799
Crossed the Cauvery river 27 miles below Seringapatam. Halted on the 31st and distributed the grain taken amongst the followers

15 April 1799
On the evening of the 31st I became so ill as to be confined to my bed and this is the first time I have taken my pen since the first six or seven days I was delirious. I had a few days before I got well of the bile and had reported myself well too soon not having recovered my strength.

Though I went in a Palanquin it grows so soon hot that I was nearly in the situation of a person in an oven. This with my disorder reduced me to such a situation that I could not lie down or get up without assistance of two or three. My resolution completely failed me and I and entreated the Palanquin bearers to lay me down under some trees or water and that all my suffering might be put an end to by Tippoo's Horse. They were deaf to my entreaties and carried me on day after day until we arrived at Seringapatam. Here my uncle had me brought to his tent to have the attention of the 1st's Physicians who in a short time cured me of my distemper but left me so weak and no flesh on my bones that I could not sit in a chair or lie in bed without a parcel of pillows or bolsters under me. I am now advancing in strength and have walked six times across the tent this morning. The second day after our arrival we took possession of an advanced fort which was well defended and lost a Major Campbell and three subalterns.[38]

The enemy regularly cannonade our trenches and have even thrown some balls into headquarters and one fell near the General's tent. Before they attempt the fort they wait for the Bombay Army which is expected every day.[39]

What ever additional pay I receive from joining the Nizam's party it is fully made up by the several advantages I have given up. With the Regiment my horses were fed gratis. Grain is scarce now to be had and even at the expense of 10 shillings per day besides a loss of ⅛th I expend owing to a difference about the exchanges.

These several other little things amount to a great deal but they cannot last longer than the war which I have no reason to wish a continuance of.

On the 14th the Bombay Army arrived consisting of 3 European Regiments and 3 battalions of Sepoys accompanied by over 5 Regiments of cavalry which were sent to meet them on the 6th. Tippoo sent many of his stable horse and a number of plunderers to annoy them which they did completely with their rockets[40] from the jungle and killed many of our horses but suffered more themselves.

On the 15th they crossed the river under the fort and from that to the 19th were employed in taking post after post so that now our position is within 400 yards of the fort. In several of the actions this was warm work and in one of them my former commander Major Mcdonald so distinguished himself that the post he took is called after his name.

The cavalry had now done everything cavalry could do in besieging a fort and suffered much from want of forage and scarcity of grain. The horses are dying every day and provisions for Europeans and natives at a great price. Colonel Read who commands the ceded district had collected a supply but no communication being possible the nearest party being 100 miles distant there was a probability of the Army suffering for want of provisions.[41] In order to bring up this supply the cavalry were ordered to the Coverporam pass to meet the Colonel. My uncle consulted the Physicians if I would

38   E. Dodswell & J. Miles, *Alphabetical List of the Officers of the Indian Army 1760–1834*, Major Colin Campbell KIA 5 April 1799. Joined HEIC 1778, Lieutenant, 1782, Captain 1795, Major 1798.

39   Commanded by Gen. James Stuart.

40   J. Earle, *Commodore Squib, The Life, Times and Secretive Wars of Englands First Rocket Man Sir William Congreve 1772–1828* (Newcastle on Tyne: Cambridge Scholars Publishing, 2010). The Rocket as a weapon was in use from the 13th century in China. In 1794 a British Officer described the typical Indian manufactured Rocket as 'a missile weapon consisting of a foot long metal tube filled with combustible and a bamboo rod, directed by hand it flies like an arrow. Some burst like a shell, others have a serpentine motion'. Major General D. Marshall used Rockets to reduce Hatrass during a siege in March 1817. The Bengal Rocket Troop with Congreves Rocket System, stored at Dum Dum, were deployed with The Army of the Deccan during the Maratha and Pindari Wars, Autumn 1817.

41   E. Dodswell, E. & J. Miles, *Alphabetical List of the Officers of the Indian Army 1760–1834*, Lt. Colonel Alexander Read, Madras Engineers. Joined HEIC 1770, Ensign 1772,

be able to travel with the cavalry as I was still very weak. He not only ordered me to leave Seringapatam but to go back to Madras for the sea air and not upon any account to miss the opportunity. On the 19th I set out in a doolie, a conveyance for the sick, but I endeavoured to ride before the heat of the day. This did very well for a few days but one day the doolie boys having run away to plunder a village, I was obliged to remain 12 hours in the sun and I for two days completely relapsed to my former situation. And Tippoo sent out his horse after us and for two days have harassed us very much and we made about 4 miles each day though exposed to the sun from morning till evening. Though our horses were not able to make a charge we should not have feared them had we not under our care all the baggage of our own detachment which are difficult to protect. However we were led to suppose that something very material had happened at Seringapatam as all Tippoo's horse went off at night in a great hurry and left only a few to burn the forage. The entire march was rather a dangerous undertaking as neither native or European with us had ever gone on the road and it was just like marching in the dark and it took us 10 days what we might have marched in four very easily. I have yet 40 miles to the pass. We are in a burning situation surrounded by mountains which prevent a breath of air and have the pleasure at night of being serenaded at night by wolves, bears and tiger. We have met Colonel Read 's detachment sooner than expected but having left his supplies with another escort we are absolutely in a starving condition as we expected every necessity on our junction.

2 May 1799

At length arrived in our own dominion and have got clear through the pass of 50 miles completely surrounded by mountains which prevent a breath of air so that both Europeans and natives die daily. Out of 250 horses we set out within the first four days 60 died, owing to the long marches to get water. In some places this newly explored pass is so narrow that we have been obliged to pass through the burning sands of a river. Last night our camp was dreadfully alarmed as owing to the loss of tents in the route, as quantities of our baggage are lost by the bullocks dying, three of us are obliged to sleep in the same tent and of course it is quite full.[42] In the middle of the night I felt a dozen of fellows tumbling over me where I was lying on my couch, making the most horrid noise possible and saw as well as the partial light of the moon would permit, the tents quite full of people running through. I immediately bounced up with the rest and arming ourselves were running to the Commandant of our detachment when we discovered the alarm was occasioned by a tiger having come close to our tent and carried off one of the followers. This was no sooner subsided

Lieutenant 1778, Captain 1783, Major 1796, Lieutenant Colonel 1796, Colonel 1804. Died Malta 1804.

42   J. Blakiston, *Twelve Years Military Adventures*. (London: Henry Colburn, 1829) 2 Vols. Vol. I p. 62. Each officer had a 'marquee, sized according to rank. A Lieuts. tent was ten feet square. Pitched with Privates to the fore, Officers to the rear.'

than another came down and carried off a child. Fires were then lighted through the camp which prevented any more casualties. We supposed we had been attacked by the Poligars, licensed plunderers of all foreigners and permitted to do so by the powers in whose kingdom they remain. They inhabit high mountains inaccessible to all but themselves and are a number of men insensible to pity in any degree.

You cannot conceive what pleasure it gave us all to meet some of our old acquaintances. Among others was Harry Montgomery one of the best people in the world.[43] We found him encamped near the mouth of the pass with a party of horse he raised and was going to General Floyd. For the first time for three months we find ourselves comfortable, we breakfasted with him, a luxury having lived so long on bad meat and bad biscuits.

Two marches more brought us to Panagra on the 4th of May where we got possession of a large house and garden with some vegetables both of which were great rarities to us. Here we halted a day to give rest to the sick and it is startling the affect it produced. Here we found a packet of European letters going to the Army. You may guess the anxiety and disappointment in not finding any for me but comfort myself some for me are under cover to my uncle and that I shall yet receive them.

Two marches more brought us to the village of Pollicode where I begged leave to quit our little detachment as they have to make two long marches to a halting place and I could get to a fort in one day, to the commander of which I had a letter from Barry which gained me a most hospitable reception. I was endeared to this also from not believing myself capable for two marches more without a halt, having a disorder occasioned by the bad water I had been obliged to drink and which has carried off more Europeans both officers and men than all the other disorders put together since we took the field.

I was not entirely by myself on this march to Ryacotta as the couzen of the commander of the place accompanied me. He had been obliged to leave the Army also on account of sickness but being more recovered than I was reached the fort at 11:00, but this day I was so weak and that when the sun got up I was forced to take up my residence under a tree until evening when I arrived quite exhausted having gone 17 miles and had nothing for 30 hours. I now enjoy wholesome food and rest and expect in a few days to be so well recovered as to proceed to Madras. If the infantry has more duty in time of peace, the cavalry are particularly fagged during a campaign. Eight Cornets joined at the time I did and six of us have now returned sick.

General Floyd who commands the cavalry is a very active and hardy man, though now a little advanced and owes his present rank to his good conduct mostly. His knowledge extends not further than his profession, is famous for his horsemanship and had been pupil to the famous Lord Pembroke. To give you an idea of him being in

---

43   E. Dodswell E.J. Miles, *Alphabetical List of the Officers of the Indian Army 1760–1834,* probably H.C. Montgomery, Madras Cavalry. Joined HEIC 1782, Cornet 1783, Lieutenant 1792, Captain 1800, Major 1804. Struck off the roll 1806.

company where an officer was much praised for his behaviour, Floyd answered in his usual gruff manner 'a good man, a worthy man but he can't ride'.

10 May 1799

This day we received the rejoicing intelligence of Seringapatam having been taken and Tippoo killed in the assault. We are ignorant of the particulars and cannot know anything until it comes from Madras. Which is hard being within a mile of the late Tippoo's country. It is surprising anyone is found to carry the despatches for if the unfortunate wretch is discovered he is hung up on the next tree and many of our hirkarahs/messengers have suffered this fate.[44] But in an Indian Army persons are to be found for everything. Not less than 2000 followed our Army in hopes of plunder. No expressions can give a more faithful idea of an Eastern Army than by some author whose name I forget 'it is the emigration of a nation guarded by its Army.'

I have just this minute heard that a packet is to be dispatched with the joyful intelligence to England as the post goes out immediately, I have only time to say that Lord Mornington is to come here to make the communication shorter. That your humble servant is so much recovered as to change his mind therefore he will not go to Madras but remain here until he is a little stronger and then join his Regiment. That the said humble servant has been rather unfortunate of late having lost two of his trunks and had a horse stolen from him which he paid a short time before 350 pagodas or £150 and been cheated by his servants. I beg all my friends will consider my sentiments to them the same as ever, so that professions are useless and agree with me that a continual correspondence is the current proof of affection.

23 May 1799

Ryacotta. Since my last which I sent by the packet to carry the news of our gallant action here which as Lord Mornington published to the Army keeps pace with those of home little or nothing worth mentioning has happened. Lord Mornington's health will not permit him to continue here as was expected for some time.

Different parts of the Army are sent into the forts we have taken so that we are indulging ourselves with the idea of soon getting ourselves settled for some time. Those of Tippoo's sons who were not taken in the fort and the famous Cuderodeen, commander of Tippoo's cavalry has surrendered. So nothing remains but to reduce a few forts to the northwards of the country and quietly take possession of the Kingdom. The road between this and Seringapatam that single Sepoys of ours have travelled without disguise, without meeting any interruption and Lord Mornington's brother is going up with a very small escort.

---

44   H. Yule & A.C. Burnell, *Hobson Jobson A Glossary of Colloquial Anglo-Indian Terms and Phrases*, Hircarrahs, Hurcarra 'person(s) employed to carry dispatches' either on foot or camel, frequently in disguise and with ingenuity in concealment of the message.

28 May 1799
This place which was a few months since only inhabited by the officers of the garrison is now become quite crowded owing to the number going between Madras and Seringapatam[45] to which the last place the communication is so clear that many of our officers have travelled there singly.

I have formerly mentioned my Uncles domestic character, let me now notice in a military point of view.

Aided by a very large share of a strong constitution and activity he is constantly fagging from morn till night and night to morn. Although his high rank would fully excuse his non attendance on several occasions, yet his zeal in the service will not permit him to take advantage of it. I have got up at different times, thrice in a night and found him either writing or his bed empty. Notwithstanding the heat of the climate at night, he always sleeps in his clothes, ready to bounce up on the slightest occasion.

His behaviour is more extraordinary, owing to the great contrast between it and every officer in camp and it may be owing to be sure to my great admiration of military genius. But I cannot help comparing him with greatest hero of antiquity. He is known from the highest to the lowest on the Madras establishment by the name of Barry Close and universally esteemed by all. The soldiery have placed him amongst our greatest general officers, in the chorus of a popular song in which they enumerate their favourites – Lord Cornwallis, General Ross, General Floyd and Barry Close.

NB A copy Letter containing extracts from the Madras Gazette (1) from General George Harris, (2) from Lord Mornington both providing glowing testimonials of Lieutenant Colonel Close have been inserted into the Letter Book.

Madras Gazette 25 May 1799
1) In every point of view I must call your Lordships particular attention to the Adjutant General of the army. His general character as an officer is too well established by a long and distinguished course of the most meritorious service to require my testimony. But the particular exertion of his talents in the present service to directing, regulating and assisting the progress of our departments when embarrassed by all the difficulties attending a deficiency of conveyance for an uncommonly extensive equipment during the advance of the Army and the ability, zeal and energy displayed by him in superintending the various operations of an arduous siege where he was ever present, stimulating the exertions of others or assisting their judgment and labour with his own claim from me to be stated to your Lordships in the most forcible terms. It is my earnest wish that my sentiments on this subject may be publicly recorded, and it is my firm opinion that if the success of this army has been of importance to

45   Distance of 288 miles.

the British interests, that success is to be attributed in a very considerable degree to Lieutenant Colonel Close.

G. Harris

2) The conduct of Lieutenant Colonel Close, Adjutant General has amply justified the implicit confidence reposed by the Governor General in Council in his extensive knowledge, approved experience, superior talents and indefatigable activity. The uniform zeal, perseverance and fortitude with which Lieutenant Colonel Close has exerted all these great qualities in every trial of difficulty and danger entitle him to the praise, esteem and respect of the Governor General in Council. And his Lordship feels himself bound by every obligation of justice and public duty to recommend the extraordinary merits of Lieutenant Colonel Close to the particular approbation of the Court of Directors and the applause and gratitude of his country.

Mornington.

15 June 1799

Madras. It is so long since I have continued my addresses to you that I scarcely recollect what passed during the interval. An opportunity offering to join the Army I found the Nizam's Detachment had marched for Hyderabad and that Meer Alumn the Nizam's representative accompanied by Captain Walker and his party of horse were coming to Madras, I thought I might go to the Presidency and wait there till they would arrive and accordingly set out without any sort of luggage or attendance except my horse keeper, trusting to the chance of finding officers on the road who were coming from the Army and as we don't stand on much ceremony in these matters here I intended to dine or breakfast with them wherever I could find them.

In this style I travelled about 200 miles leaving my baggage to follow on and I was fortunate enough by some forced marches I made to dine every day. I am now in Madras greatly disappointed at not receiving a single letter from Europe though there has arrived two fleets. I cannot conceive how you could have neglected me so much as every person else here has received letters. I sincerely hope I maybe now fortunate next fleet as my happiness in India depends on my frequently hearing from home. With a correspondence constant I shan't do well with what interest I have here but what is that to happiness if the other is wanting. I have already made such advances in the Hindoostan language as to enable me to converse pretty fluently and am now busily employed at the Persian. I believe the Colonel is perfectly pleased with my advancement in the languages and if I am to judge by his conduct to me with my behaviour altogether. You will excuse my mentioning what looks so like praise to myself but indeed half the pleasure of it is lost if not enjoyed by you. Ever since my arrival my uncle has behaved to me in the most affectionate manner possible, relieved me in every difficulty and now got me this appointment in the Nizam's Cavalry not so much on the pecuniary account as that I may have an opportunity of learning the court language.[46] I shall go in about a month to Hyderabad to the Nizam's Court, a journey to which place was published just I left England as a great curiosity in a book entitled Ausley's Miscellany. I wrote some time ago an extract from general orders relative to the Colonel but since I have got a collection of Gazette's relative to the campaign and which I shall send with this. A ship sails in a few days with the Seringapatam Colours. Guns were fired here today June 27 in consequence of the definitive treaty being concluded by which I understand we have reserved to ourselves Coimbattore country and Seringapatam. A country of five lakhs is given to the Nizam and the same to the Marathas. Tippoo's son's are completely cut out and one of the former Mysore family put on the throne at whose court Barry is made Resident, this is what I have heard, it is not yet made public and may not be true in all parts. If I find that such is the case before the ship sails I shall mention it.

This will be taken charge of by Dr Connolly the Surgeon General on this establishment who is an acquaintance of long standing of my uncles and now going home. He says he will pass through Chester on his way to county Monaghan and requested I would give him a line to you which I have accordingly done. Indeed he was good enough to offer to carry home for me any of the jewels belonging to my prize money but as I have not yet got them could not take advantage of his offer.[47] The first dividend of my prize money amounts to about £500 and the next it is said will be equal, that is if we receive it and that is not always the case. You may guess how busy Barry is always now when his three or four last letters to me have been written by one of his clerks which he dictated whilst engaged in other business. I am going back in a few days to Seringapatam and if you have any commands and from thence to Hyderabad. No one's name is to be heard of here but Colonel Close. Some offer bets that he will get a piece of ribband and a handsome salary to support it.

Others are so very violent in his favour as to say that 'Timenshaw' the Arab horse who saved his life should be excused any further service and kept at the company's expense.

I need not tell you I suppose how anxious I am to hear in what manner you all proceed. Whether you still propose remaining at Chester, what are William's views,[48] and for what you intend for St. John, in short what all my acquaintances are about as it is now more than a year since I have heard concerning anyone I know in Europe. I beg you will remember me most affectionately to my grandmother and all my aunts my brothers and sisters and believe me most affectionate yours, VB.

---

46 The formal language of the Mughal Court was Persian, replaced by Urdu which is still one of the 22 languages in India. Phonetic similarities with Hindi.
47 *Concise Oxford Dictionary*, 'Prize' normally a reference to a captured ship but also treasure and valuables seized as the 'spoils of war' then sold, often by auction and the money distributed eventually amongst participating troops. Many such artefacts were later displayed in museums or stately homes.
48 Valentines third brother. 1778–1850.

27 August 1799

Arcot. I shall not attempt my dear Father to express my joy and surprise at receiving a letter from you today. What my disappointment was at not hearing from you before I believe my former letter showed, how it came I do not yet know as my uncle enclosed it to me from Bangalore,[49] letting me know at the same time he was too busy to tell me particulars but he expected to see me in a few days being in his way to Madras. Your letter has no date which I suppose to be owing to many hands being engaged in it however by the matter I am led to conclude it is nearly contemporary with Wms. which I rec'd about a week ago. May I request my dear correspondents you will never entrust your letters to passengers coming out without you know they are people who will let them lie in the trunks a couple of months after their arrival or not ?

Williams letter has been in India three months ere I received it and one month within a mile of my camp, what is provoking is that the fleet is just sailed and I cannot answer your letter until by the November Fleet. The surest mode of directing to me is under cover to my uncle. Not withstanding I have seen a quantity of beautiful scenes during my peregrinations through this country, I can't help in envying you your trip to the lakes and I think I shall do the same at the end of some four or five or twenty years. We have had the same information you have heard respecting the death of Bonaparte but in this you are no doubt undeceived as it was one of his officers that suffered in his place. I think however this of small consequence as he will never make his way here especially on account of our late brilliant success. Since my arrival in India this is my fifth package I have sent off so that you will be able to let me know if all have arrived as there was a regular connection between them. I have discontinued till now partly wanting until something of consequence to begin on but being now roused by yours behold the business commenced, which will henceforth no doubt go on regular.

On the 18th of July I arrived here and thanks to my Commanding Officer Captain Walker for the good opinion he had of me was left for the purpose of forming the new Regiment to serve with the Nizam: and he went down to Madras to enjoy himself after the fatigues of the campaign. I am happy to say that almost everything having been left to my own guiding they are daily improving which furnishes me with employment from morning till night. As to the public transactions here they are brilliant and successful as to satisfy than most sanguine expectations. Shortly after the fall of Seringapatam, a man called Rhoodia who made his escape from prison during the storm appeared in arms to the northwards having gathered together a number of Tippoo's horse and others of desperate fortune resolved to run any risk for the sake of plunder during the state of confusion incident to a newly conquered kingdom.[50]

---

49   E. Thornton, *Gazetteer of the Territories under the Government of the East India Company.* Bangalore, after the defeat of Tippoo, became the chief station of the military in Mysore with barracks for over 800 European Cavalry troops.

50   J. Weller, *Wellington in India* p. 88–92 Not Rhoodia but Dhoondia Waugh. A notorious Poligar Chief whose army was destroyed 10th September 1800.

They shortly appeared of consequence enough to oblige the Army to march towards them and there was no reason to suppose, that several strong forts to the north would submit to a small detachment whilst such a detachment remained under arms. About the middle of July a detachment of the 2nd Regiment of Native cavalry by forced marches came upon him and put a number of them to the sword. This act, however cruel it may appear was but right when you consider they were rebels in every sense of the word having been as troublesome to Tippoo formerly as they were to us. And they had been summoned as well by Tippoo's heir apparent as by us to lay down their arms before any hostile steps were put into execution against them. Add to this the very day before they had put the inhabitants of a mud fort to the sword, men women and children because they had refused to give up their all to be plundered.

Since that he has been now been much harassed in every quarter till the middle of this month when he had collected so large a body of horse as to attempt standing a charge of the said Regiment which had annoyed him. You may guess the success. There were 600 killed upon the spot and the rest were obliged to precipitate themselves into a river in which numbers were drowned whilst Rhoodia (sic) made his escape towards Bednore. This is the last intelligence that has been received of him. With respect to the strong hill forts they have all surrendered or been taken except a few that our troops have not yet arrived at.[51]

29 August 1799

Today I had the singular satisfaction of a letter from Sam; I scarcely know what say of this said Miss Fleming and the irregularity with which she delivers out her letters, perhaps if I may judge of by the past she may tumble out a few more letters for me. I am beginning once more to think myself in the world in consequence of these three letters and trust I shall never be 10 months more in India without a letter from one of the family. Sensible by experience of the pleasure of attending a regular correspondents I shall be regularity itself on my part sincerely hope to my friends at home will let no opportunity slip on their part towards the production of it. Notwithstanding my uncle being appointed Regent with the young prince, his talents were of too much consequence with the Army to be dispensed with till things were in some matter settled. This obliged him to accompany the Army to Chittledroog,[52] but Lord Mornington having resolved on an increase of Native cavalry sent for him as the only one who can arrange it properly. It was on his way down that he enclosed my father's letter from Bangalore and saying he expected to see me at Arcot. However he passed through it

51   J. Salmond, *A Review of the Origin, Progress, and Result of the Decisive War with the Late Tippoo Sultan* (London: Cadell & Davis, 1800). There were thirty seven hill forts in twenty districts of Mysore.

52   E. Thornton, *Gazetteer of the Territories under the Government of the East India Company*, Chittledroog, 130 miles north of Seringapatam. A fort used by Tippoo as a prison was above the town.

during the night and had no time to stop and you may guess my surprise at receiving his letter from Madras enclosing same when I was looking out for himself.

If what the general report says turns out true I shall be one of the most fortunate dogs breathing as the two new Regiments of cavalry will make me 3rd or 4th Lieutenant in the Cavalry Regiment, what some unfortunate men cannot boast of who have been 25 years in the service.

You have asked me if I have any intercourse with either of the Hawkins here. I have been in company with them on this establishment about 1/4 hour coming down the Cauveriporam pass, mentioned in one of my last letters. I met him going up as Paymaster to the Southern Division, a very good situation but did not know he was the Bishop of Raphoe's son. Montgomery I shall see in a few days having been appointed to raise a new bodyguard for Lord Mornington and in consequence of an order will come here. He is a remarkable fine little fellow and has made me a present of two camels and a horse which are on their road from Bombay and will be very convenient to me.

18 September 1799
Again let me resume my pen and need not tell you all worldly expectations are short and fleeting: all my hopes with his Highness the Nizam are at an end. His old excellency thought that a few Regiments of cavalry and infantry in the British style would be too expensive a concern, which provoking idea he signified to the Governor General and an unfortunate order for all Europeans serving with the Hyderabad forces to repair to their respective Regiments was in consequence issued. Therefore behold me reduced to a common subaltern.

20 December 1799
Harwelly.[53] Three months since my last date during which time I have travelled about 2000 miles. The day after I had written the foregoing I have a letter from my uncle desiring me to prepare for the long journey that was going to take a tour of the conquer'd country put under his care and that I was to accompany him in command of the detachment of cavalry ordered as his bodyguard. Though this is no money making situation you must allow it to be a pleasant one. No Commanding Officer over me, sole commandant of the party, obliged to keep no table, no house. To accompany the Regent of Mysore wherever he goes, which generally being at a hand gallop I am necessitated to increase of the number of my chargers to five. Having the charge of the Residents household, sit at the head of his table, etcetera. During my peregrination I have crossed the Peninsular of India from one shore to the other and at last after a variety of adventures arrived safe at Seringapatam, in course of which have visited the remains of many cities and palaces the owners of which were either put to death by Tippoo or his father.

---

53   Ibid, *Gazetteer of the Territories under the Government of the East India Company,* Probably Harnhully a town in Mysore state 60 miles NW from Seringapatam.

It is Tippoo's grand palace that is alloted solely for the use of the Resident, extremely large and in the style of the grandeur of the east and situated in the midst of an extensive gardens. The pillars very lofty and superbly ornamented with gold. When the Resident rides out for an airing in the morning he is only attended by your humble servant and half a dozen troopers but going in his palanquin on business or out to dinner he adopts the Indian style, is surrounded by chobdars, men carrying long sticks covered with silver, pikemen, hircarrahs or messengers and swordsman. The rear is brought up by your obliged servant and my troopers. Sometimes he goes out to dinner on an elephant and when travelling is always attended by his full bodyguard. He has 4 civilians attached to his household who help him through business and the surgeon to take care of his health. His establishment will still be larger but affairs are not so far settled as to allow of a final adjustment.

After our arrival at Seringapatam some affairs required his presence at Bangalore about the settling of claims which Tippoo had silenced during his reign and it is from a fort halfway to that place I write at present.

24 December 1799
Bangalore. It now approaches the time of the ships sailing by which I mean this to go. The June fleet not arrived yet. I mentioned in the beginning of my letter many unpleasant things of Miss Fleming having kept yours so long in her trunk. I have found out since it was a mistake of mine and that the lady was perfectly innocent of all I said of her as she arrived later than I said she did. I hope this retraction will do away my fault.

As you wished my dear Father particularly to knowing uncle's sentiments towards another from the family coming out to him I broke the matter and found him as well disposed to receive St. John[54] as the most sanguine expectation could desire, indeed he said he felt himself quite hurt that you could suppose he would find it any inconvenience. As to the time St. John should arrive here, about eighteen is the best age as generally reckoned that is owing entirely to the advanced situation that education may be in. If St. John is kept to business he may very well leave England at 16 and by that means gain more rank in the service. None of the things I brought from England were superfluous except the writing desk, for that there is no necessity. Scarlet cloth is useful but not made up in coats or cashmere waistcoats and breeches such as you get in the shops at the India house. Anything he can learn of Persian is so much gained as though he cannot learn to speak it there he may well perfect himself in translating it and make the characters of the language familiar to him. I do not know of anything else to mention relative to St. John coming out. To get what knowledge he can of Persian in England and not to forget that what ever education he has must be received at home.

---

54   Valentine's younger brother and his anticipated recruitment into the HEIC army.

1800

1 January 1800
Dascottah. I recollect my dear Father the injunction contained in your last letter to me when in England, that I should give it a perusal the first of every year and depend that I shall never be neglectful, I have but this moment done reading it and feel in full force everything it contains. I know nothing more to say that I enjoy my health very well much more than upon my first arrival and that I am as happy as possible so far from all that is dear to me in this world. Be good enough to let me know everything that takes place in family concerns. It being particularly interesting. How long I shall remain in my present situation I don't know of course till I get something better. My present mode of life is certainly active enough having been now 15 months in India, never two months in one place and since my arrival I write by the same conveyance to most of the family. Give my love to all my relations. Believe me dear Father ever your affectionate son.

I sent off my last in a great hurry, hearing that the fleet was to sail immediately I have been today informed that they are to wait perhaps a fortnight or three weeks longer till Lord Mornington's despatches are ready therefore I continue on account of a proceedings during the interval that may happen.

Since my last dated 2nd Inst. at Dascottah we have been travelling by easy marches through a wild uncultivated country in many parts of which no European has been before, in order to put under some sort of system a large tract of the conquerd district occupied by Poligar Rajahs who cause considerable trouble. They have been offered handsome pensions by Government to reside at headquarters which many have accepted: but there are still some who seem resolved to sacrifice anything for their independence. Their love of independence can't be held blameworthy, but when they possess it they never fail to infest their neighbours by frequent plundering parties, the effects of which is well known by experience to every power in the peninsula of India. In short they are a bad resemblance of the English barons of the 13th century. On our arrival at a wild corner called Gounwnair Palah we found one of these Rajahs with a force near us amounting to upwards of 1000 men. As this was infinitely superior to our force we thought it prudent to get an addition as fast as possible to our assistance but this was so inconsiderable that we lay two nights on our arms.

We came to our present situation in order to settle a difference caused by Meer Cummerud Dun Khan the former commander of Tippoo's cavalry having taken possession of some towns without authority for the Nizam under whom he at present holds a large a district.

Nizam Ali Khan therefore sent an ambassador to meet my uncle here to negotiate the matter.[55] He arrived within ½ mile of us this morning and sent information of

---

55   C.E. Buckland, *Dictionary of Indian Biography*, the Nizam, Ali Khan Asaf Jah II of Hyderabad 1734–1803. Described as 'a weak ruler,' he eventually ceded territory to the British for the payment of a subsidiary force at Hyderabad.

his approach. Had my uncle's rank been less than his he would have waited on the ambassador to conduct him to our encampment but that not being the case, while it was necessary that someone should go your humble servant was pitched on for that honour; and accordingly set out with all of the Resident's retinue. After all the Indian ceremony of embracing etc was concluded I conducted him to the Resident, where the same thing being repeated he took his departure for the day and I mine to write so far.

1 February 1800

Chintomine. We remained for days at where I dated the foregoing from during which time we had frequent conferences with the ambassador each of which was conducted with suitable state ceremony. He is a man of highly polished manners and speaks Persian with great fluency his father having been a native of the nation. When he took leave we had a grand collection of great people, the Rajah of Mysore's prime minister, the ambassador from Hyderabad and two Rajahs. We delivered over to the latter as the country's possessed by their families became now a part of the Nizams share of the conquered country. After this there was distributed as a sign it was time to take leave beetlenut rose water, attar of roses, shawls and gold cloth by which you will no doubt conceive that it is a serious thing being visited in form: as I suppose that presents given as liberty to take leave amounted to about £200.

We experienced about four days ago the shock of an earthquake, it commenced with a trembling noise like a carriage at a little distance and increased till we felt the motions which were strong enough to overturn a vial bottle on my table and continued shaking everything in my tent about a minute, after which it ceased but the noise continued for two or three minutes longer. We were in a situation very favourable for an earthquake being in a deep valley which it is observed is generally where they are felt more frequently.

7 March 1800

Mysore. I was mistaken in my information about the time when the ships should sail they were gone before I had an idea of it so that the supplement to my last despatch must be continued as the beginning for the next.

We kept traversing the country backwards and forwards for many days till we arrived at a bungalow again and having halted there for some time set out for Seringapatam. The road we came was very much cultivated once on a time and possessed a strong fort about half way which had cost Hyder Ali an immense sum in building it but his son Tippoo on coming to the throne and finding it was the direct way from the Carnatic to his capital destroyed the fort and laid the country waste, permitting the underwood to grow over it and the tigers to take possession of it. We are now cutting down the woods to expel the wild beasts notwithstanding which they will make their appearance sometimes on the road and carry off the poor post which in this country always travel on foot.

There are people who are remarkably expert at killing the tigers. Their mode is to tie a sheep in a place haunted by them and six or seven men armed with matchlocks take post in the neighbouring trees, on the beast making his appearance they all fire and seldom fail of killing him. Our camp has been disturbed by them but once and then there was no damage done but to a buffalo. It caused however a considerable uproar as the people attempted to frighten him away by shouting and hallooing.

On our arrival at Seringapatam we found a detachment forming for some expedition but its destination quite a secret. Colonel Wellesley who now has the command of all the forces above the Ghauts is ordered to accompany the detachment,[56] where it is going is only known to him and Colonel Close here. As I had been thrown out of the last business with Dhoondia I asked my uncle to apply to Colonel Wellesley for leave for me to accompany the latter on this service which he has promised to do for me. After spending a few days at Seringapatam we left it to come here where we have now been five days it's but 10 miles distant and occasionally the gentry from Seringapatam come over before breakfast. There is a tract of ground laid waste by Tippoo for hunting and it is well stocked with deer and antelope and such are hunted once a week by the tiger cubs. They are taken when young and trained for the purpose.Their manner is as follows; the tiger cats are brought out blindfolded on cots and when they get in among the herd of antelopes one is let loose after them. At first he crawls along the ground till he gets near them and then springs off with amazing velocity and soon overtakes the deer he has fixed on, which is generally the largest in the herd, it often happens that this animal is so terrified as to lose the entire of its faculties and instead of bounding off with its usual speed tumbles down two or three times. We ride out and regularly every morning sometimes start a fox or hare in which case we indulge in a chase as I have got a couple of smart greyhounds that accompany me in a morning rides. We shall probably remain here for a few weeks as this is the Residence of the young Rajahs and consequently my uncle has a good deal to do here.

13 April 1800

Seringapatam. Having heard that the fleet is to sail shortly I sit down to continue my letters. My uncle made the aforesaid application to Colonel Wellesley and it being granted I was ordered to do duty with the 2nd Regiment of Cavalry. I immediately joined the detachment and having made two marches we were ordered to halt the next day to our former ground. It was supposed that the reason of our being recalled was the season for the rains to set in as near as our destination was to a hilly country it was thought too late for the undertaking. I then applied to return to take charge of the Resident of Mysores escort which being accomplished I am again doing duty in my former capacity. It is now five days since we arrived from Mysore and have at

---

56   E. Thornton, *Gazetteer of the Territories under the Government of the East India Company,* the Western Ghauts, a mountain range that runs parallel to the western coast of the Indian peninsula.

last taken possession of the palace of the Lal Baugh or Red Gardens. The Sultan had three palaces, one in the fort, one in the Dowlah Bagh or Garden of Happiness and the one that my uncle has which is by much the more elegant. You may guess the size of it when it takes 22 globe lamps besides many wall shades to light up the dining hall.

17 May 1800

My dear Father what was my pleasure when my uncle delivered me last night your letter of the 10th of September. It came in good time and I was actually going to respond this being the third fleet that has arrived since your last of the 28th of December 1798 came to hand. I shall now set every article in your letter in its own order. You do my correspondence great honour forming it into a book as you mention which I am sure will cut but a sorry figure if you don't correct its style considerably being unfortunately rather ill connected. It will be no doubt be a spur to my constant writing but dear Father I can tell you a much more effective one, letting me hear from you more frequently as I am very sorry to say this is but the second time I have experienced that pleasure during a residence of near two years in India, besides dear Father it will have the effect of strengthening me in my resolution to abide by many things you so strongly advise in your letters. Poor Mr Temple that you say I have interested you for is no more after having stood out the dangers and fatigues of a campaign died about three months since of a bilious fever very much regretted by everyone who knew him.[57] I assure you I find a considerable loss from that unfortunate event as we were very intimate friends and no rivalship subsisted between us except in our progress at the Hindoostan and Persian languages. You mention obstacles to St. John's entering the King's service. They are all forcible and even were they done away I would advise his coming to India. There are 10 appointments that can be held by military men here to one there is in England. Besides the appointments that are common to both on a detachment or Army taking the field which now frequently happens here than in England. There being fewer officers' to Regiments here than on the King's establishment too. It is not an uncommon thing for a subaltern now and then to have charge of a battalion and it frequently happens that he commands two or three company's sent on detachment. In short that are many advantages and so great attention paid to merit and application that you never hear of a clever man remaining unnoticed. When you run into any of my friends about Donegal pray remember me. I have not heard anything of Hill Morgan more than except his safe arrival at Bombay. My respects to the Bishop of Raphoe and Mrs Hawkins. I have not met with Frank Hawkins since my arrival, should I in future I shall not fail to remember you to him. I have my dear Father covered most of the articles mentioned in your letter of the 10 September it

---

57   E. Dodswell & J. Miles, *Alphabetical List of the Officers of the Indian Army 1760–1834,* John James Temple, joined HEIC Madras army 1797, Cornet 1798, Lieutenant, 4 Sept 1799. His death is not recorded but must have occurred early 1800.

was a long time coming to hand owing to the Mornington packet/the ship in which it came having first gone to Bengal. I will now give a little account of myself.

The latter end of last month, April, business of importance carried my uncle to Vellore I applied to accompany him but he said he should not remain there more than three days and as he was to go post all the way in a palanquin and I would have to ride, it was more than probable he would meet me in the road on his way back. That being the case I thought it was prudent to remain at Seringapatam till his return which I did. As nothing happened in the interval worthy of mention except a few dinners I give you an account of them. On the 4th of May the day of the storming of Seringapatam Colonel Wellesley gave a grand dinner to the officers of the garrison. They sat down at the table, 90 almost all of whom had been present that day. We had many appropriate toasts to each of which the band played appropriate, till we came to drink the health of General Baird and the storming party and growing warm on the subject stopped the band and brought into the midst of the assembly ten drums and as many fifes when they played the Grenadier's march, pretty instruments for a room you will observe and the evening ended with fireworks and dancing girls. Our next great dinner was given by the Dewan/Prime Minister to the Rajah on account of his sons marriage, it was also very magnificent. My uncle returned from Vellore on the 11th of May and on the 15th invited the gentlemen of the garrison to come and visit the Rajah at Mysore to congratulate him on his having removed to his new palace which was fitting up for him. On this occasion there was a grand breakfast prepared and the next day a feast given to all the gentlemen and principle natives of the place by my uncle in the Lal Bagh which was no doubt very magnificent. Another expedition now fitting out for the northward where Dhoondia has again appeared in great force, I applied to accompany it but my uncle told me he could not spare me at present as he was going shortly to march himself and in the same direction the detachment would go when perhaps I might have an opportunity of joining.

1 August 1800
Bangalore. All earthly projects are vain. I have told you immediately above of my expectations to join the detachment going on service. On my arrival at Bangalore I was seized with a bilious fever which obliged my uncle to leave me behind, but he left me in good hands. Lady Clive had just arrived at Bangalore to escape the land winds at Madras and I was a delivered into her care and attended by her Physicians.[58]

About a month afterwards I arose from my bed when her ladyship was preparing for a tour of about 15 days. She behaved in a most polite manner, if I thought I could accompany her she offered me one of her palanquins and a set of bearers and if I was not strong enough to travel she offered to leave some of her servants and furniture that

58   223 Henrietta Antonia Clive, 1758–1830 daughter of 2nd Marquess of Powis she married Edward Clive 1st Baron Clive who was appointed Governor of Madras in 1797, museum <wales/articles/2012-01-31> (accessed August 2017).

I might not be at a loss for my dinner as I had none of my own things with me having left Seringapatam in my uncle's family.

To accept of the first I could not, having only got up from a months habitation of my bed and the last would be imposing too much on her ladyship's goodness: so I proposed taking up my quarters with an officer about 15 miles off who is employed on the Survey of the new territory and I accordingly arrived at Dascottah,[59] his residence where I remained till Lady Clive returned to Bangalore. She then sent me a pressing invitation to go with her to Seringapatam where I proposed staying till my perfect recovery as I had a relapse. After spending a pleasant week with her my uncle who knew I was going to Seringapatam advised me against it on account of the rains which might bring on a second relapse. I of course altered my resolution and preparing again to go to Dascottah. But I have entered into a very particular detail of this business. The fact is I could write sheets in her ladyship's favour, how her behavior is so fine and affable and she was so obliging in furnishing me with books and want of a record contributes to amuse a convalescent.

I must now go back about four days to mention a most disturbing situation the receipt of your letter of the 6th of December put me in. My uncle enclosed it to me from Chittledroog and arrived just as I was at dinner with Lady Clive and there was I obliged to sit 2 hours knowing I had interesting news in my possession from all I hold dear for I had opened my uncle's letter and her ladyships company never appeared a burden to me but then, I must insist on your all condoling with me on my truly to be pitied situation and in reward I'll allow you to enjoy the idea my happiness on escaping to my own room where I devoured the pleasing intelligence of your all doing well. I shall now answer your letter article by article. I should have written to you by the last fleet but the fact is I was waiting to the last that you might not have an old letter, till at last the ship sailed someday sooner than I have expected.

I have confessed my faults in one extreme that I may warn certain persons against getting into the other extreme, for example my dear Father your letter is dated early in December and the ship which brought it sailed from England in March. 3 months is a great interval I now suppose after a first letter was sent and the ships not sailing immediately another letter as a supplement had been forwarded two months after-wards. I should have late news of you all and flatter myself I set a good example in this respect. Many thanks for the attention you payed Colonel Massey: by his hasty marriage on leaving you it seems as if all had been prepared. Had he been at the siege of Seringapatam his share of prize money would have amounted to about £1700. The subalterns share of prize money would have amounted to about £400 nominally, in this was included jewels valued at £150 but which sold for about half the money.

My dear Father I agree with you that persons who separate themselves from every relations they have, do it in expectation of being able to return to their friends in

---

59 The Great Trigonometrical Survey of India. Valentine was to be appointed in charge of the Survey 1823.

process of time in affluent circumstances. Those who do it are very few with respect to the numbers who intend and those who are enabled to do it are also very few. What makes the fortune are the appointments. I will venture to say that the number who have gone home in but moderate circumstances acquired from their pay are very few indeed. That I am comfortably provisioned in necessaries and not in debt I have first to thank my uncle and afterwards when I lost everything in camp I have to thank my prize money.

About one third of those who came out to this country remain in debt the first ten years and many much longer. I trust that I shall never be of either description or in debt at all. I give you my word as soon as I can lay by without acquiring the name of a stingy fellow it will be done.

How I can well conceive the pleasure and the high encomium so justly merited by Barry must give to all his relations by the affect it had on myself. Singly his public character is great but when with that his privations is considered what a man does it make. I can assure you that when he was fagging so hard, going perhaps down to the trenches under a heavy fire frequently both day and night: he has several times arose from his couch at night when perhaps he had only a few hours to sleep and offered me water during my sickness or anything else I might want. What a happy thing it is, St. John coming out to me being so good. May I request that particular application may be made to every branch of mathematics above all things it is requisite to an officer's education in all countries but particularly advantageous in this. My uncle wrote to me that he had expected his two nephews out next year.

How came my aunt Marge to become ill before her arrival at Chester but I will forgive her as you say she is perfectly recovered. I must insist on Cath: giving me a particular of the trip to Elm Park which commenced in so many disappointments. You are very good my dear Father in returning me such warm thanks for being regular in my correspondence I Trust you will never have occasion to find fault with me for the contrary behavior as I assure you I feel my resolution now as strong to continue it as they were at the hour of parting and I shall pay particular attention to your cautions concerning my health for in fact I have met with some serious disappointments by unfortunately falling sick on the eve of execution. I put your message to my uncle informing him how high he was at home and as I am now arrived at the close of your letter I shall inform you what Colonel Wellesley has been doing who commands the detachment with which I was to have gone. As soon as he got a sufficiency of supplies for his Army he marched into the country the rebel Dhoondia had appropriated to himself, took the fort of Raucebed and put the garrison to the sword. He then marched towards Savenore where the rebel was who retreated on his approach and following him took another fort called Dummeul in which was a garrison of 1000 men. They were put to the sword as well as those of another fort. This is bloody work but it is a esteemed proper by the laws of nations when towards a rebel.

My uncle often leaving Bangalore went to Nundydroog where he was detained a considerable time in the trial of emissary's of Dhoondia who were endeavouring to corrupt the principle inhabitants of the country. Some of them were hung, after which he preceded to Serra and was there detained by the inspection of revenue accounts.

He has now left that some days and I suppose has nearly arrived at Chittledroog ere this.

In Madras there are two churches and I believe one or two to the southward which are all the establishment can boast of. We have got however a clergyman in Seringapatam who reads prayers to us in the open air.

I assure you I can't help envying your jaunt to Mr Floyds in Yorkshire and should like to have transported myself to England to form one of the party and perfectly recollect Miss Floyd, to all of whom I beg you will particularly remember me at the first opportunity.

How unfortunate the two adventures in Miss Ellis's gig, I sincerely condole with you on the consequences and hope dear Father you and Mary will not wear yourselves any more with runaway horses.

Notwithstanding Maxwell's turning about to Bath, Bristol, Dublin and Rochester except for all his business at the bar which I am truly rejoiced to hear is so prosperous, I think he might have contrived to let me have a few lines. I think I will take a bet with him whether he is a Judge or I a Colonel first. As there are none above me in the Regiment but have been here upwards of 12 years in the service and having been sometime past in a sickly situation and now being on again for service, there is but one officer with the Regiment, so that I think there is a probability of some going home to preserve their lives. I was going to say of some dying but I thought it was too much bordering of levity of expression. That such things are very common here where a gentleman will say to his senior officer, 'I wish you would either die or go home as I am very anxious to get into your place'. It cannot be expected however that a soldiers feelings can remain long as tender as those of other people where you lose perhaps in a day many of your too intimate acquaintances. There are no less than five of those who came out in the ship with me since died. The late campaign put an end to three and two from not living as the climate requires. Was a soldier to feel acutely the loss of every friend he would be suffering continually on account of others and be unfit for his own duty. Not that I would say a man should be hardhearted, on the contrary I think it is both amiable and the sign of a good disposition to feel for others. But such is the effect of custom that you frequently hear a soldier express much sorrow for the misfortune of a companion and very little for his death.

I have no doubt of William advancing in his line and his prosperity so far is what I expected and happy and I to find my expectations fufilled. I hope though he had no time to pay attention to Sam and Maxwell when at Belfast, he will to let me hear from him. I wrote him a long letter also to every one of the family accompanying my last to you and was disappointed not to hear from any one of my brother's by this fleet. Dear Father use your influence with them to let me hear frequently from each of them.

I am perfectly sensible of the good effects arising from an uninterrupted correspondence which you have so clearly set forth to me.

Give my love to my aunt Margaret and also my thanks for the hope she gives on a cadetship for St. John and I hope you have no doubt of the sincere pleasure of I should take in acting the brother towards him. Nor is there in my opinion the slightest doubt as I judge from experience that my uncle will be a father to him. In my last letter I mentioned particularly what I thought necessary for his equipment as well as his education, nor do I think it of the smallest consequence his being idle now, as you say his abilities are good provided only he is kept a little strict as attention will come of itself in a few years.

Steadiness is requisite in a counting house because you must acquire character there, but a little giddiness in the Army is of no consequence nor is one considered a worse officer (I am a subaltern) as he will have time to cool before he comes to be a General. I grieve much for the ill state of Bess Gervaises health, she is certainly very nervous but I hope will recover. You ask why buffalos are not made use of for carrying baggage. They are very slow and lazy and apt to take a fright and throw off their burdens. They are employed in carrying manure and drawing loads of stones and such coarse material on rough made carts and so insensible that you frequently see the driver belabouring them with sticks without any effect.

The Sanskrit language you inquire about is almost never studied and now known to very few among the Brahmins or anyone else. It never was a spoken language but contained in it a system of astronomy and many other sciences, also algebra several hundred years ago. In this however are numberless defects. Their astronomy is I believe the Ptolemean System.[60] Their writing of the miscellaneous kind consists much of pastorals and any history they can boast of and is so mixed with palpable falsehoods and superstition as to merit no respect. Some who have studied the language affect to find beauty but any translations they have given are very flat and contain either vulgar or unnatural ideas. As for my attaining any proficiency in it there are many impediments and no advantages. In the first place there are no grammars or dictionaries of the language, books there are, but not in the reach of Europeans, as they look on your attempts to learn it with a strange degree of jealousy and keep the writings as sacred monuments. The Gentoos and Brahmins have different set days in the year but not so frequently as once a week and have no amusement but what are connected with religion which in the present time is gross idolatry whatever it may have been formerly when Brahmins were intelligent and the Sanskrit language flourished. Notwithstanding the ignorance of the generality of the Brahmins of the present day they contrive to keep the several castes of the Hindus in pretty good subjection by the power of superstition except such as have been much accustomed to the English. Those Brahmins who have not been accustomed to Europeans conceive themselves to be contaminated by their touch. The grand distinguishing feature of the Hindu religion is that it admits of

---

60   Ptolemean system. A series of tables produced by the Greco-Egyptian mathematician Ptolemy to calculate the movement of planets <http//www.britannica.com> (accessed August 2017).

no proselytes. I went some time ago with my uncle to see a famous festival at a great Hindu temple. The image was brought out and placed in a car, near 100 feet high and covered with different carved ornaments and white linen cloth with with flags of different kind so that at a distance it had the appearance of a ship sailing when moving along, to effect which I suppose there were not more than 500 or 600 men. Numerous were the Pilgrims who came to perform penance and some are so enthusiastic that it is not infrequent for them to throw themselves before the car and be crushed to death beneath the wheels.[61] That did not happen however when we were there. The penance I saw was after they washed and purified themselves, to measure a certain distance about a mile with their bodies and afterwards roll themselves three times round the walls of the temple. At this employment there were hundreds of men women and children and many so faint that not being able to roll themselves any longer they remained insensible and their friends who accompanied them roll them over till the completion was effected.

The Brahmins know nothing of Zoroaster nor have they any particular respect for fire. There are however many fire worshippers in the Peninsula but chiefly near Bombay where they settled on being expelled from Persia by the Mohammadans. They are a handsome fair race of men and chiefly follow the mercantile line. Where the Brahmins first originated is a matter of great doubt and has been much investigated by the Asiatic Society to no purpose. The most vague conjectures have been formed without any foundation by these gentlemen except perhaps some distant similitude in two names or terms. There has been a paper lately published by the society to prove that they originated in Egypt and they have gone so far as to say that England and Ireland were once peopled by Brahmins. It is pretty clear they did not originate in the Peninsula as they have it on tradition and its said on record could the records be found that they expelled the giant worshippers of which there still remain some but a few hundred years ago. The name of the last mentioned image is Boad. I believe that there are only three in India, one I have seen and it is about 60 feet high of one solid rock. There are however among the Brahmins some so intelligent as to suppose the images merely objects to fix the attention and have the most sublime idea of the supreme being. One of their favorite appellations is 'without beginning middle or end.' The transcription of souls they know little of and if you ask them why they do not eat meat they give you as a reason, because it is not their custom. The opinions held of the Brahmin in Europe is agreeable to its original tenets. It is a much sunk however in the present day and the followers of that worship decreasing as is also the Mohammadanism and in the same proportion that Christianity increases. Many

61   H. Yule, & A.C. Burnell, *Hobson Jobson, A Glossary of Colloquial Anglo-Indian Terms and Phrases*, Juggernaut, from a Sanskrit word 'Lord of the Universe' a euphemism for Krishna, a Hindu God. An idol is annually dragged from its shrine in the Jagannath Temple, Orissa on a huge wheeled structure. The modern definition is similar 'a huge, powerful vehicle.'

thanks for your offer of sending things out to me and should I take advantage of it but that it is 10:1 if it is ever received here.

It is true I gave up a Lieutenancy in the infantry to come in as Cornet of cavalry notwithstanding that the latter establishment I found of such considerable use during the late campaign that there may be two new Regiments added which lifted me up to the fourth lieutenancy from the top and am now the third by the death of our major a few days since and I may look out for another step very shortly. For the regulations of the service is such that if the first major or lieutenant Colonel or Colonel of cavalry gives up the service no matter of what Regiment, the promotion goes on in our Regiment being the oldest on the establishment.[62]

Many thanks your kind intention of civility to Colonel Massey who will be able to tell you a good deal about your friends here. If you had doubts about my being able to bear the prosperity my uncle has heaped on me you may all increase them for he has heaped more on me since. An Adjutancy is the first employment must be held before you expect anything else, this I mentioned in some of my last letters I have held seven months so that I am ready for any of the superior appointments, Quartermastership or an Adjutancy in one of our own Regiments my uncle could have no doubt for me. But he thought, I presume it more for my advantage to be attached to him where I would have an opportunity of acquiring a greater efficiency in the language and of learning the manners of the great natives of this country with whom he has so much connection, than if I was to remain with a Regiment.

26 August 1800
Nulledel Droog (Null Droog).[63] I have just received intelligence of the ship leaving ready to sail I must therefore conclude lest my letter should be left behind as the last was. I received a few days ago since a letter from William which I shall answer by this ship if possible though I'm not sure if this will be time enough at Madras. I have mentioned in this how much St. John should apply to mathematics, as an example I have the prospect of an appointment for what I know of them. Many thanks to my father for the foundation he gave me of Euclid and astronomy: I have been enabled by the assistance of it and that the practical part of the latter I earned on board ship to perfect myself in the art of surveying during these two months that I have been keeping house with a gentleman employed in the survey of the conquerd country, as I have already mentioned. It is carried on in a most scientific manner not a measured distance in the whole but entirely from computation which is an advantage that even England has never enjoyed except along the seacoast. On my finding myself capable I

---

62   There were no specific rules governing at what age HEIC officers should retire and promotion was by seniority. The system created a stagnation for younger more ambitious officers which lasted until 1860.

63   E. Thornton, *Gazetteer of the Territories under the Government of the East India Company*, a hill fort in the district of the Nizam of Hyderabad.

wrote to my uncle who promised to apply for me if I thought I was equal to the labour of it. This I conceive I am though it is an amazing image? I have not heard from him since but if he applies there is no longer any doubt of getting it, the salary is equal to a Captains pay in the infantry, independent of my present pay.

Colonel Wellesley sent forward all the cavalry in pursuit of a division of the rebel Army: they came up and had an engagement after a march of 25 miles in which they cut to pieces the enemy and took all the guns, elephants, baggage and many horses. This happened about a fortnight since. I know of nothing more to say at present that I am sure you are all very well convinced I am yours most affectionately Valentine Blacker. 26 August 1800.

29 October 1800

Bailoor.[64] Instigated by a letter from Maxwell I again resume my pen and after more than a month's cessation. After dispatching my letters for Europe I returned to Mr Warren the officer employed on the survey and taking advantage of his instruments surveyed part of a district in order to find (as a sample of my abilities in that line) to the superintending surveyor. This is in a much more scientific foundation than what is generally understood by surveying in England. The general acceptation of the same term there, applying to the measurement of fields and the several constituent parts of estate, whereas what I mention is termed by the French, geographical engineering or the survey of a kingdom. After the conclusion of this of business I proceded to join my uncle who said he was anxious to see me if my health would permit the journey and sent me an order from the Rajah's Dewan enabling me to prepare provisions on the road as I proposed taking of the shorter route not abiding by the highway. In the course of my journey I visited a famous hill (Shivaganga) well known in India now I am the first European who has ever ascended it. It is a famous place of Hindu worship and has some most elaborate works. The village at the foot of the hill or rather mountain contains nothing but Brahmins and cows, (the sacred animal with them) and enjoyed a romantic situation in a small valley formed by the Shivanga mountain and a huge pile of rocks. To enter it at either end tis requisite to pass through a closed grove which admits not a ray of the sun for near a mile and is as gloomy as the fervour and super-stition of Brahminical religion which in some respects resembles that of the Druids. You pass through an idol temple in one entrance into the town which has almost as many places of worship as habitation. The grand temple is on the side of the mountain and cuts a very conspicuous figure from below. On advancing further up after passing several gateways, is another pagoda containing a large figure of a bull and on different parts of the ascent you are shown large wells neatly built round with cut stone and each the property of its respective deity. The latter part of the ascent is extremely difficult and in some places nearly approaches a perpendicular, except a few yards there are neither built or cut steps the whole way up. On the summit is built a small temple

64   Ibid, Ballapoor, a town in Mysore 90 miles NE from Seringapatam.

from the foundation of which larger segment of the rock has fallen but agreeable to the Brahmins account the influence of the deity inside prevents the building from falling. Two large pillars were erected on the marriage of one of the gods and ever since about the month of January every year water oozes out of the solid stone a drop of which is sold at a great price to the poor pilgrims who come to visit the shrine. Another conspicuous work of the idols which is shewn is the hanging of a few bells to the under part of a large rock which projects from the summit the height of which above that part of the hill immediately under it cannot be less than 300 feet. From Shivagunga I proceeded through a wild part of the country in a western direction through jungles of a wild date trees till at length I found the Colonel at a fort called Caroor. In my search of him I frequently varied my course according to the intelligence I received on him from of the natives to whom he is known by the appellation of 'Close Bahadur' or 'the brave.' This route of mine was about 150 miles in many parts of which no European had before been seen. In two places the villagers almost all retired within their houses to give the idea of it being deserted and therefore not a fit place for a traveller to halt or encamp at, so ignorant and easily frightened are the natives. Tis this which gives the English the notion of the peaceable and innocent dispositions of the natives here, an idea completely false and likely to continue so, as any writer who from being in this country attempts to undeceive the English who have not been out of Europe is immediately stamped a prejudiced person and you need not be listened to. The English Government is still at home oppressive but is so popular among the natives that they come from other parts to enjoy freedom under us which they do not deserve as they are treacherous, servile, ungrateful and dishonest. There is a very remarkable mountain near where we are famed from the earliest age as one of the highest in the country, and from having been a place of Hindu worship now is become sacred to the Mohammadans. Of course as no other white man had ever been upon it I was determined to visit it.

'A lengthy Hindu legend has been omitted which described how the mountain was formed
The Hindus believe the world has been 4 times created. The 1st 1,728,000 years ago, the 2nd lasted 1,296,000 years, the 3rd 864,000 years and the present one 4,320 years.

29 December 1800
Camp near Mysore. We arrived by easy marches to fort Chinroypatan where there is a curious statue about 70 feet high cut out of the rock on the top of the hill, there still remain in the peninsula a few of the worshippers of this sort of image of the great bulk having been supplanted by the Brahmins those inoffensive creatures who have punishments among them which would make even an inquisition shudder. Many of those images are in Tartary, Thibet and Cashmere and the worshippers of them called Jains.[65] The one I now mention is the only one south of Delhi. The Asiatic Society

---

65   Jainism, a non violent belief in re-incarnation and the universal welfare of all living creatures.

have spent much time and labour in the investigation of everything concerning it and conclude that it is the *illegible* of the Chinese and the *illegible* of the Goths. After four more marches we arrived at the Lal Bagh[66] near Seringapatam with the intention of halting 10 days. Six were spent very pleasantly but then the Colonel and I were seized with a fever and ague, a disorder frequent after the great rains. We remained six days and were then commanded to move to Mysore for a change of air. But this had no great effect, the force of bark after a month's illness brought us about.[67] As we fell ill and recovered together we also relapsed at the same time but the connection terminated, The Colonel recovered immediately and I am still upon the sick list. It was the intention after the 10 days wait at the Lal Bagh to proceed on a tour to the south toward a direction which it has not been traversed by the English. The sickness of the Colonel however prevented its being put into execution and another expedition being on the point of marching it was conceived necessary that he should accompany it. I say another expedition as you will have heard of the masterly manner in which Colonel Wellesley put an end to the last by killing the rebel Dhoondia.[68] He is at present on an expedition supposed to generally be against the Mauritias as the French privateers from the island have very much annoyed our trade here of late.

The expedition we accompany is against a Rajah who has been hostile to us upon many occasions particularly by assisting Dhoondia against us. We lost a detachment from Bombay sent against him formerly.The particular caste of men consisting the inhabitants of this Rajah's dominions are termed Nairs,[69] they are a most cruel, barbarous set of people in the Peninsula, their arms consist of a matchlock, sword and a large knife with this latter of which they execute the most horrid murders. Their country is an entire jungle and every house fortified with a sound hedge and ditch which is sufficient to give some idea of the disposition of the inhabitants.

We are encamped with the Army and have been under marching orders these three days but owing to the quantity of rain which has fallen always we have not moved ground. Six marches will take us into the enemy's country where probably the communication may not be any longer open. We have our tents pitched near headquarters but have a separate Union flag for ourselves with our escort consisting of half a troop of cavalry and a company of infantry commanded by your humble servant, who is

66 'Lal Bagh,' translates as the Red Garden.
67 Fever Tree Bark from a species of twenty three plants of the Cinchona genus. Also known as Jesuits or Peruvian Bark contains Quinine used to reduce fever.
68 J. Weller, *Wellington in India*. p. 251. Waugh was allegedly killed 10th September 1800 but this is not confirmed. He had a son, Salabuth Khan who was adopted by Colonel Wellesley. When he returned to Europe, Wellesley left an annuity of 1000 pagodas for Khan's education and maintenance with the Magistrates at Madras. Khan died of Cholera 1822.
69 H. Yule & A.C. Burnell, *Hobson Jobson, A Glossary of Colloquial Anglo-Indian Terms and Phrases*. Nairs, fighting men, a ruling caste. A group of warlike castes in Southern India who were hostile to British rule. By 1809 they were being recruited into the HEIC Army.

not to be, I believe a surveyor, as the Colonel seemed not forward in talking on the subject. I conceive he did not like the plan so I dropped it. The Military Secretary to Government some time ago paid the Colonel a visit and he told a friend of mine that he did not think the employment of surveying adapted to my active disposition. One comfort however is that now some of the men in power know that I am fit for such employment, besides it is almost absolutely requisite in many other military affairs.

1801

14 January 1801
Manentwaddy. Capital of the Rajah of Wynaid.[70] My dear Father, agreeable to your former desire I did not neglect to peruse your letter of fatherly instruction at the commencement of the new year which was the day of our first march. On the sixth we halted and sent on a detachment to seize a fort the enemy had erected on the borders of their country. This was carried in a masterly manner with very little loss and the next day the Army marched unmolested. The next was also a peaceable day. The third, orders were issued for our brigade too halt for the preservation of the park and stores and the rest of the Army to march without tents or anything but one seer of rice each man. In this state we advanced about 4 miles when we came to the bank of a river on our flank and a deep trench cut in our front. Here we have to halt till the Pioneers had cut a road across the trench and immediately a heavy fire of musketry opened from behind an embankment on the opposite side of the river. From our side we poured in grape shot until the road was finished and then having room having to draw up a part of our line and gave them such quantities of a musket balls we obliged them to retire to the wood in rear of them. Our Grenadiers attempted to cross a river but found it unfordable. As for your humble servant, perceiving that there was no possibility of bringing his troopers into the business drew them up in a secure situation and got leave to attend the Commandant as an intelligence officer during the action and was employed running about with orders. As soon as opposition to us ceased we proceeded cutting a road for our guns through a wood expecting to meet with some smart work in crossing a river to get at our present situation as the ford was completely commanded by the town: but we were agreeably surprised in finding the place deserted and we entered without opposition.

This is the eighth day since our arrival during which time several detachments have been sent out, none of which have fallen in with the enemy with various success carrying on what the French call 'petit guerre'. We shall probably remain here five or six days longer as we are busy erecting a small fort here which will require some days longer to complete it. We are now in a straight line within 12 miles of the western Ghauts and the Bombay detachment as near it on the other side. The pass is where we expect the most opposition as it is narrow and they have got some works constructed.

70   Now Mananthavady, Waynadad, Kerala.

However we form very sanguine expectations from our bomb shells and red shot especially as their defences are mostly constructed of bamboo formed into stockades. This will probably make way for the introduction of a few bayonets which will ensure success.

The climate here is a most unhealthy, scarce a person in camp but is troubled occasionally with fever and ague owing to the cold and damp of the evening and morning. I suppose you will scarcely believe that within 13° of the line the thermometer has seldom been above 50 degrees since we came into this country in the mornings.

I have dear Father delayed my letter so long that I fear to keep it any longer lest it might be too late. It goes in the same ship with Lady Clive who returns home with her two daughters as they have been very unhealthy of late. I shall however some days hence write to some of my brothers, if too late it cannot be helped, if in time it will give some further account of me. No one who's affection for their relations and love of their country has not been effaced can be happier so far from home than I am. These two passions exist strong in my breast and that the first is mutual affords one of the greatest comforts in life to your most affectionate son.

Rec'd 13th Nov 1801

Undated[71]

My dear Father, extreme pleasure and your letter arrived together yesterday. I am grieved however that I mentioned my anxiety at not having heard from some of the family in one of my last years letters as it appears to have affected you much.

No, I have received sufficient proofs since of the continuing affections of my relations and promise not to complain anymore. St. John will now be shortly leaving England and I shall anxiously wait his arrival when, if possible, I shall meet him at Madras. It will be fortunate if they come out with Major Darby as Colonel Close says he would pay attention to their behaviour as they are both young. Depend upon it my dear Father that any aid or assistance that brotherly affection can prompt or parental love can desire shall not be omitted towards St. John whilst I have the power to confer it.

Extreme youth is frequently averse to instruction and I am fully sensible that in most cases the influence it may have depends in a considerable degree on the manner in which it is conveyed.

I have reason or so to suppose that these are the Colonel's ideas on the subject as in no one instance yet has he given me direct advice: but took care that I should occasionally learn his sentiments from his genial conversation. As to anything respecting

71   E. Thornton, *Gazetteer of the Territories under the Government of the East India Company,* in the next letter 5 March 1801 Valentine refers to this camp stop as Peria. Periapatam nr. Coorg 4000 feet above sea level. Destroyed by Tippoo Sultan, a ruin in 1800 'infested with tigers.'

tactics and St. John's military education I think that I could assist him after the foundation he will have received from you which without doubt will be moral and religious.

The latter holds very little in general in this country among Europeans and I think the good conduct here must be most generally attributed to their morals. I think my brothers are all in a promising way though I look upon my profession to be as one room or as any in the world yet it is not the one for making a speedy fortune. The greatest number of large fortunes that have returned are owing to little debasement that a perfect upright mind does not submit to. Meanness which though not pleasing are the slow and sure steps to a competency: such methods I think my father is too well acquainted with my principles to suppose I would stoop to. The first authors having endeavored to make the military contented with their situation by epithets fit to catch an open heart as 'Honourable poverty, discipline, proud submission and Honourable obedience.' Without the assistance of either Gibbons or Burke I am so enamoured of my profession that was I not so far away from my native country I never should think of leaving my profession while fit for service.

I am sorry for John Floyd in not being remembered in the will. I remember him perfectly well and hope that Miss Floyd, his sister has been handsomely dealt with. I think I recollect something about your summer residence on my approach to Corwen where I fell in with James Nebitt and his sister if you remember her. I did not strictly adhere to the high road.[72]

Many thanks for your attention to Colonel Massey he is a very good sort of man and I should think a steady friend. Your direction to me with respect to politics I am glad to see you observe we have the Europe News overland about two months at least before we have it by sea, which latter is a conveyance of letters not to mention the general gratification the communications with those we love. There is another benefit attending letters from my friends at home which operates very strongly on me. Human nature is weak and the good resolutions I make at the desire of my well wishers and my own ideas of the propriety of things do sometimes grow dead in a certain degree. A single letter from the suggester revives them with all the vigour they ever possessed.

You enquire concerning the number of troops in a Regiment of cavalry, there are six. At the time you allude to I wanted five gradations to make me a captain/lieutenant. Sam to whom I have written to desires an account of my uncles appointment, that will make Sam's letter too long I must therefore reserve it for Ms Nobles from whom the Colonel showed me a letter yesterday. This epistle goes in answer to yours of the 1st August and is written as you will perceive after that from Manentwaddy, I wrote many more letters this fleet if in time, believe me dear Father …

5 March 1801
Ardenhilly. After our arrival at Peria from where I wrote last we proceeded southward and after cutting our way through a close jungle and swampy ground we arrived

72   Corwen, Denbighshire, Wales.

at a pass in the Ghauts called Jambucherry. Here we were quite at home as all the low ground between that and the sea shore is our own country and we get fresh provisions from Calicut.

The Colonel however has been seriously indisposed quite alarming and he wrote to the Presidency for permission to leave the Army. An answer arrived when at Jambucherry and we accordingly set out for Seringapatam from halfway to which place I now write after a march of 16 miles. We have got clear of the Wynaand country which I never wish to see again. The Army has been so active in establishing posts that we have already appointed Collectors of the district in spite of the Rajah. There are three separate races of people in it. One set Brahmins, another warriors and the third cultivators; Mere slaves of the land that are transferred from one proprietor to another like the trees that grow upon it in short they are what was in old feudal times called villeins.

There are no tigers in the woods but it is thickly inhabited by wild elephants, hundreds of whom will come in a body and destroy the cultivation of rice which they particularly like, you may guess there is a no standing against such an attack as this. However they are easily frightened and so harmless that it is with great difficulty they are taught to act the part of an executioner though so docile in other things. Their males are very wicked about a month every year yet even then they show great sagacity. An elephant in one of these moods broke his chains, got loose, ran through a village, put the inhabitants to flight overturned the huts and whatever obstructed his passage. There was a poor old fellow so decrepit that in order to get away he attempted to scramble on all fours. It was to no purpose, the mad creature came up and the poor man expected to be crushed to pieces, when to the surprise of the beholders he uplifted him in his trunk, surveyed him from head to foot laid him to one side out of danger and pursued his career. Their spirit is such that no commendation is too extravagant for it. A six pounder having stuck in the mire on the line of march an elephant was brought up to extricate it, he made several efforts but all proved ineffectual, at last summoning his whole strength he lifted it out, running a few yards from the road, dropped and expired instantly from the exertion.

Now that I am in the natural history of the elephant allow me to conclude with an account of a tiger hunt at which I was present. One day sitting at breakfast when encamped at Mysore there was an account brought of two royal tigers being in a grove about 2 miles distant. I was sent out by the Colonel with a part of his bodyguard to destroy them. We posted armed men on the skirts at one side and sent in men with a noisy instruments to frighten them from the other. This had the desired effect, they came towards us where the armed men were and hid themselves under a thick bush unknown to us, so that advancing to the spot, they both darted out and laid two of our men on the ground. They were much wounded but not killed. The animals retreated so suddenly they only received a few shots some of which no doubt took effect but was not sufficient to bring them down. In short after pursuing them from one thicket to another during which they wounded some more men they were at last killed. The velocity with which they dart and the force with which they strike is the most surprising part. When pursuing any animal they trot like a cow but when near advanced take a short pace and a spring of several yards and absolutely fall on the animal. The men whose profession is to take tigers, tie a sheep at the beasts haunt and take post in a tree near by. The bleeting of the sheep attracts the tiger and on his seizing his prey the men fire from the tree and seldom miss to effect their purpose.

27 May 1801
Camp before Panjalum Coorchee. Having travelled about 600 miles since I wrote the beginning, I continue my letter having an idea that my Regiment was going on service and knowing there were many new things practiced which were introduced since I last served with it, I requested leave to join which permission I received with the further latitude of returning to my situation with the Resident when I thought proper. I accordingly set off with my baggage to join them at Arcot. On my arrival there I found the Regiment had marched to Trinchinopoly, upon my arrival there I found they had marched from thence to form a small Army to the southward and after following them about 100 miles I arrived and overtook them here a few days afterwards. We came down along with some Regiments of infantry and a battering train as a reinforcement to a detachment that attempted to take this fort but were beaten back with considerable loss about 400 killed and wounded in the breach.

After our arrival the necessary steps were taken to a breach again and a hot bombardment opened, this produced on their part an action that has nothing I believe of a similar nature in history. They absolutely hollowed out caves in the fort, sufficient to hold 22 to 50 men in order to get out of the way of our shot as their artillery was not equal to ours. When the breach was made practicable the troops were paraded to storm and the cavalry were posted to cut off the retreat. It was a most interesting thing. This fort belonging to a Rajah Kattabomia,[73] who was fond of committing depredation on his neighbors had been three times attempted before, once by the French, and twice by us and always a made a gallant resistance which all obliged the besiegers to retire. However the enemy still took care to evacuate it as soon as they got a another place that they retired to. On this we would always destroy the fort and leave the country, then they would return and build it up again. At present I understand a more eligible plan is to be pursued viz. to put a strong garrison in it. As the people are superstitious I believe they thought it could not be taken. They were however mistaken for we stormed it, though to do them justice they made a vigorous resistance and killed many of our men and officers. When they saw we were masters they attempted to escape in a column of about 2000 men from one of the gates to a post they had about 8 miles of a distant. This was the time for the cavalry and no doubt they took advantage of it. There were but 250 of us and with this small body we charged through their column repeatedly backwards and forwards until our horses

---

73   A Poligar later executed by hanging <http://www.rjisacjournal.com> (accessed August 2017).

could gallop no more and that we had killed three times our own strength, 700 being counted on the field of battle. But this was not executed without much loss on our side and I had the fortune to have my charger killed under me and to be wounded myself in the leg.[74] I must pay a tribute to the memory of my poor horse by giving you some account of him. He was a most beautiful as well as the best tempered creature, had cost me 200 pounds though no sum could have purchased him from me, as I put great trust in him, I always rode him when I had anything particular to do. He had his neck laid open in the first charge by a sword cut and in the third charge was run through the body by a pikeman and when I received a wound in my leg. After this he carried me at a gallop ½ mile when I, perceiving the quantity of blood that continued to gush from his wound, mounted a troopers horse and my own dropped instantly down. His noble spirit kept him alive as long as he was mounted. Pardon this digression. I expect soon to recover as my wound is a very clean and I am attended by the surgeon who belonged to our Regiment, a Mr Best.[75] He surprised me very much a few days since by asking me if I had any sisters in Chester. On my replying in the affirmative he said he had the pleasure of dancing with two of them occasionally at the assemblies there. At that time he belonged to the Worcester Fencibles,[76] he is a very good sort of fellow.

16 June 1801
Ramnad.[77] The camp arrived here a few days since and during our progress here have been harassed in a most troublesome manner, attacked in our outposts almost every night and much annoyed by an active enemy every march. Since the last date we have had two smart actions by which I must say we did not gain much by attempting to effect our object with too small a force.[78] I had so far recovered my wound as to be able to mount my charger again and during one part of the action was ordered to charge with my squadron. This I am happy to say I effected with much success, so as to break the party I attacked and put them to flight, in which we killed many but not withstanding my success I received a second wound by a musket ball which however

---

74   J. Welsh, *East India Journal* 1830 vol. 1. Welsh, an officer in the Madras Army was a witness to Blacker's injuries.
75   *Asiatic Annual Register 1803*. John Best listed as Assistant Surgeon Madras in Military Promotions 1803. Valentine uses the phrase 'belonged to our Regiment.' It is clear that the regiment he is referring to is The Hyderabad Contingent, Native Horse. See extract in letter dated 8th October 1802.
76   Worcestershire Fencibles. Several regiments originally raised as provisional Cavalry in 1796 for service in Great Britain only. On 13 August 1799, converted to Fencible Cavalry. March 1800 disbanded <www.napoleon-series.org> (accessed August 2017).
77   Ramnad now in Tamil Nadu.
78   J. Welsh, *East India Journal.* 1830 The two actions were against the Poligars at Naglepoor 29 May and Tripachetty 7 June when they 'were attacked and completely routed, in gallant style' by Lieutenant Blacker and his troop 'cutting up 60 to 70 of the enemy.'

found its way out again without the assistance of the surgeon's instruments. There are no bones broken I expect therefore to perform duty in a very few days again.

I had a letter yesterday from the Resident requesting I would return to him as soon as circumstances would permit which I certainly will comply with as soon as this business is over. He has, I am sorry to say, been so unwell with that fever and ague as to force him to the Carnatic for change of air where he is now something recovered. I understand there is a ship to sail immediately, and as you know I make a point of missing no opportunity, I now close my letter with a request that you will remember me affectionately to my brothers and sisters and believe me your very affectionate son. (NB by the last fleet which sailed between two or three months ago I wrote to almost every person.)

Rec'd 1st December 1801

15 September 1801

As I have now given some account of myself I shall proceed to answer your letter line by line. H. Montgomery seems to have no idea of returning to Europe immediately, indeed I should think him rather foolish for so doing, as he is in great reception at present more so than ever before. I should have liked much to have accompanied you and Maxwell into South Wales as you know I have a great taste for the romantic which I understand abounds there particularly. Indeed my brothers must have very pleasant trips occasionally across the Channel and William gives a very ludicrous account of his meeting with Grace on Chester walls. I have received a letter from Sam mentioning his jaunt by Scotland to Ireland after leaving you. Indeed Sam, is a most affectionate brother and wrote to me a long letter.

I intended to have been at Madras at the general time for the arrival of the Spring fleet, no doubt expecting St. John and Robert Close would come by it.[79, 80] But this southern campaign quite overturned my arrangements, luckily for the lads it was of no consequence as my uncle happened to be there who, as St. John will inform you took, immediate steps for their reception and I am happy in admiring St. John's prudence in refusing pecuniary supplies from the Colonel which his own good arrangements had rendered not absolutely necessary. Government are now so attentive to cadets on their arrival that they can scarcely go wrong owing to some excesses which have been lately committed by young men on their landing. But I leave to my brother to give you a full account of the regulations of which they are subject to before joining their Regiment and I am well convinced his behaviour will be such as to render their strictness unnecessary, if I may judge from his commencement. The Colonel in his

79   E. Dodswell & J. Miles, *Alphabetical List of Officers of the Indian Army 1760–1834*, St John Blacker, 1786–1842 Cadet, Madras Army, Cornet 1801, Lieutenant, 1804, Captain 1819, Major 1823, Retired 1828.

80   Ibid. Robert Close, Valentine's Cousin. Cadet Madras Establishment 1800; Cornet 29th sept. 1801; Lieutenant 1 May 1804; Captain 27th Dec. 1816; Major 28th Aug. 1821; retired to England, 5 June 1826; died on 5th Jan. 1857, aged 71.

letters to me says, my nephews are delightful boys; I am still in hopes of being able to see them at Chinglepat before they leave that place and if I do not they will be either appointed to some Corps before they leave that place to the southward, where I will make a point of meeting them or to the northward and then most probably my uncle will contrive to take them up with him.[81] He wrote to me some days ago desiring my opinion respecting the line best for them whether the cavalry or infantry and I recommended the cavalry which I think is the most rising line now. I have found it so and if fortune favours me as much as it has done heretofore I shall be a Captain ere long being now the oldest Lieutenant in my own Regiment. I show you Dear Father of my favourable prospects as soon as they present themselves but as nothing human is certain we must expect occasionally to be disappointed. Witness the Surveyorship in which you all wished me joy and which there is now no probability of my ever possessing. Indeed I do not now wish it and so far my disposition is a happy one, that I generally discover some consolatory circumstance after a disappointment. I have had letters from all the family and shall be busy answering them every halting day till I get through them by which time I think it is probable the ships will be ready to sail. It will afford me something to do when not on duty as it is impossible to carry about many books in campaigning this last article is the most unpleasant consideration for otherwise I like campaigning very much, there is something in it always interesting in the variety attending success and victory to its opposite. I believe I mentioned in one of my letters last here that I had been two years in the country without two months halt in any one place. I can say the same at the expiration of three years. Certainly summoning together all the times I have been at Seringapatam it will amount to a

---

81 W. Wilson, *History of the Madras Army.* Vol III p. 78–82 and IOR/F/4/96/1948 Africa & Asia collection British Library. Arising from a concern over 'the youth in general of the Gentlemen Cadets' a Madras Military Cadet Seminary had been established by General Order Fort St George 15 July 1800. The Seminary, strictly a 'Cadet Company,' was formed in vacant barracks at Chingleput, a district of the Madras Presidency now Chengalpattu. A later GO dated 24 July 1800 published Rules and Regulations. The regime was strict with military instruction and teaching but particularly Hindstanee. 58 Cadets attended initially and on successful completion of their studies were recommended (or otherwise) for a regimental commission. The uniform was 'a scarlet jacket made to fit close and to button down the front, with yellow cuffs and collar; three rows of small white with twist, the colour of the jacket down the forepart; twist also to substitute for shoulder straps; a round black hat with white cockade and red feather. White linen waistcoat and pantaloons; half boots and side arms- a bayonet.' Muskets and Fusils were also issued. Captain Charles Armstrong was appointed as Principal and in charge of 'The Cadet Company.' Also in attendance was Mr Surgeon Ainslie. The Cadet Company moved to Tripassoor in 1803 and to Cuddalore in 1806. A similar establishment at Baraset in Bengal was closed down owing to 'the reprehensible conduct of cadets refusing to learn native languages.'
In 1809 Addiscombe Military Seminary nr. Croyden was established for the instruction of East India Company Army cadets obviating the need for such establishments in India(see later footnote).

longer period. But separately I have never been more I believe than about five weeks at any one time at the Lal Bagh. St. John and his cousin will have an active life for every Corps almost is on service now in the field and will most probably continue sometime on the Madras establishment notwithstanding the Honourable the Court of Directors say we ought to be at peace now that Tippoo Sultan is no more. Our faithful allies the Marathas are ready with an Army collected on the frontier to make an eruption the moment any part of our Northern Army in the field is at all withdrawn though they affected to assist us until we destroyed the rebel Dhoondia. To the southward an Army of 15,000 men is actively engaged and since the last assumption of the Nabob's country there are a number of discontents and spirits ready to follow the first daring leader: a character never wanting in this country when an opportunity offers. It's but a few months since our Western Army was sent into quarters yet the Honourable Court of Traffickers,[82] who know as little about India and a great deal about the pounds, shillings and pence as can be, pretend to say what should or should not be in this country. Thank the Fates the Government, particularly since Lord Mornington came out and acts on more liberal principle indeed had they followed the advice from their masters in reducing the force in this country we might be confined very near Madras now. His Majesty is taking us every day more and more out of the Company's hands and in the same proportion do we advance in liberality of Government. I dare say a member of the opposition at home will amuse themselves in descanting on the injustice of taking the management of the Nabob of Arcot's Dominions into our own hands. It is a very easy using a little sophistry to justify it. For example, all tenure of property in the Carnatic under the Nabob's Government was uncertain, any unfortunate native who by honesty, industry, frugality, and rascality or oppression had collected more money than his Highness was immediately disencumbered. Informers are never wanting here and false witnesses are as abundant as Mosquitoes and exercise a very reputable profession in this country. They are so accommodating that they will give false evidence through thick and thin, provided it is not against any of their own particular caste. If a man is so silly as to say he has no hidden treasure they very gently squeeze his fingers between a couple of bamboos until they coax him out of his secret. The only people who will suffer from this new arrangement are the Musslemen (sic) about the several departments under the late Government. But what are they in comparison with the large body of the people existing in a state of witchcraft and apprehension owing to the maladministration of affairs and that short sighted policy arising from the extreme uncertainty of all worldly events in India which induces a power to provide for the present by heavy acts and actions rather than for the future by encouraging cultivation and manufacture. That the system of Government adopted by the Company in this country is diametrically opposite to the above picture. Impartiality must allow that such plan of administration is better for the great body of the inhabitants is equally

---

82   'Traffickers', people engaged in trade: a term of abuse for The Honourable Court of Directors.

evident. Ergo, the Company should take the wilderness of the Carnatic into their own hands and convert them into so many gardens. The successor to the Nabobship is allowed a handsome salary and to retain all of the parade of a court about him.

There is now no room for digression. I have just received a letter from St. John mentioning that the ships will sail the middle of this month and I have not yet commenced a letter to any of the rest of the family therefore I must make brief work.

Since of the 15th ult. the date of my first sheet I have been marching about with my Regiment on detachments, conducting convoys, making forced night marches and ever at other grand feats during which time the infantry have behaved themselves so well that our forces have now got possession of Callacoil and every stronghold in the enemy's country.

Undated (October 1801)
Hearing that a ship was to sail about two months ago I wrote, giving you some account of our campaigning to the southern of the peninsula of India. Since that time until the present we have been so much engaged in the centre of the enemy's country that not the least communication has been opened with the civilized part of the world here. I therefore do not know if the ship has sailed or not and very probably that letter and of the present may have some of those of the 24th of December 1800 and the 24th of February 1801 namely to go in one and the same ship and be received together.

I have received the several letters you mention except that dated the January 3, 1800 but before I answer your letter regularly I must give you an account of myself these last two or three months.

After leaving Ramnad from the neighborhoods of which place I last wrote we made a peaceable march to Madura. Both these places you will see in your large map. After a halt of 20 days for reinforcements, having found our original force insufficient, we marched in the direction of Callacoil. Though I ought to have surmised that I was detached with some others to relieve some of our friends who were obliged to take post by the enemy and as it was a business of emergency we made 80 miles in two days which is no trifle in a hot climate. This being accomplished and our Army increased after two days fighting not in the grander scale however, we arrived at Chiswail the capital of the Rajahs country and he, finding he could not defend it against us, burnt it to the ground. We encamped closer to the remains and commenced our operations against Callacoil about 6 miles off: a fortress surrounded by an almost impenetrable jungle or wood. This you will conceive the more probable when you consider that no trees grow wild in this country but such as are covered with thorns and so close do they intertwine there is no possibility of beating them asunder. The road through this jungle was so well defended that no attempt was made by us to proceed by it and we commenced the arduous undertaking of cutting a road through the wood itself though so thick that there was no possibility of seeing the distance of 10 yards. This plan was pursued for the length of 5 miles which occupied 30 days but in the execution of it we suffered such a loss that we were obliged to abandon the idea. There was now so great a scarcity in the camp that the followers were starving and but a few days of provisions for the fighting men and that was bad quality and to be declared unwholesome by the surgeons. Half of our troops were sick from fatigue and wounds so that we found it difficult to send out foraging parties which at first was a great relief. It would be impossible to enter into the detail of every little action with the enemy which took place almost every day for the month. Suffice to say that they were of the most disagreeable sort viz. a good deal of danger and that a very moderate share of honour to be acquired. As in England they never trouble themselves about what might happen in this country without the fate of an Empire depends on the operations.

There is some satisfaction of fighting in Europe. There every action is detailed and if an officer happens to do a meritorious piece of service his name is mentioned with applause and heard of by his friends. Whereas, in this country we may be wounded, knocked in the head and no consololatory eulogium consequent. This digression being concluded let me return to camp where they were in such a doleful situation. We had provisions and ammunition collecting in the country of about 40 miles of distant and there a detachment was sent to conduct them in. Our Regiment went as a part and where we had the satisfaction of receiving a few newspapers and we rejoiced in and the success of the British navy at Copenhagen.[83] This I assure you was a great treat for we had heard no public news for two months. Still however there was a great disappointment. I knew the fleet from England had been arrived about a month and I expected St. John and a larger packet of letters by it. The letters I expected to have received and my anxiety on St. John's account was raised to a considerable pitch by the uncertainty of my uncle being there at Madras and it were not in my power to write to him. We returned to the Army in three days of harassing marches when the enemy used their utmost endeavour to cut off the supplies we were escorting, knowing of the distress it would reduce us to. Our troops received new spirits with the supplies and as the ground we occupied was grown sickly from our long stay we fell back a march into an open country where a force could act with more probability of success.

How affairs took a turn in our favour and many of the enemy came over to us, which induced the inhabitants to return to their towns and villages and finding how lenient our treatment was, brought in quantities of provisions for sale so that plenty once more reigned in our camp. We soon after this got possession of all the open country and in one day all our letters that had been collecting two months and all the Europe letters by the Spring fleet. If you can Dear Father conceive an ecstasy continuing from morning until night I beg you will do so and on this occasion this one day fully paid me for all the fatigues and campaigning and I was moreover happy in receiving letters

---

83   A naval battle on 2 April 1801 where the British defeated a Danish fleet in 'The Sound' at Copenhagen. Primarily to prevent The League of Armed Neutrality i.e, Russia, Denmark, Sweden and Prussia from assisting France during the Napoleonic Wars. It was during this battle that Nelson coined the famous phrase 'I see no signal' <www.britannica.com> (accessed August 2017).

from St. John written in great spirits and from my uncle giving an account of the favourable state of his health which was so bad before as to oblige him to go to sea.

Indeed he suffered a great deal and many people despaired of his recovery, I am told however he will be kept at Madras as long as possible. Government can find an excuse, as otherwise they he would immediately return to Mysore and run the danger of a relapse. It was found so difficult to get him to the coast before, that Lord Clive was obliged to make business an excuse to order him down to save his life most probably. Two or three days after receiving our letters I was ordered off with another detachment to bring in ammunition from Madura. This you are to consider accomplished and I have once more arrived in camp.

5 October 1801
Yesterday I accompanied the Commander of our Army to examine many of those works in the jungle which had formally given us so much trouble and cost so many lives. By the nearest chance in the world we surprised a party of the enemy who had also come to reconnoitre. We had two companies with which we pursued and after continuing this for some miles in the closest underwood you can conceive came up with their rear, killed some and another lieutenant who had come out through curiosity and as well as myself advanced in front with me and we had the good luck to take prisoners all with our own hands: The Rajahs two son's, the almost entire instigators of this war, the Rajah himself being a decrepid old man nearly doting. As they struggled we were obliged to wound them and immediately four more of the family came to their assistance. All was gone thin, if at that very instant some of our own party had not come up so and we took the whole set prisoners. This is to be hoped will put an end to the business and our commandant had the goodness to return us particularly his thanks in General Orders. No small the reward let me tell you as our General Orders are published through every station in India.

By the promotion of our eldest Captain the gram agency of our Regiment, an appointment generally held by the senior Captain has become vacant.[84] The next Captain would have got it had he been in the country but he is on leave to Europe and my uncle requested it from Government for me. The person holding it has the superintendency of the grain for the horses of the Regiment which in this country is called gram. There is a salary of £250 a year attached to it but in general there is much money made by it though not honourably. I hope you have no doubt of which line and conduct I shall pursue. St. John tells me in one of his last letters he has fixed on the infantry, of course he is right as my uncle seemed to wish it. Thank you dear Father for the razor and a razor strop which St. John says he has for me, you mention some cards from Major Eyre which do not accompany. I now My dear Father arrive at that part of your letter when you mention of the change likely to take place in your situation.

---

84   Gram Agent. The officer in charge of orders and funds to purchase gram (grain) from the bazaar for horses and animals. A lucrative role for the less than honest.

It is most natural that one who experiences much conjugal felicity as you did and for such a considerable length of time should find a great change and vacuity in sustaining a loss of those numberless satisfactions of conferring and receiving obligations and kindness which in general constitute happiness. Nor is it less natural my dear Father to desire a repetition of the same enjoyment, concurring circumstances rendering it equally eligible. Residing so far from home as I do, it can affect me but as it affects my father and the rest of the family, and much pleasure do I receive in this satisfaction expressed by my brothers and sisters at the prospect, and ardently do I wish and hope that your happiness and consolation on your new union may equal what you have so much reason to expect. This to accomplish and preserve my dear Father no person knows better how than yourself.[85]

I recollect perfectly the two Miss Messiters at Major Eyres and during the period I had the pleasure of their company I had every reason to admire their amiable manners and perfectly coincide in the opinion formed of them by Maxwell. As I have many letters to write to Europe by the present fleet I must conclude sooner than I otherwise might have done. Having written that I hope you will allow it to be tolerably close. I have but five days more and the prospect of active service which is very much against writing Europe letters.

Yours most affectionately I am dear Father yours VB.

7 October 1801

My uncle has been removed from the Court of Mysore to the Maratha Court at Poonah and will set out in a few days most probably. Indeed his former position was too severe, his present is equally honorable and advantageous. In his letter to me on the occasion he says that now considering how far it would be eligible to take me with him the result was that I ought to remain on the coast. As there was no captaincy open for me to go in, equal to the gram agency and that he wished to have me near his other two nephews who have so lately arrived.

From Colonel B Close

My dear St John, I have unfortunately neglected writing to you so long that in commencing this letter I have scarcely the means of referring to any communication of former date but although silent myself during the lapse of so large an interval, my friend Valentine will have informed you from time to time of my movements in Mysore. After having made a tour of the country for the purpose of promoting the revenue I returned to Seringapatam in November last and, although I had previously experienced excellent health above the Ghauts, I had scarcely taken up my abode on the island when I was seized by a fever which continued to visit me till the beginning of the year, when I found myself so far recovered as to be able to accompany the troops in a little expedition to the western Ghauts which overlook Malabar where a

85   The Rev St. John Blacker had re-married.

rebellious chieftain had long kept the province in a state of disturbance.[86] The service terminated favourably and in a shorter period than had been expected which enabled me to return to Seringapatam by the end of April.

Here the fever again visited me, and as by the end of May it seemed to have laid fast hold of me Lord Clive gave me an earnest invitation to pass a few weeks with him at the Presidency doubting not but I would benefit considerably by a change of air. In June I came to Bangalore: and pursuing leisurely I arrived here in the beginning of July. The sea air soon helped to restore me and much of the month had not past away, when some of the leading ships of the March fleet came in to anchor in the roads.

I now began to look out for my nephews, who I had learned had certainly embarked from England. My anxiety to see them was not of long continuance, the remaining ships of the fleet having soon made their appearance I lost not a moment of getting the young men ashore. I could not entertain them myself being at that time a guest of the Governor, but I managed to accommodate them suitably at a comfortable habitation close to my neighborhood. A seminary for the instruction of the cadets had been established at Chinglepat, a pleasant spot about 40 miles from hence and the two young men were ordered to proceed with all possible dispatch. They were allowed to continue here however for eight or ten days and in this interval, they were provided with the few things they had occasion for: I saw few as you had fitted them out in a most judicious and ample manner. St John who is a very handsome fellow promises to be at least as tall as his brother. They left me in good spirits and reached their destination in good health. I hear from them both frequently. Captain Armstrong who presides in this seminary and to whom I gave them a letter of recommendation is kind to them in every respect and speaks of them in the warmest terms of approbation. Although the discipline they observe at the seminary obliges them to practice the duties of the inferior ranks, they are both Lieutenants of some standing and will accordingly proceed to join a Corps the moment that Captain Armstrong reports them perfected in their present course of instruction which he will probably be enabled to do in a month or six weeks.[87] They are both studying the Persian language and as they are young and, possess good parts, I expect that their progress will be rapid. I need not say that I shall not be unmindful of them when they step forth to join a Regiment. I have now

86   The expedition to Wynaad (Waynadad) against a rebellious local Rajah.
87   E. Dodswell & J. Miles, *Alphabetical List of the Officers of the Indian Army 1760–1834,* Charles Armstrong appointed cadet 1783, Ensign 7 Sept. 1783 Lieutenant, August 1790, Captain, December 1799. Brevet Major whilst i/c Cadet Company at Chingleput. J. Cotton, *List of Inscriptions on Tombs or Monuments in Madras* (Madras: Government Press, 1946). 2 volumes. Major Charles Armstrong d.10 July 1806. Formerly Captain in charge of the 'Cadet Company' at Chingleput. He resigned in 1802 to resume a command in 2nd Madras Infantry. Murdered by mutineers during the Vellore Mutiny July 1806. IOR/Z/E/4/38/B587 Armstrong had been replaced at Chingleput by a Capt. Box. *Asiatic Journal 1800.* There is a warm letter of thanks to Armstrong from Officer Cadets dated December 1800. See Blacker letter dated 10 October 1804 and undated letter post 7th October 1801 from Colonel B. Close to Rev. John St. Blacker.

to speak of Val: he continued with me till May last, when finding that his Regiment was likely to be employed in the field he hastens to join it and he expected to find it at Arcot but before he arrived there a part of the Corps including his troop had marched to Tinnevelley Province to the southward to be employed against a powerful tributary who had shown himself in rebellion in that quarter. He therefore pursued his troops in all haste and overtook it before it reached the scene of action. The rebels were now attacked in their stronghold and on one occasion our Cavalry amounting only to about 400 were ordered to charge a body of these not less in number than 3000. The attempt was arduous but the Cavalry succeeded beyond all expectations, our loss was moderate while that of the enemy was very considerable.

In this affair Val received the wound of a musket ball in his leg and lost a delightful charger which carried him through the action but expired of his wounds immediately after. The wound soon took a favourable appearance and before it was quite healed he again took to his duty, which bringing him upon a rear guard he had occasion to charge with his troops a strong party of the enemy in which he had complete success receiving however a another wound in his leg but so slight as scarcely to have confined him. From these exploits added to his many military qualifications I now consider him as a very distinguished officer and I assure you I am not a little proud when I have occasion to mention him as my near relation. He still continues on the same service which I trust will terminate successfully ere very long. Your letters for him and all the others that come for him by the fleet were forwarded to him but I am a little uneasy at his not having acknowledged the rest of them; they may have met with interruption but I think they must be safe. He has been extremely fortunate in rising well in his Regiment and I have the pleasure to add Lord Clive has just given him the gram agency of his regiment which is a very desirable appointment. This improvement of his circumstance gives me the more satisfaction as you must know that Marquis Wellesley has lately inimated to me of his intention of taking me away from Mysore, employing me at the court of Poonah, so that if I be now removed to so great a distance from this Presidency, Val I trust will be able to watch over and assist St John and little Robert in my absence. At all events I think their interests will not be neglected. I am greatly obliged by the interesting picture you have given me of political appearances at home. Some events have since happened however which I hope have helped clear up the forbidding prospects which hung around you. The death of the Emperor Paul,[88] Lord Nelson's exploit in forcing 'The Sound' and our success in Egypt can scarcely fail to accelerate the negotiations which seem to be on foot for a general peace.[89] I was delighted to hear of my mother's recovery; she is now far advanced in years and

---

88   Russian Tsar Paul I 1754–1801. Reigned for 5 years until assassinated <www.britannica.com> (accessed August 2017).

89   J. Walsh, *Journal of the Late Campaign in Egypt* (London: T. Cadell and W. Davies, 1803). Napoleon invaded Egypt in 1798. He returned to France in 1799 but his remaining Army was defeated at the Battle of Alexandria in April 1801. All French forces capitulated to the British in September 1802.

you may suppose that I contemplate the moment that may permit me to see her with increasing solicitude. From what you have said if I may venture to congratulate you on your recent change of situation, if the event has taken place of which I do not doubt, I sincerely hope it is attended with all the comforts and advantages which under your circumstances it promised to bestow. A very few years may allow me to witness the ease and complacency of your domestic society.

8 October

My nephews have now finished their course of practice at Chinglepat and are accordingly preparing to join their Regiments. They have both been appointed to the Cavalry which I think is the preferable Corps of the Army, although in the infantry they would have had more rank. St John goes to the 1st Regiment to join his brother and Robert goes to the 4th Regiment which is commanded by Colonel Dallas[90] a particular friend of mine. Valentine continues to the southward but the service in that quarter has terminated most successfully, I have not heard from him since he got his late appointment or rather since he got information upon the subject. I expect to receive orders daily from Lord Wellesley directing me to proceed to Poonah. I have the pleasure of using the saddle you sent me every morning; the razors are excellent. Yours my dear St. John most affectionately, B. Close

14 December 1801

Tiagur.[91] Since I last wrote to you my dear Father many circumstances of consequence have happened here. The contest which existed between the Company and the southern Poligars is now completely concluded in favor of the former. The rebel chiefs have lost their heads and we have put new men in their places.

After marching to and fro a good deal in the enemy's country we were sent off in a most expeditious manner to the very south of the Peninsula within some miles of Cape Comorin there to prevent fugitives getting possession of some places it was thought they would attempt. We might have been spared the trouble as they were taken before they got half so far. We spent about eight days at Palmacotta where there is an excellent English Society and we really had a very pleasant time whilst we remained.

We were then directed to proceed to Trinchinopoly where we arrived after many difficulties having marched 200 miles in the midst of the monsoon through a country

90   E. Dodswell & J. Miles, *Alphabetical List of the Officers of the Indian Army 1760–1834*, Thomas Dallas, commanded 4th Madras Native Regiment. b.1758, Cadet 1778, Ensign 25 April 1788, Lieutenant 15 January 1782, Captain 1 June 1786, Major 18 December 1798, Lieutenant-Colonel 7 May 1799, Colonel 25 October 1809, Major-General 1 January 1812, Lieutenant-General 27 May 1825. Knighted (G.C.B.) 7 April 1815. Died 12 August 1839.
91   E. Thornton, *Gazetteer of the Territories under the Government of the East India Company*, Tiagur, a town south of Arcot.

intersected by numerous large rivers, but what made it particularly unpleasant was the state of ground. Also that part of the country being the more famous in India for cotton manufacture and the ground which grows that plant being of the softest kind it obliged us frequently to make marches of five or six miles a day. But here we were again recompensed by the height of gaiety. It is the station of one of our Generals and this being a large English Society of both males and females we had fine dancing every week. I confess we were not in dancing order, our cloaths being very much the worse for wear just coming out of the field. As the grand river, which you may see in your map runs close under the walls of Trinchinopoly is at this time of the year so deep as to render it unpassable. It was necessary for our Corps at all events to make a halt of most probably some weeks: and my own impatience, seconded by a hint of my uncles as he left the coast induced me to think of applying for leave of absence to see my brother at Arcot the regular headquarters of our Regiment. I was dissuaded however by the General of the station telling me that most likely the dismounted men of our Corps, who had lost their horses in the last field service would be ordered to Arcot shortly and the serviceable part of our Regiment cantonned at Trinchinopoly, in which case I might be ordered to proceed to the former station. This was the more desirable as the less one is on leave the better, and on my arrival at Arcot, though five of our officers with about 300 men are there yet they are all junior to me and I shall command and have an opportunity of forming my brother the more according to my own ideas.

You are now to suppose me after this long preamble if I may so call it, sitting in a Choultry at Ranganagur three marches on my way from Trinchinopoly to Arcot at which I am feasting myself with the expectation of arriving about the 21st Inst. Today being the 13th of December 1801.

I have met with nothing curious so far except the manner in which the natives crossed the Cauvery River when it happens to be full. They set off from the opposite side considerably above the landing place in a float made of bundles of sticks and empty earthen jars which are so light that when stopped at the mouth they bear a very considerable weight. Thus they drop down the stream one by one, men and women. Even when fordable for men it is frequently too rapid for women to attempt crossing in which case they set the female on a bundle of wood or drag the little float after them through the water.

It is a needless to say with what impatience I am actuated at the near prospect of meeting with St. John and Robert. The 1000 questions I shall have to ask and accounts I shall receive concerning the family and friends at home will be quite delightful and though many of them are frequently supposed too trivial to communicate by letter yet I often find them more interesting than those of more general consequence.

Nor is it more necessary to say with what anxiety my uncle is actuated for the welfare of the two lads, was it not that I am well persuaded that however thoroughly you may be convinced of the fact yet still instances give the highest satisfaction to a mind nearly concerned. In a letter I received from the Colonel just before he embarked from Bombay he says provided I could not proceed immediately to Arcot, if you have any acquaintance at the station who you think may have the means of being careful to them you must endeavor to interest him in their behalf, they are so young that they require the aid of discreet friends. And indeed he urged it as the reason for not wishing to have me with him to Poonah, that he did not like the idea of leaving them entirely to themselves on their first arrival. But previous to his letter I had taken the precaution of writing to a few of my steady friends there and one of them an old Captain and one in the true style militaire. I expect to see them both shortly well mounted, as two horses each is absolutely necessary, and hope they will be more lucky in that article than I have been, as towards the close of this late service I have lost a horse by hard labour that cost me £150 besides the charger on whose fine qualities I expiated on so much in my last and for which as being killed in action the Government allowed me not quite half of what I paid for him.

The number of Mussulmen sauntering about the country through which I am now a travelling is quite distressing to see. Their power in India which they have enjoyed in great splendour these last five or six centuries is now completely overthrown and the only vestige that remains is the Nizam. Even his country is preserved for him by our troops and were we to withdraw them the Marathas would pour in upon him immediately. The Great Mogul is now but the name and had his city Delhi taken from him and his eyes put out some years ago by the Marathas.[92] For them and the English, India is not quite large enough and there's every reason to suppose that a rupture must take place not long hence now that Tippoo is dead whose existence caused a balance.[93] But two great powers don't long retain an equilibrium. Now that the several Mohammadan states have been overturned there remains no longer sufficient employment for that race of people and they wander about in all directions not knowing what to do. They would consider themselves downgraded should they stoop to cultivate the ground or do any handicraft work and are taught to conceive all employment as disgraceful but the sword and dishonorable but destruction. This is the only time I write by this ship which I have heard of by chance and to depart immediately. Ever dutifully I remain your, etc etc

I finished the first sheet of the present packet to my father on the 14th Inst. expressed at the close of it an intention are sending it off by a ship supposed to sail very shortly but on arriving yesterday at a post office station I was informed there was not the smallest chance of it being in time and therefore did not make the experiment. As my account of the present state of the Mohammadans in this country was very contracted I shall take up the subject again and expiate on their concerns a little fuller.

As originally, force was found requisite to give the stability to the foundations of the Mohammadan religion so has it continued to prove necessary to its existence in any

---

92   C.E. Buckland, *A Dictionary of Indian Biography*, Shah Alum II, 1728–1806 the House ot Timur. Eventually he was taken under British 'protection' in 1803.

93   Prophetic words. The 2nd Maratha War 1803–05 and the 3rd Maratha War 1817–19 were some time away. Ed.

extensive degree. For owing to their extreme sensibility and debauchery in private life with the uncommon numbers that have been swept away by the sword when acting in a public capacity it was not surprising that they should not increase and multiply in the same proportions with other nations. Finding that the regular course of nature did not increase the prevalence of the Mussulman faith and that their religion itself did not possess any of that attractive amiableness so particularly the characteristic of Christianity which requires but persuasion and an introduction to the unbiased mind they enforced the ceremony of circumcision on millions leaving it to the next generations to become true believers. As therefore their religion requires the hand of power for its support it may be supposed it will fall with their sovereignty. The Moguls influence is no more nor is Tippoo Sultan's country, or the Carnatic any longer receptacles for the cultivation of Mussulman principle. What proselytes they once had in the eastern islands when their trade to these countries was in the zenith have not been able to keep it pure and unmixed from the customs of their surrounding neighbours and if it is scarcely to be observed in their manners now but by the peculiar degree of ferocity. The Nizam is not so great a cipher as scarcely to deserve mention and in short they may be safely said to be confined to the Persian and Ottoman Empires. The Persians never were famed as a military nation. In modern history they never even were mentioned in that light and I am sure they cannot be said to have gained much credit in ancient history from their wars with the petty states of Greece. They were not then Mohammedans or for admitting the Roman Armies into the heart of their dominions. In the present day their endurance and want of spirit is more excessive than ever and was a horde of Tartars to come from the northward in their former degree of irresistibility they must in all probability fall a sacrifice.

What a pity that no man of ability in the descriptive accompanied our late envoy from this place. He is returned about eight months since having gone through the very heart of Persia from the Gulf to the Caspian Sea, passed through their most famous cities in the historic page and visited the ruins of Persepolis. But need there be a more conspicuous instance of the very depressed state of mark on the and than that lately exhibited in the western part of their Empire? No longer do the Turkish Army's penetrate into European Russia or pass the boundaries of Hungary; and so far away are their fleets from presuming to enter the Adriatic Sea or navigate between the Pillars of Hercules that perhaps their very existence in their present even reduced condition arose from the heroic exertions of the crew of a single British ship HMS 'Le Tigre.'

But this is a wonderful digression when I proposed to confine myself to India. The Moors of the peninsula are of a remarkable, handsome well made race of people. Their features generally inclining to the Roman style and you regularly meet among them with figures that would make the most respectable appearance in an historical picture. I speak as to the males, the females fall very short indeed of my fair country women in exterior and exterior beauty, the very mention of a companion is ridiculous. Any qualifications, but merely the power of exciting sensual desires, are esteemed masculine, out of character and even indelicate and their most extended education proceeds no further than learning to repeat a very few forms of prayer and the interior regulation of the house. In marriage any mutual affection is entirely out of the question; the parties never see each other until the ceremonies are adjusted past retraction. From the very great idea that a woman is defiled if even seen by one of a contrary sex and among the higher orders, the matrimonial ceremony generally takes place when they are infants. If a woman is not fortunate enough to be married in her prime of youth she is not expected to remain virtuous, indeed such is the depraved state of their ideas that the parents would almost be unnatural to enforce a chaste life. It is quite amusing sometimes to meet with an English newspaper containing a paragraph concerning this country as such absurd things are regularly invented e.g. I met with an account of the dress of the Sultaness of Seringapatam and it was exactly the habit of a man. There was such an elegant description of her turban whereas the females never wear a headdress of any kind other than a few ornaments of precious stones. The late Sultan's Government as well as the present Nizam's is so lax that little or no attention is paid to what passes in the interior of a man's family; a parent may put his children to death and perhaps nothing more is heard of the matter. The killing of a concubine is merely exercising a proper authority, supposing her to be unfaithful and their wife under the same circumstances treated in a like manner affords an example which every true Mussulmen will rejoice at even to her parents if some enmity has not subsisted between their families. This is what takes place under their own Government but under ours in the country we are so meddling and officious as not even to permit a Mohammadan to put a slave girl to death without inquiring into it, such is the oppression we are guilty of in India. The Moors conceive it a very sacred duty to marry and much more incumbent among them than it is held with us, in which perhaps they are right and therefore instead of seeing so great a proportion of the inhabitants unmarried as in England you scarcely meet with a person who is single. When they lay aside their arrogance their own likeness is a caricature of the French so they appear always perfectly at ease and unabashed but there is not that delicacy in their civility nor the same proportion of kindness which characterizes the English. Would they pay you a compliment, it is not presented with the delicacy which nicely shows the application and then desists for fear of offending sensibility; on the contrary it is explained in the most glaring manner and plastered on in the broadest, though frequently in the most ingenious style. However they may resemble the French in their politics they have not the smallest of the frivolity and gaiety which characterizes that nation. Their gravity of the deportment and gait differs widely from the flippant step of the French. And their proud ideas of the superiority of the male part of the species would be offended at the thought of dancing. I cannot account for this admiring so much and a vein of gallantry which runs through their romance is when the smallest shades of it is not to be found in their manners and when I mentioned above their paying compliments it must not be supposed they are addressed to women. No that would be descending below their dignity. None of them can read or write either among the higher or lower orders except such as are to earn their bread by it and therefore when they find it requisite to correspond with any one they are obliged to have recourse to a third not only to perform the part of an amanuensis but also to arrange the language. I have thus my dear Father given you an account of the character and manners of the Moors of the present day in this country as they have struck me. I mean those that are not immediately in our military service, these latter owing to European discipline have got over many of the prejudices of their sect though still I believe they would be very happy did an opportunity to show their inveteracy to Christians.

Dated 18 Dec 1801 Trincomalee

28 December 1801

Arcot. Behold me arrived and situated for the present in command of half the Regiment and here have I found St. John and Robert Close as promising young cadets as I could have wished. They are both practicing to enable themselves to take charge of troops and are generally out every morning. I have had some very interesting conversations with them and intend introducing a little regularity in their studies of the language. I have Robert in my house: St. John and Mr Tucker as acquaintances of Mrs Nobles live together. Mr Tucker is a fine young man and will shortly leave the place with his Regiment which is expected to march.[94]

The little casket I promised to send Mary, St. John tells me there was a funny resolution of putting into the bank, that being the case I will retain it here and by the 7th January fleet send a couple of fine gold chains, more valuable for their workmanship than their materials which, with their low prices would render it absurd to make use of them but that for which they were intended viz. an ornament for a lady's neck. They are common presents from this country to females at home and notwithstanding many attempts have been made to execute them at home they have commonly failed.

I was particularly surprised to find St. John such a tall handsome young fellow, he is positively the most conspicuous that way of anyone I have seen in India. Robert will be exactly the same figure of the Colonel in person and is certainly as sweet a tempered little fellow as I ever saw. He is reported fit for duty and I suppose will shortly be ordered to join his Regiment. This letter will go by a ship from the Malabar Coast and as I am acquainted with no one going from thence I could not send them with this. I hope however I shall be more lucky next fleet. I have received accounts from the Colonel at Bombay when he was in good health and have since seen a paragraph in the newspaper mentioning his having left that place under the salutes due to his diplomatic character. That is what I've heard of him lately. I shall most probably, dear Father write to you again very shortly and remain with the utmost duty and sincerity your affectionate son.

94   E. Dodswell & J. Miles, *Alphabetical List of the Officers of the Indian Army 1760–1834.* George Tucker joined HEIC Army 1800 Cornet August 1801, Captain October 1803, Died August 1804 in Camp at Poonah.

1802

2 March 1802 (*Received 27 August 1802*)
Camp near Ongole.[95] My dear Father, although a fleet has sailed from the coast within this week for England, yet as I had written but a few days I may say, before by a ship proceeding from Anjango, and that St.John was writing I knew by the lately sailed one, I deferred communicating my proceedings until the next.

The Fates have decreed I believe I should not have any rest, for I had scarcely been a month in Arcot when I was ordered off with a squadron of the Regiment in a few hours warning. The cause of this unexpected order was an information received at HQ of a party of marauders to the number of 3 or 400 who had made some incursions into the Vellore District which you will perceive in your map lies about 100 miles north of Madras, destroying villages and putting to death the inhabitants. As they were merely a banditti of plunderers the squadron was considered as sufficient and I was directed to proceed with all convenient expedition.

The distance from Arcot to Vellore is 140 miles which I marched in seven days, but as the report of an approach of some troops to march against them had made them draw off, I found nothing to do particular and therefore pitched my little camp near the Collector of the district, who was at this period making a tour, the better to ascertain the amount of his revenues. After remaining about a fortnight with him information arrived of the same party of marauders assembling on the borders, on which I left him and proceeding in a northwest direction towards the Ghauts and presuming that your map is Rennels, I shall henceforward mention the name of towns which he has inserted and as he spells them, for in the letter there are so many different ways as the pronunciation strikes the ear of different people. Frequently the entire name, generally the termination and always the pronunciation differ with the caste from one of which you receive information, which is the cause you may suppose of many mistakes. Having separated from the Collector and thus finding myself without an European near me, to supply of the deficiency I resolved to commence the present letter which has the consolatory effect of making me at least ideally present with those so precious to me.

St. John I left in very good style at Arcot learning his duty and who promises to be a good horseman and smart officer. I can say the same for Robert Close, he departed a month ago for the ceded territories to join his Regiment at Belharee. My last letter from Poonah gave no good account of the Colonel's health and his having arranged everything comfortable about him.

<hr>

95   E. Thornton, *Gazetteer of the Territories under the Government of the East India Company*, Ongole, Ongol, a fortified town in the district of Nellore, Madras. Described as 'wretched' with a population of 31,000.

On the 25th of February I arrived at Soondy,[96] the seat of a petty chief who keeps a force of about 500 men: he is on the same footing with the ancient Britons of England. He has got his little castle in the hills, besides his estate which supports his little army and he calls himself a Prince among his own Clan though he is not permitted to make use of that title in any transactions with the Company under whose Government he is. On my approach he sent out his Prime Minister as he calls a man who manages his affairs (such is their fondness for the imitation of princely grandeur) with a message that he would call on me provided I had no objection to his coming in all his Glory, drums beating etc. You must understand that it is a privilege never granted to an inferior and this was as much as to say that he looked upon me as in no way superior to him. Such is their love of distinction that there have been instances of some wealthy nobles giving some Lakhs of Rupees to pass their Sovereign with the Naqquara drums beating.[97] You may perceive from my being treated with so much ceremony how highly the English name is here. He had perhaps a higher idea of my situation and influence, there being so very few Europeans in this district, which is one of those the Company has got some months after the death of the Nabob. All matters being settled about the style in which he was to come and the manner he was to be received he came to my tent with all his force after him, horse and foot, himself in a palanquin and his drums and trumpets making a most hideous noise. I met him the regulated number of paces from the door and embracing him in the Eastern style led him in. Here we had a great deal of ceremony and the most barefaced flattery and compliments on both sides, when I handed him some Betel nut and spices as a signal for him to conclude his visit and he took himself away with his horse and foot performing a mock skirmish in front the whole road to his house, about 2 miles. Next day I returned his visit with fewer attendants and was received as I had entertained him. He requested leave to give a dinner to my squadron which I permitted, after letting him know that he was not to expect it would be of any affect towards influencing the Collector for or against him with whom he had heard I was on intimate terms. Such is the venality of the Eastern Governments that it is required a considerable time to persuade any native that he can have justice without giving a douceur after he comes under the English jurisdiction. He requested I would go to hunt with him which I consented to do. I met him with all his followers and getting into the jungle very shortly raised a wild boar which his men put an end to very shortly with their spears. We afterwards raised a hare and all his people, even that are scattered about on a signal, that the game was sprung, they formed a large ring with the poor animal in the center and by degrees closed in, the hare laid down in grass and they threw a long net round it at some yards distant and threw stones into the bush and the hare jumped into the net. This you may suppose gained but little interest as the animal has no chance of escaping but is killed almost as soon as discovered. In this manner we killed three or four and then took the diversion of hawking. This was also stupid enough

96   Ibid. A town in Nellore district Madras.
97   Drums that precede a dignitary and indicate rank.

for instead of letting out the hawk as we do they first let off the hawk and afterwards throw up a poor bird they had caught in a snare by which it had not the smallest chance of its life and indeed all their sports the amusement with them seems to consist in the game being caught and killed, not in the pursuit as with us. And of the three I liked the wild boar being hunted best. The present duty I am on, I can't call it service as there is no likelihood of any fighting, is reckoned of the most disagreeable an officer is subject to in this country, being cut off from society in a great measure for there is a little satisfaction in the company of a native; our manners differ so much and also our ideas arising from the very great differences in the Governments we have been bred up on.

The widow of an Asiatic is what an European would call cunning and has been found absolutely necessary under their own Princes in order to preserve what ever property they may be possessed of which if they would behave with openness they could not long retain.

Though Soondy is the point nearest to which I had reason to expect marauders would come, yet seeing they were completely dispersed again, on finding a party was coming so near them, I moved for greater convenience towards Ongole from whence this first sheet of my dispatch is directed. It is a place of great resort being on the great road from Madras to all the posts to the northward as well as to Hyderabad. I shall find myself more at home whilst I remain here as there resides a Commanding Officer and a Collector in the fort and many Europeans are continually passing.

Adieu ever yours VB.

24 March 1802 (*Received 12 Dec 1802*)
Ongole. My dear Father although but a few days since I have closed a letter to you yet I can't refuse myself the pleasure of communicating to you by the earliest opportunity a difference which has taken place in my situation. I received some time since a promise of the appointment of Persian Interpreter to Headquarters on its being vacated by the officer holding it who proposes going to Europe for his health. I did not inform you of this my prospect as I have had reason to entertain so many heretofore which never took place, that I considered it probable this present might meet with a similar fate. It so happened before the ship in which the gentleman had taken his passage was unexpectedly delayed behind the rest of the fleet to take a cargo which was not prepared in time and in the interim the Persian Interpreter so far recovered as to make the voyage unnecessary. To add to this untoward circumstance, by Order of the Court of Directors the appointment of Agent of Supplies was abolished and of course I lost my situation with my brother agents but by the assistance of my good uncle I was nominated by the same order Secretary to the Commanding Officer of the Southern Division, Brigadier Patton,[98] having been lately appointed to the command in room of General Bridges,

98   E. Dodswell & J. Miles, *Alphabetical List of the Officers of the Indian Army 1760–1834*. Probably Brigadier John Pater: Captain 1784, Major 1790, Lt. Colonel 1796, Colonel 1798, Major General 1805. Retired 1813. d.1817.

gone home. I now wait only for another officer from our Regiment to relieve me that I may proceed to my station, Trinchinopoly about 400 miles from where I am at present and then perhaps I may experience a little rest. The last Commanding Officer had an Aide De Camp and Brigade Major attached to him but as the rank of the present is not sufficient to admit me of an Aide de Camp the same situation and pay is given under the name of Secretary. We have however a Brigade Major in the family. The appointment of Agent of Supplies was abolished owing to the unconscionable peculation which were practiced by the holders. To satisfy you of that I was not of that number I transcribe to you part of a letter I received from a friend of mine who commanded the Governors bodyguard shortly after I was nominated Agent – 'your conduct in the office of agency does you the greatest credit, Maclean (secretary to the military board) and the military board have already remarked that they have discovered a phenomenon, viz an honest agent of Regimental supplies.'

Impute not to vanity the foregoing extract but derive it from the purer motive of communicating to my dear Father the same pleasure it has occasioned to his most affectionate and dutiful son.

Henceforth I am Captain Blacker.

15 July 1802 (*Received 26 February 1803*)
Madras. My dear Father, I have a delayed in writing to you from day to day this week past in hope of receiving from St. John your letters of October 1801 and January 1802 that I might proceed in my reply regularly and circumstantially. I received them about 10 days since and forwarded them on the Inst. to my brother who has detained them for the purpose of taking a copy. As they have not yet arrived and the despatches from Bengal came in yesterday which will oblige the *Swallow* packet to sail by which this goes in less than 48 hours I must not wait in hope of receiving your letters from Arcot. About five days ago I wrote to Catherine in which I complained of my bad luck in not having got at that time your letter of October last as from the tenor of your favour of January I had reason to imagine there was still one to come to hand. Thank my lucky stars it has since made its appearance to my exceeding joy with it also came one from Sam and William but my answer to them I must delay until the next opportunity it being rather uncertain whether this may be in time or not. My last letter was from Ongole dated the latter end of March informing you of my appointment to the Secretaryship of the Southern Division the headquarters of which is at Trinchinopoly. In April an officer was ordered from the Regiment to come and relieve me in charge of the squadron I commanded and St. John requested he might be sent that he might have an opportunity of seeing me before I preceded south. He came and we passed three days together at Vellore since which time he has returned to Arcot. From the conversations I have had with him and the reports of his uniform, correct conduct I have received from different persons who have seen more of him than I have since his arrival in India I have not the smallest doubt of his success, on the contrary my confidence is of the most satisfactory kind.

I had a very long letter from him five days ago in consequence of yours of the 5th of January I sent to him, he requests in the most earnest and anxious terms that I would assure you on many heads regarding his demeanor as well towards himself as me on which you appear to harbour doubts and I must in justice to him as also for your satisfaction testify only that his conduct is universally remarked by his acquaintances as the most amiable and gentlemanly; and with regard to me his attention to my advice or recommendation of any particular circumstance in general behaviour I may have hinted has been flattering to my judgment and gratifying to my fraternal feeling.

The changes that have taken place in family arrangements are highly interesting and I make no doubt will continue to prove highly satisfactory nor can I sufficiently express my happiness to find that Sam has abandoned the dishonourable state of a bachelor for the more holy one of matrimony and I ardently hope the remainder of my elder brothers will take into serious consideration to follow his example. To talk gravely upon the subject I think is a considerable a defect in the custom of the present age in England that so few marriages take place in society and a large proportion of those which do happen to have a disparity of years by no means to the next generation. In no other country is so large an establishment requisite for a wife as in England which circumstance renders it ruin to the prospects of any young man who is obliged to improve his fortune in the world and this serves as an insuperable bar to his entering into the conubial state. I hope to have shortly from some of the family more particular accounts of my fair sister than what I have as yet receive or they have been enabled yet to give me. I am sure they will not neglect a point which must be so interesting to me. How needless must it be to express my happiness and joy that my dear Father's late connection has continued to give that satisfaction and comfort in the family that he so justly expected as the consequence. Consider me grateful on my sister's account and present my love and duty to my mother on my own. I am now on the point of leaving Madras where I have been remaining near three months, leading a gay, pleasant life enough. As I have been living in Lord Clive's family I have with considerable attention and civility from the whole society in Madras where I was before scarcely known on account of my having been always up the country. My residence in Madras should not have been so long but that I had some accounts to settle connected with my late appointment in the Regiment which met with many unexpected delays in their adjustment. My letters from Colonel Close continue to rejoice me by the most favourable account of his health, the precariousness of which he is so insensible of that he omits not to use the proper precautions to ensure its continuance. This attention of us all is of that steady affectionate nature which lets not an opportunity slip of being useful. He has lately made presents to Robert and St. John of a horse each which mounts them in good cavalry style and he warns them of the great efficacy of studying the language. St. John has got a most excellent Munshi now which I found him from hence and if he duly attends he must succeed from his years.[99] I never lose an opportunity depend on it to keep strongly impressed on their minds of the necessity of it.

16 July 1802

I must leave this place tomorrow morning and am now so busily employed in packing up my baggage that I must cut short my letter and send it to the post office. I may be able to write more particularly to some parts of your letter when I receive it from my brother and that most probably soon for the present being an extraordinary one I have no doubt, but another ship will also leave shortly when I shall clear off my debt to all the rest of the family. I must therefore request my dear Father you will present my love to my brothers and sisters and make them perfectly easy with respect to St. John under the idea that most unremitting attention will be paid to him by your most affectionate son. V B

8 October 1802 (*Received 24 March 1803*)
Adams Bridge.[100] In my last letter which I believe has not yet left India, I proposed to write more particularly to your letters and to St. John and Mary, the same cause which prevented me from putting that intention in execution then exists still. For the Cornet has a not had an opportunity of forwarding your letter since until lately and as from my present vagrant state I shall not receive it until my arrival at Trinchinopoly. I fear to delay on that account for the present which if attention be paid to the Government advertisement will not itself be in time.(see below. Ed.) For some unaccountable reason the *Swallow* packet was prevented sailing these last three or four months and another ship is now under orders; report which is ingenious in discovering the cause of every event asserts that our present administration, if I may so term our Principals in our Government here, is going home in her and wait but for the prospect of a new Governor's approach. But to more intimate concerns, I received a week since your letter at Palamcottah dated in April and immediately afterwards forwarded it to St. John from whom I have not since heard. To say my dear Father it affords me much pleasure must be so unnecessary that I should omit the declaration was it not for the handsome testimony it bears of my uncle's satisfaction as to my conduct, it's a piece of information I could never obtain directly from himself and one that carries with it in my estimation the greater value particularly from its coming through so interesting a source. It makes me wish I had not said so much about myself as I think it must weaken the effects of what my uncle may have been good enough to say in my favour but it is now past and cannot be helped and I console myself under the consideration that the earnestness my

---

99   Munshi, a language teacher, usually of Urdu.
100   E. Thornton, *Gazetteer of the Territories under the Government of the East India Company*, Adams Bridge. A geological feature of shoals or reefs between the South East Peninsula of India and Sri Lanka, formerly Ceylon.

friends have shown for particulars, assisted by little partiality upon their part will make at best a lame excuse for me.

From the Colonel I have not heard lately but make no doubt of his being in good health as was he otherways I should certainly hear of it through some channel; that he is immersed in business to such a degree as scarcely to have to think up on any subject but his diplomatic concerns is the result of the delicate situation of affairs between the English and Marathas. They are our grand rivals now and the only one we shall shortly have any severe struggle with in case of a misunderstanding occuring. I propose commencing a study of their language as soon as I am strong enough in Persian to admit of my directing my leisure to any other pursuit.

Within these three months I have written to most of my brothers and sisters and in some of them mentioned my being on the point of going on a tour of review with my superior. I am now upon my return and enumerate the names of the principle stations we have visited that you may see what a round we have had. On leaving Trinchinopoly we proceeded to Errod about 90 miles in a NW direction, thence to Dindigal, Madura, Chaskanacoil, close under the mountains from whence we were to have gone had time permitted to visit a waterfall reckoned of one of the highest known, that of Niagara in America not excepted. Thence we struck east about 40 miles to Palamcottah and to Tutacorim an old Dutch settlement on the seacoast. Without abandoning the beach we arrived yesterday at the strait dividing the island of Ceylon from the Continent called Adams Bridge and tomorrow we go to Mannad lying inland. Our route from thence to Trinchinopoly will be by Gallacoil so that I shall again pass through the scenes of our last year's campaign. A number of small islands lie between this part of the coast and the opposite shore which however is distant some 50 miles; these must have been very convenient for Adam to get to his bridge, the stones of which are scattered many miles to the southward. That they were for the before mentioned edifice every inhabitant of the neighborhood does not entertain the smallest doubt. However a person who may be absurd enough to argue from evident and external appearances which I confess I was might conclude they were formed on the very spot they still occupy. Owing to some local circumstances or mixture of some particular sorts of clay with the same, the latter in many places cakes and becomes as hard as firestone which it very much resembles. It is washed off and slaked by the forces of the sea in large flakes which form the scarred ruins of the famous bridge. It is almost a pity to spoil the popular story by proving those stones must have been formed thus from the circumstance of the separating in the same manner every instant and large lumps lying within a foot of and forming exactly like the part they were separated from. At all events Adam had never anything to say to the building of it and how it got its name it is hard to guess but the tradition of its action in this place is that attended with so many particular and minute circumstances that a candid impartial mind cannot withhold its belief of the truth of it.

Several lines of native legend omitted.

I had a letter from Robert Close lately who is doing very well as when I last wrote, St. John being nearer to him I heard more frequently and I have in my last letter to him been insisting upon his giving me a regular account of his progress in the Persian which I recommended his immediately commencing.

I know not what can possibly be done with Mr Deveux, he has been now been nearer one and a half years at Chinglepat, nor can he be reformed by a gentle or coercive means.[101] He is stubborn to a great degree and wishes to be sent home in any manner, he will never answer for this service. If an opportunity offers on my arrival a fortnight hence at Trinchinopoly I shall write again myself, the pleasure of answering my mother's kind and gratifying letter for which make her my kind thanks and assure her of my love.

Mr Dodwell whom you inquired about lived in the Resident's family as the youngest assistant while I was there and remains there still he has the best interest in the country but in a great measure defeats it by his own unsteady conduct for this last half year I know not how he has come on. I hope my dear Father that you will be able to read this and believe me ever sincerely yours, VB.

An Extract from the India Register published in 1803 The 1st Regiment of Native Cavalry:

Name	Rank	Date of Appointment to Regiment
Lieutenant Colonel	Charles Rumley	20 May 1801 on furlough
Major	John Doveton	20 May 1801
Captain	George Neal	30 July 1800
Captain	David Foulis	2 September 1801 2nd Brigade, Brigade Major
Captain lieutenant	H. O'Donnell	2 September 1801 on furlough
Captain lieutenant	Val: Blacker	4 September 1799 (Secretary to Officer Commanding Southern Div).
Lieutenant	John Collet	4 September 1799
Lieutenant	R. Otto Bayer	8 May 1800
Lieutenant	Robert Bryant	17 June 1800
Lieutenant	Edward Lyne	13 July 1801
Lieutenant	John Moore	2 September 1801
Cornet	J.W. Morgan	20 August 1801
Cornet	St. Martin	20 August 1801
Cornet	St. John Blacker	29 September 1801
Gram agent	Valentine Blacker	8 September 1801
Adjutant	John Collet	23 September 1800

---

101 E. Dodswell & J. Miles, *Alphabetical List of the Officers of the Indian Army 1760–1834*, Lieutenant Arthur Desveaux. Cadet 1800. Lieutenant 1801, pensioned 25 Sept. 1804. Possibly Lieut. Desveaux had a 'medical' issue as he received a pension on his discharge.

Name	Rank	Date of Appointment to Regiment
Quartermaster	Edward Lyne	19 September 1801
Surgeon	James Johnston	26 November 1799
Assistant Surgeon	John Best	
Lieutenant Colonel	Barry Close	29 November 1796. 3rd Regiment Native Infantry at Poonah and Honourable Aide de Camp to Governor General.
Robert Close:	Cornet	4th Regiment Native Cavalry 3 October 1801.

15 October 1802 (*Received 1 August 1803*)

My dear Father, I have at last procured from St. John the many letters I lately forwarded to him and have now an opportunity of noticing many articles in your favour which from not having them before me during the writing of my last letter I was not before enabled to do.

From the account you give of your house at Wells I shall make no scruple of helping myself to a bedroom as one will be scarcely missed out of so many. And indeed the whole concern appears to me most eligible whether we advert to the annexed grounds, to the convenience of situation and beauty of prospect.

I believe in a former letter of mine I had occasion to observe that the number of fortunes made in this country were very few, at all events in the present day, although I can well conceive the contrary to be the prevailing idea in England. Now they are much rarer than they were formerly and those that are acquired are known at home whilst the number of persons who come to this country without ever returning from want of the means are never heard of. Thus in England the fair side of the prospect is only seen and from that partial view alone is of the character of India taken. I might further observe that setting aside the instances of people of extraordinary interest who thus make immense fortunes in a short time, a number of those who enjoy the means of returning home owe it to the possession of some little property in England which they draw into this country and I know many young men in that situation at present who otherwise would never be worth anything.

My friend Temple was of that number and had he lived would have reaped very considerable benefit from £3,000 he possessed by putting it in the Company's Biennial Loan.

I have been led to the consideration of the circumstances from reading that part of your letter relating to your will which I think dear Father you express a degree of consideration that it only requires a moderate portion of diligence and frugality to acquire a sufficiency to go home on. This is a prejudice I am inclined to contradict in my own justification for I should conceive myself inexcusable as also would my friends under such a prepossession was I not to exert the above intended two requisites to enable me to return to the enjoyment of that happiness so intimately connected with the society of my dearest relations, could it be by this means obtained.

With regard to the extract from your will which you have been good enough to send me I can easily enter into the feeling and sentiment which prompted the recommendation accompanying it. There appears to me remaining £400 of the very equitable division my father has made among his sons and I would trust I shall not be accused of treating anything lightly, anything assigned me from that quarter when I say that the above sum can make very little difference to me either one way or other whilst in India. On the contrary I am a most heartily grateful for it but as a further obligation I request it may be made over to my four sisters viz £100 each as the only means I at present possess of testifying to them the sincerity of my brotherly affection.

In all my marches through the country I invariably ride but if I find it necessary to go quick the most convenient way is to have palanquin boys posted during the night and saddle horses during the day. When it is necessary to be accompanied by baggage a traveller of course can go no faster than they can. This was my predicament going to join the Army to the southward, concerning which you have demanded the account you mention in an overland dispatch of the Panjalum Courchy affair is the same I wrote to you about and agrees with mine I fancy, as much as any two accounts of a battle generally do, for I never knew of ten spectators, any two give exactly the same description of an action.

I am enabled to say that my health is improving every season and that I believe my constitution is such that having once weathered the grand tryal of the first two years residence it is more congenial to the soil of India than most others. Indeed I have acquired by experience so thorough a knowledge of it that I can in cases of indisposition in general much better prescribe for myself than any medical man and am so well acquainted with the approach of the bile that I am always able to prevent its further progress by the necessary precautions and preventatives. English conquest in this country by no means excites the same conduct in native powers that it does in European ones. That policy called 'balance of power' is but ill understood in India and a grand bar to it taking effect is opposed by the difference of Castes – a distinction which the many revolutions that have taken place in Hindoostan has never been able to destroy. It is the system of the English Government here to indulge and humour the native in these points not only as it attaches them to us in a manner but as it is the cause of supporting those jealousies by which they are conditionally actuated against one another to their own weakness and our strength. Their shortsightedness in this cannot be more strongly evinced than in the instance of the Marathas who at this moment are slaughtering one another (the three powers Holkar, Scindiah, and the Peishwa) instead of joining to keep a watchful eye upon the English.

The state of civilization in India scarcely authorises us to look for any theoretical knowledge of this important secret in modern European policy – for if only we advert to the era of its commencement in the West we shall find it comparatively speaking very recent. Perhaps the Earliest instance is the combination formed among the Italian states Maximimillian and Ferdinand of Aragon to expel Charles VIII of France from Naples. The early struggles between France and England wherein the latter was on the point more than once of becoming Master of both kingdoms does not afford any example of the other states in Europe coming forward to prevent so alarming a progress, nor do they appear to have given more attention to the continual hostilities the various kingdoms in Spain were engaged in and of the successive occurrences which evidently tended to unite them all into one great monarchy.

As the same conduct however will not answer for the French that does for the natives there are many salutary steps taken and arrangements made to prevent their ever penetrating into the interior parts of the country or forming cabals to our annoyance among the Rajahs. These latter we are fast depriving of the means to harm us, by making them as many as possible, new pensioners with only a small party of troops to each by way of an honorary guard. The whole executive and legislative powers are vested in the English nor are they permitted to collect the most trifling revenue in their former dependencies.

The information you wish regarding the extent of the British possession in the Peninsula of India is more easily afforded by enumerating the exceptions to entire proprietary there by giving the names of actual possession. Draw an imaginary line from Goa to the nearest part of the Toombudsha (a river which falls of into the Kistuah) and accompany it to the sea by which means you will have cut off that part which contains the English possessions with the long stripe of land which running up the Eastern side from the last mentioned river to near the head of the bay is called the Northern Sircars. In that vast extent of country so cut off there are independent two small patches Cochin and Travancore on the Western coast and a trifling province about half of what is termed Marawar, opposite them on the Eastern coast. The tributaries are Mysore and a few districts belonging to Poligars that are of little or no consequence and you would not probably find them in the map.

We march through them all our troops, except the two first independencies I mentioned and indeed all the rest are lately disarmed and precautions taken which completely annexes impossibility to their ever possessing firearms or ammunition in future. The places which will be ceded to the French are Pondicherry,[102] Caracal and Mahe but the grounds attached are only what the guns and their forts command.

British possessions in the Bengal side are the same they have been many years past with the addition of the kingdom of Lucknow annexed about three years ago and of which Lord Wellesley's brother is Governor. If you have not got Major Rennel's maps and memoir of his map of India you should procure it as the best and most satisfactory published; he has made an appendix to it since the war of '99 which shows all the partition of the country after the Mysore conquest.

It is pretty near as the British Territory now stands at except that which was alloted to the Nizam has since been made over to the English in lieu of the expense we

---

102 E. Thornton, *Gazetteer of the Territories under the Government of the East India Company*, Pondicherry a French coastal settlement within British India, once described as 'the handsomest town in India: Mahe also within British India formally annexed in 1793 but restored to a French settlement in 1815.

incurred by depriving him of his independence which always requires a field establishment. I have scarcely conscienced to regret you will excuse this long political not to say learned discussion however now that I have got through it I think it may as well go to Europe as be torn (sic) especially as I have but few incidents at present to make up an English letter. I am rejoiced to learn that you have not had the Gout for such a long period and entertain sanguine hopes that the air of Mount Roy may be found salutary enough to keep it off in future.

26 November 1802

I must impart to you now dear Father that I have lost my appointment of Secretary to Brigadier Pater for the more eligible one of Captain Commandant of Guides, a situation of particular confidence during war and permanent at all times with a handsome salary. I must attempt to describe its functions so that you may know how I shall be employed. The Corps consists in time of war of a Captain Commandant and his deputy who is an officer with prospect to succeed as circumstances may allow to the command: all the rest are guides with different roles, men intelligent in the roads of the country and all invariably Brahmins. All detachments and parties marching are furnished with a guide, to remain with them until their return, from the captain who is answerable for the man's fidelity and intelligence. The General in Chief has always to consult the Captain of Guides concerning the country he proposes marching through in order to obtain the necessary information about water, roads etc and everything local and this it is which makes him a man of consequence. On the Continent when the geography of the country is better known the Guide belonging to the Quartermaster General Department and owing to that circumstance he is accounted the Head of Staff as he must be acquainted with the proposed march of the Army in order to give him time to collect his own minute information. In this country where the Guides is a separate department of itself the Quartermaster General is sending to the Adjutant General and is only required to take up a good position for the Army and distribute the ground to the different Brigades, his office is an office of record of routes and he always furnishes Government with any new intelligence he may require. He must be a piece of an astronomer and a good military surveyor, in time of peace he may be employed by Government in gaining local information respecting country that is not well understood or measuring out new military roads which may be required.

I must conclude it with a remark that every Captain of Guides who has been on the coast has succeeded to higher situation and their names are in general mentioned as authors of geographical information in all English maps of India.

30 November 1802

As I have through want of information not treated of the subject properly I must again take it up, indeed the circumstance must prove to you how impatient I am always to communicate my good fortune to you and that I always write under the impression and influence of what ever occurs instantly. When I first commenced the subject I had not received the orders appointing me. I have since discovered that an entire new arrangement has taken place regarding the Guides and that they are henceforth to be considered in the Quartermaster Generals' Department. This is certainly more systematic and to improve the matter your humble servant is also appointed Assistant Quartermaster General in consequence of which he expects to succeed in less than 100 years to be Quartermaster General himself.

1803

20 February 1803
Camp of the Grand Army, Chittledrooge.[103] No opportunity having occured to send this letter written some months ago, I alone among them have kept it by me until now that I hear a ship is on the point of sailing. Our ally among the Maratha powers has been dethroned by one of the others and we are obliged to come forward and assist him.[104] This it is to be hoped will afford an opportunity of establishing a subsidiary force at our allies' court and of obtaining some territory which they have a long refused us on the Bombay side. The Army has now advanced near the frontiers and I am with it in my official capacity and the further charge of Superintendance of Bazaar Supplies for the Army. This is but temporary until the Army is Brigaded as it is of itself sufficient business for any one man. I hope to let you hear from me soon. Believe me dear Father your most affectionate son VB

NB I was near forgetting to mention I have sent home by one of the present ships my portrait by way of a refreshing all your memories. You may either impute it to this cause or to vanity what ever you think proper, I am told it is very like, on making the proper allowance for flattery, what ever the risk you must allow that my staff uniform is pretty at least.

I have further sent 4 gold chains which my female friends here say is the most acceptable present can be sent to a lady from this country. They cannot be made by an European and are reckoned curious. One is intended for each of my three elder sisters and one for Mrs S. Blacker which I request my Brother Sam will present with my most profound respects and well wishes. I shall take the Earliest opportunity of writing to my brothers and sisters but hoped that the present may be found sufficient until then.

The whole is consigned by my agents here, Messrs. Harrington Burnaby and Co to the agents in London Messrs. Bochm & Co. to be forwarded to the Rev. Dr St. J. Blacker, Wells, Somersetshire. My brother St. John is with his Regiment in camp and getting on vastly well, I hear the same of little Close. My uncle writes to me in good spirits and in a great measure the fate of the present armament must depend on his

---

103 E. Thornton, *Gazetteer of the Territories under the Government of the East India Company,* Chittledrooge, Chittledroog, described as 'unhealthy,' a town in Mysore at the foot of a rock on which was situated a fort. 1200 Troops rebelled here during the 'Tent contract' dispute in 1809. See background & letters 1809.

104 C.E Buckland, *Dictionary of Indian Biography,* a reference to The Peishwa Baji Rao II 1775–1851.The use of the word 'ally' proved to be a misnomer.

negotiation, he has an active situation since the Peishwa has been unfortunate. Yours most affectionately VB:

24 June 1803 (*Received 6 February 1804*)
Camp near Moodgull.[105] My good fortune has been such my dear Father that since I last wrote to you I have received your three letters of 2 October, 17 November and 9 January. My last letter was dated 23 February and then I had become a little impatient about the arrival of news from home, but they have since followed one another very close and two of them came in one ship. I shall proceed to answer them regularly from the very first. I rejoice My dear Father at the good effects with regard to your health produced by your labours in your garden of which the plentiful harvest of fruit is certainly, however pleasant the least benefit. And it is no doubt a considerable argument in favour of the situation at Wells, that whilst its society and other local circumstances are so superior, that its salubrity should also be so uncommon.

I do not know of the Major Clarke you mention and suppose he must have belonged to the Bengal or Bombay establishments.

How kind is the Bishop of Raphoe in his recollection of me, he is a most excellent old man and I hope my respects may be presented to him. I know nothing whatever of Mr Francis Hawkins; his brother on the Madras establishment is an eccentric man but in neither extraordinary 'rec.ts' (sic) or likely to be in them. He is considered a man of the best heart and purest principles but took up an idea that it was necessary to his independence to differ in opinion with Government and he has continued to think opposite to them on every subject for several years. You will conclude that this conduct would not procure him the patronage of Government and the fact is that had he been a young servant instead of one of an old standing he would have a lost what appointments he had, long since. He is by no means a man of business and latterly possessed such bad health as obliged him to go to sea.

I agree in your observation that attention may be paid to all great events which occur in India in England but what I formerly complained of on that head is the fate of the soldier who may exert every possible zeal and enthusiasm in the execution of his duty and never reach the consolatary reward of being brought forward to the notice of his brother soldiers or countrymen: in that respect the service in India is a melancholy confined field.

The son of the late Nabob (or viceroy) of the Carnatic was not permitted but another relation was put in his place, and at the same time that the son's succession was proposed by the English Governor to the principle natives they said they could not think of submitting to the authority of an illegitimate child. Now the circumstances of which excites the indignation of the people at home arises from of the exertion of a lawyer fuelled by the man deposed, to go home and attract the interest of parliament

---

105 E. Thornton, *Gazetteer of the Territories under the Government of the East India Company,*
      Moodgul, a town in the state of the Nizam of Hyderabad later sequestrated by the British.

and the people at large. The prince never wrote the letter in question nor is he a young man but Mr Stewart Hall the lawyer who is a clever man knew well the circumstance is likely to touch the feelings of an Englishman.

It is impossible to give a general answer to your queries regarding the seasons, as they differ with the change of situation without leaving the same degree of a latitude. Six days ago it was so hot that our Commander in Chief who is an elderly man was so affected by it as to be obliged to leave camp and get into the nearest garrison:[106] at those times the thermometer, of which 32 is the freezing point, used to rise to 108–110° at two o' clock in the afternoon.

It is now so cold that I rode yesterday in a greatcoat such is the difference produced in a few days. Heavy rains have set in here and will continue for several months whilst in the same latitude 150 miles to the eastward the hot season exists with winds which have the effect sometimes of striking a European dead on the spot. Numerous are the instances of soldiers who by exposing themselves to it have been killed instantaneously. All along the eastern coast the rains set in during the month of November and then comes on the cold season.

To give you a more pointed example of how much more the climate depends upon local circumstances than on the seasons, at the moment the heat is insupportable at Ambore and all along the foot of the Ghauts whilst by making one march to the top of the Ghauts a fine bracing cool climate is to be enjoyed. Since we have had the Mysore country under our protection we have improved much in gardening. I have ate at Seringapatam, strawberries and cream, apples and potatoes, the latter of which are become so plenty as to be had occasionally at the common market.

You testify only my dear Father anxiety lest St. John should be given to slothful habits. Make yourself easy on that head; he is one of the most active young fellows I know and though I consider myself entitled to entertain some interest in his future welfare I assure you there is not any circumstance in his general conduct that I can in the smallest degree find fault with, on the contrary by the line of conduct his natural propensities have inclined him to adopt, he has only anticipated what I might otherwise have recommended.

Bob Close is as I mentioned before a great favorite grown much taller than I expected he would be and his uncle speaks in high terms of him. He will have written home that on his arrival at Poonah he was permitted to leave his Regiment to meet the Colonel coming from Bombay and to remain with him whilst the Army halted in the neighborhood of Poonah. He has now marched North and it remains to be seen how far they go.

I have as yet been allowed nothing for my charger, owing I believe to some mistake in an order sent to this country. In His Majesty's Service a Cavalry officer is not only handsomely recompensed for the loss of his horse but also for his camp equipage if lost. My Brother Sam is an excellent correspondent and truly do I rejoice at his happiness

106 Sir John Braithwaite, aged 64 years. He died two months later in August. See previous fn.

which I have the pleasure to hear of from all my correspondents. Grace has ere returned from Stewartstown and is enjoying the gaiety of Wells after the domestic scenes she has for some time witnessed. William, I have not heard from for the length of time but expect to be much more fortunate in future. I wrote to him last I think the latter end of the year after my arrival at Trinchinopoly. It is at all events satisfactory to hear that he is doing well though I may not have it exactly from himself. I have received the Maxwell's letter containing his interesting tour through France and propose writing to him by the first ship. I have also heard from Mary, Catherine, Grace and Char. Our last accounts are of the 11th March and by them we learn that war had not been actually declared but there is scarce a possibility of it being otherwise. I have this day understood that the 'Avant Courier' of the French fleet has just arrived at Pondicherry with General Delains aide de camp on board The force coming is not exactly known yet but in the present state of affairs it will be probably sufficient to give us much to do.[107] I am not sorry for it, I must confess, as I conceive it may be the means of bringing the Indian Army into more notice than it has hitherto enjoyed. The French have so much Gasconade in all their publications that I think they must call the attention of Europe to everything connected with their movements. Whilst every action, however trivial it may be if performed in Europe, is brought forward to the notice of the people, the most successful exertions if performed in this country are never heard of. If by them a kingdom is gained or some other similar advantage the effect may be known but the means are never inquired into it though it may involve the most heroic conduct in Corps and individuals. Such apathy to this part of the Army because it is so far removed forms one of the most disheartening reflections to the soldiery, however enthusiastic he may be in the love of his profession, and becomes one of the most grating circumstances incident to his absence from his native country. What an advantage it is the King's troops enjoy over us that they can return to their home without prejudice to their military rank whilst the Company's must bid adieu to it West of the Cape.

Allowing that an individual may possess the means of returning home he may be prevented by his love and entire devotion to a military life which must be given, if in the company's service, in order to leave India entirely. Indeed I cannot well conceive how a soldier, if possessed of that warm and zealous ardour, that devoted love and that enthusiastic admiration of a military life, can coldly calculate on the time of abandoning his profession. I believe I have said enough upon the subject. You may rest assured my dear Father that any service in my power to perform shall not be neglected towards your neighbour Mr Maunsell's son as I am well convinced you would not recommend any but creditable persons.[108]

107　R. Wellesley, *Despatches, Minutes and Correspondence of The Marquess Wellesley* (London: John Murray, 1836) Vol. 3. June 1802. After the Treaty of Amiens, Pondicherry was returned to the French. Valentine's fear of trouble with the troops was not realised as they had received 'permission to disembark and to be treated with respect.'

108　E. Dodswell & J. Miles, J. *Alphabetical List of the Officers of the Indian Army 1760–1834*, gives two Maunsells joining the Madras establishment in 1800. Philip O. Maunsell, 1800,

I am so much rejoiced to hear that the Nobles are comfortably situated where Maxwell left them, I suppose however if the war breaks out again they will be obliged to return. The day your letters with others from the rest of the family arrived St. John was on a grand guard sitting under a bush to shelter himself from a hot sun which even in a tent raised the thermometer to 108. As soon as I had them I sent them to him when he was sitting by himself and I fancy made happy for that day notwithstanding his disagreeable situation. We now be encamped in a part of the Nizam's territory called the Doab or two Rivers situate between the Kristnah to the north and the Toombudra to the south; in this tract you will find the place from whence I date my present letter. We loiter here ready to support the Army in advance in case of any failure, but the instant that official accounts arrive of a declaration of war in Europe we must start for the Carnatic as there is scarce a single battalion to be disposed of from any of our garrisons to prevent the movement of the French after their landing. It will astonish the new Governor Lord Bentinck when he arrives with,[109] I believe positive injunctions to reduce a considerable portion of our force, to find no part of it within 500 miles of him and two thirds distant about 800 miles.

I have now enjoyed thank God for a length of time excellent health and am now in a handsome situation laying by money what I could never do before. I have received much civility from the Commander in Chief and live in his family. He surprised me not a little by giving me an account of many particulars relative to my own family, however it is before I was born. General Stewart tells me that when he was a subaltern in Ireland between the years '60 and '70 he served against the rebels (Hearts of Oak Boys) and he speaks as familiarly of Connor Blacker's house on a terrace at Landiage, and Mr Close's at Elm Park and of Mr Maxwell's at Tynan as if he had lived there all his life. Remember me to most of my brothers and sisters to most of whom I shall however write by this ship and give my affectionate love to my mother and Mrs Messiter. Sylvester Daggerwood is a character very first in my recollection nor shall I forget him in a hurry, he was such an entertaining fellow. With fervent prayers my dear Father that your domestic happiness may increase every day if possible, I remain your very affectionate and dutiful son VB.

4 September 1803 (*Received March 12th 1804*)
Madras. Your favour dated March 7th I had the pleasure to receive a few days since and immediately sent it to St. John whom I left on the banks of the Toombudra, who has since crossed it into the country called the Doab or that situated between two Rivers the above mentioned and the Kristnah. Your former favours alluded to under

---

died at Asseerghur Feb.1804. George Maunsell, Lieutenant, 1801, Captain 1811, Major 1823, Lieutenant Colonel 1825. Died at Sea 1828.
109 C.E. Buckland, *Dictionary of Indian Biography*, Lord William Bentinck, 1774–1839 appointed Governor of Madras in 1803 but as a result of the Mutiny at Vellore was recalled in 1807. In 1828 he returned to India as Governor General.

dates October 2nd, November 17th, 1802 and July 10th, 1803 are acknowledged in my last dated the beginning of June. You mention being disturbed at my appointment at Trichinopoly. It would be no doubt pleasant that we should be together in the Regiment but that is attended with disadvantage. In one affair which falls heavy, in one Corps the two brothers run a greater risk of being both cut off and than when there are separate not to mention many others. With regard to your query concerning our happiness in our present situation, I am sure all my letters must have expressed mine and I think I might also answer for St. John. You are perfectly right in not harbouring any fears respecting my getting into debt so far from it that I am now laying by about £500 a year. St. John I believe is not in debt and I am sure he is perfectly convinced of the inconvenience of being so.

   Captain Henry Montgomery has certainly made a most uncommon large fortune and perhaps there will not be found a similar instance of good look for many years to come as there has not been for many years past.[110] He is indebted to his own industry, a certain tenacity at making money and ingratiating himself into the good graces of people in power, to perform which the mode is not always by public zeal and devotion to your duty. I am only surprised that Mr Nisbet of Kilmacredan should have lived so long. Has Mr Morgan changed his parish that he lives at Killybeg ? I have not seen Hill Morgan since I have come to India although I have been at one time within 10 miles of him when early in 1801 I was in the Malabar country during the Wynaad expedition. I continued to change a few letters with him afterwards but when I was so near him no communication was open to less than 500 or 600 men. I shall take the earliest opportunity of paying my attention to Mr Godley mentioned in your letter.[111] At present he is at Mirzapore where all the younger men on their arrival learn the rudiments of their profession. What is provoking is that I was there six days ago on my way here and did not know of his being there also. On a new plan of operations being resolved on, when the French made their appearance on the coast, General Stewart and most of the General Staff of the Army were ordered to the Carnatic, I among the rest, but was directed to come by regular marches in charge of the Quartermaster General Department in company with the troops of the Carnatic.

   I arrived here therefore on the 28th of last month just in time to see the ceremony of installing the new Governor and to take my leave of the old one. Lady Bentinck appears to be an amiable woman but I hope to be able to speak more fully respecting her in a few days. I have been introduced to his Lordship but have had no opportunity of being acquainted with him yet. I left St. John as I have mentioned on the banks of the Toombudra with his Regiment where I am sorry to say he will not have an

---

110 See previous fns.
111 E. Dodswell & J. Miles, *Alphabetical List of the Officers of the Indian Army 1760–1834*, William Godley joined HEIC 1802, Ensign 1802, Lieutenant, 1804, Captain 1817, Major 1826, Retired 1829. *Thorntons Gazetteer* makes no mention of a Mirzapore in the Madras Presidency although there is one in Bengal. There is probably some phonetic error in pronunciation or spelling.

opportunity of seeing any actual service. He has been unfortunate in that respect to have been kept behind whilst the Corps are employed in advance as you will have known before you receive this. The fall of the famous city of Anudnuggin[112] by a British Army will form quite an era in British history. I shall not speculate on what will be the consequence of a further advance into the Maratha country but there is every reason to hope for the best from an Army commanded by General Wellesley. With regards to myself I have not the smallest idea of what is to become months hence, it will now require that time however to enable me to bring up old accounts connected with my late appointment in the field of Superintendent of Supplies. I wrote so lately that I might have apologized to myself for not writing again so soon but I cannot let go of the opportunity of the ship which sails with Lord Clive. I ever remain, My dear Father your affectionate son. VB

9 September 1803 (*Received 7 April 1804.*)
Madras. My dear Father, this will be delivered to you by a Mr Knowles who goes home by the same ship which carries my letter of the fourth Inst.[113] He is an intimate acquaintance of mine and a worthy man, he has been patronized in some degree by the Colonel and is acquainted with some of our connections.

He is obliged to return on account of sickness and I take the liberty of introducing him to you as one well acquainted with my style of life here which I have the vanity to suppose some account of may not be uninteresting to you. He is a but a Lieutenant in the Company's service, however he has almost always held a Staff appointment which I fancy has enabled him to return with ease until he recovers his health. I can say nothing of more of myself having so lately written, believe me etc

15 October 1803 (*Received 10 April 1804*)
Madras. My dear Father, my letters I think you may perceive followed each other pretty thick. I take this opportunity of a ship which is to carry home the French prisoners to let you know how we come on. I still continue at Madras and am likely to remain a few months longer. St. John is still within a few marches of where I left him and Robert in the Maratha Company with General Wellesley, one of the most brilliant characters the British Army possesses.

I am induced to mention his late action with the combined forces of the Marathas, because Robert was in it and had his horse shot under him. The Battle of Assaye was fought on the 23rd September in which we gained a most signal victory, slept on the field of battle, captured 113 pieces of the finest ordinance almost ever seen with an extensive supply of ammunition and so completely overcame them that they

---

112 Not identified.(Ed.)
113 E. Dodswell & J. Miles, *Alphabetical List of the Officers of the Indian Army 1760–1834*. Lieutenant Joseph Knowles, 3rd Regiment Madras Native Infantry, Captain 1804, Major 1812, Lt Colonel 1818. Awarded CB.1818, d.1824.

did not halt until the third day afterwards. But woeful was our loss. Upwards of one third of our men killed and wounded, near half our officers, nor was there a single mounted officer in action who had not his horse killed or was not wounded himself. The General had no less than two killed under him. I think this is a pretty good initiation for Robert, I wish St. John had been there also. This is a greater loss in proportion to the force we have engaged than either the French or Austrian armies suffered at the Battle of Marengo in Italy, which is reckoned the most bloody fought last war. I have heard from Robert since in high spirits and he gives a very clear return of the business as far as he could know, acting as he did with his Corps. He is certainly an uncommon fine young man and well merits to be the favourite as he is with all his acquaintances. The Colonel still preserves his health and spirits and writes to me occasionally when there is anything of consequence, but he is by no means so regular a correspondent as he was formerly. Indeed he has not the same occasion as he need not be so anxious about me now that he has procured for me an excellent appointment that allows me to lay by so handsomely out of my pay. I wrote to you lately by a Lieutenant Knowles who has been obliged to go to Europe for the recovery of his health, and I send you another letter (not the present) by a Captain Shawe (sic) who proceeds as Commissary in Charge of the prisoners taken at Pondicherry.[114] I propose also giving him letters to Sam. and William as he proposes in having spent a short time at his father's in the County of Wexford to make a tour of Ireland. You can mention it in any of your letters to them but they are so much in my debt all of them that I should give them a little time to clear off old scores before I write to them fully again. My letters by Captain Shawe as there will probably be a delay in delivering them shall be merely introductory. He is a plain man, has suffered much from bad health which obliges him to return to his native country. He has always held a Staff appointment in this country and has been the latterly Aide de Camp to the Commander in Chief.

In England an officer on the personal staff to a General Officer is generally the 'Pink of the Fashion' however you must not expect that in the present instance nor is it the case in this country on most occasions. The new Governor and his lady are very affable people but not particularly gay – and they appear desirous of being as much domesticated as possible. She is an uncommonly amiable woman and he is a very attentive man to business. I am by no means intimate with them, though I have been at the house to their partys (sic) two or three times and on bowing terms, nothing more. Make my love to my sisters and tell them I shall take an early opportunity of writing to them, present my respectful duty to my mother and believe me my dear Father your most affectionate son

114 Ibid, *Alphabetical List of the Officers of the Indian Army 1760–1834,* Captain William Shaw, joined HEIC 1790, Ensign 1791, Lieutenant 1794, Captain 1800, Major 1808, Lt. Colonel 1813, d. 1814. French prisoners were removed from Pondicherry when the Treaty of Amiens 1802 broke down.

1804

16 March 1804 (*Received October 1804*)
Madras. My dear Father, I have delayed for a considerable time commencing my letter to you in hopes of receiving some intelligence from home. Ship after ship has arrived but no letters, so that I have to console myself with the idea that either you have not written to me last season or that all epistles for me are on board the *Admiral Aplin*,[115] lately captured and taken to the Isle of France – in case of capture the packets of private letters are frequently transmitted to their place of destination and on that account I have put off my writing to you day after day but as the ships are now preparing to sail I can no longer delay. My last letter was dated Madras 4th September 1803, since then I still reside at the Presidency and see no immediate probability of my leaving it. You will remark that hitherto I have never continued so long in one place since my arrival in India so that I have been obliged quite to collect a new set of habits for myself, more suitable to a resident in Madras than my former vagabond ones were. I now begin my dear Father to please myself with the expectation of one day of seeing my native country, a prospect that hitherto I have with the but most solicitude avoided dwelling on, never having had a well founded hope until lately of having within my reach. Whilst I could not flatter myself with the expectation of attaining such an object, I ever used every effort to shun the thoughts of it and endeavoured to please myself with painting in the most glowing colours the honour and brilliance of my profession and arraigned in the most fascinating dress the pleasures and variety of a military life. I am still equally sensible of them but they no longer hold the undivided sway in my mind of the bond and wish of again seeing my friends, hitherto sedulously suppressed, again bursts forth with a redoubled violence. Without a young man has the prospect of uncommon interest he should not too long delay his coming to India. If he is to spend his life in it let him come out as soon as he can have finished his education and not wait until he acquired too strong local attachment which will ever be followed by endless regrets. My acquaintance at Madras is just as extensive as I wish it to the, I am in the habit of dining out about four times a week and going in the evening to whatever gaiety is stirring: by which means I get on remarkably well. I at present keep house with a friend of mine who was once serving in the same Regiment with me and is now the Adjutant of the Governor's Bodyguard.[116] I shall however shortly manage matters by myself for as we have been living in a magnificent house, the seat of Sir B. Sullivan

115 '*Admiral Aplin*' 550 tons built in 1801. In May 1802 she sailed her maiden voyage to India commanded by Captain Rogers.
116 E. Dodswell, & J. Miles, *Alphabetical List of the Officers of the Indian Army 1760–1834*. Lieutenant, R. Otto Bayer, joined HEIC 1797, Cavalry Cornet 1799, Lieutenant, 1800, Captain 1805 Major 1819, Lt. Colonel 1829. Retired 1831. On 8 May 1800 appointed Adjutant of the Governors Bodyguard (see also Extract October 1802).

my friend's uncle, who is now on his return from Bombay.[117] As soon as he arrives I shall be obliged to turn out and my present inmate will no doubt prefer residing free of expense with his relation whilst I shall have to look out for myself.

Besides of the common detail duties of the Quartermaster General's office, which I have to attend to daily I am employed in making local and military survey of the vicinity of Madras to the extent of about 10 miles round. As it is a very confined and intersected country and having also other employment it will be a considerable time before it is finished. I have lately been quite set up in surveying instruments having got them from home to the amount of £150 prime cost. Had I purchased them here I should have been obliged to pay about double that sum and still not be equally certain with the respect to the goodness of the instruments. I have written home for the Encyclopedia Britannica and shortly expect it, I have however already a very neat library which adds much to my satisfaction. It is collected at the several auctions of the books of gentlemen returning to England by which means they are acquired pretty cheap.

The Colonel is now at Bombay having been obliged a few months ago to remove from Poonah on account of ill health; he certainly should go home now if ever he proposes it. Never can he have a better opportunity with credit to himself perhaps, however he may be waiting for the periods of Lord Wellesley's retirement which certainly would be as eligible a time as he could wish he having been so very instrumental in carrying of the Governor's projects into execution. I am happy to say however that the Colonel is quite recovered again and I shortly expect to hear of his return to Poonah. He has now passed certainly his prize (sic) and his constitution is much worn out. He has risen to the highest post he can possibly attain in India, his progress has been marked by incidents of the most honorable and creditable nature to himself and by this time he should be possessed of a competent fortune. On the several accounts the present is the most favourable time for him to return to his native country, yet I doubt much if he would be happier there; his habits here both of body and mind have been the most active and his 'mind time' might become irksome to him when unaccompanied by the anxiety of a responsible situation. He left home young and this having been the country in which he has formed his ideas of men and things, his earlier habits and mode of thinking, it must appear to him much in the light of his native country. Many of his intimate friends however have gone home and the remainder will shortly leave him very little social enjoyment here as he cannot be expected to make many new interesting friendships.

St. John is still nearly in the same situation as when I last wrote to you. I need not lay many particulars as he informs me that he has written himself to you; I need only to observe that he is doing remarkably well. Robert Close I presume has also written, he is a universal favourite wherever he is known. I have had some very manly and

---

117 Sir Benjamin Sullivan, 1747–1809 Puisne Justice of the Madras Supreme Court <http://www.thepeerage.com> (accessed August 2017).

spirited letters from him after the Battles of Assaye and Argaun. His last informs me of his having been put in charge of the escort with the Resident at Nagpore.[118] I cannot proceed without returning to my disappointment in not having received letters by any of the ships of the last fleet by which means I have none to acknowledge since I last wrote – what are my sisters about and how does my mother do? Make my most affectionate remembrance to all, Charlotte must be a fine bouncing girl now and I expect to have some entertaining letters from her. Upon my word if my sisters give over writing to me I shall be quite inconsolable. I have exhausted all I have to say and must prepare for a party Lady William Bentinck has desired my company at. Believe me dear Father your affectionate son, VB.

2 August 1804 (*Received February 10 1805*)

My dear Father I have to congratulate myself on my good fortune in the receipt of several Europe letters lately. I have not received them above a few days, and now find that a ship, '*The Glory*' is to sail immediately,[119] an opportunity I must take advantage of or perhaps wait a considerable time. St. John is at present at the distance of several hundred miles from me, and as I have sent to him some of the letters I received and he has not returned them I may not perhaps answer them with the same regularity I otherwise might. I did not take the opportunity to compare the dates of the letters you enumerated to have written before I sent them to my brother, however from the number I consider I must have received them all. In my last letter dated the (*word missing*) I mentioned my fear that packets for me might be on board the '*Admiral Aplin*' which was captured and carried into the Isle of France.

My fears were well founded but the letters arrived a few months afterwards having been opened and sealed up again. They moreover translated all those that touched upon political subjects into French and sent them directed to different persons here along with their own letters, agreeable to an example we had given them when we had interrupted their correspondence from Egypt. I only saw some of them as they were at several times and active measures were taken by Government but to suppress the circulation. Among others I did not see one from Mrs Blacker to Colonel Close, but the gentleman who had seen it told me he was surprised the French should publish it as it was of a quite contrary nature to despondence.

I am sorry to hear that the picture and gold chains which I thought I had arranged to go free of expense should become so heavy an article as they appear likely to be from your letter. I shall wait until I hear what your costs have been and shall then

---

118   C.E. Buckland, *Dictionary of Indian Biography* Josiah Webbe, 1768–1804. Appointed to the Indian Civil Service 1783. British Administrator who held various appointments in Madras Presidency. Described by Wellington as 'one of the ablest men I knew and … the most honest.'

119   '*The Glory*,' a 550 ton East Indiaman which later sank in a hurricane November 1808 together with six other ships.

attack my agents to whom I left the whole economy. I must at all events insist on being the only person affected on the occasion, otherways my intention is wholly defeated.

I cannot well express my satisfaction on finding one of the females married and rejoice much that the match should be so eligible a one. On this subject I must reserve further explanation to my letter to Catherine herself whom I propose writing to by this ship. My brothers it would appear get on in the same way as formally, that outset is established and there is no danger to be apprehended, two them also I shall write by the present opportunity.

I presume the young man whom Mrs Vereker may have recommended to my protection is a passenger in some of the ships lately arrived, I have not yet received any letter from him; of course as soon as I do I shall take the Earliest opportunity of interesting myself about him and rejoice in an occasion of testifying my gratitude to one who has behaved in so liberal a manner to my sister. Having now alluded to the several parts of your letter I shall now attempt to give some account of myself since my last. I was then keeping house in a very comfortable manner with a friend of mine at Madras in a house belonging to an uncle of his then residing at Bombay. Shortly after that the uncle, who is one of the three judges here, returned and I was obliged to turn out. I took a house for myself at the rent of £20 a month which you may rather think too high for me as it was not in the least furnished. Such however is the state of society in this place that one in my situation could not with respectability inhabit a mansion to be procured for less, nor could I have invited any of my friends to a meaner one. This circle in which I have associated in the Presidency has always been the first, as I have always made it a rule there to move in the best society or in none whatever

I had lived in this manner about a month when I received an unexpected order to prepare for the Charge of the Quartermaster General's Department with some troops assembling to quell a rebellion breaking forth among some tributaries in a part of the country well known to Colonel Massey and indeed I am now writing from a place where he commanded a long time. The chief town in these districts is Chittoor which you will observe in your map near 30 miles and north of Arcot and Vellore.[120] I consequently equipped and set out in a day's warning and on the 25th of last month came before one of their posts containing about 2000 men: as they refused to give it up it was to be stormed next morning at daybreak and the arrangements for it were just concluded about 7:00 pm when I received all the Europe letters.

I of course read them all that night, least the chance of war should prevent my being able to do it again, the precaution was however unnecessary, for during the night it was evacuated.

I hope the business will be settled in a short time after which by the by my labours are not over, as I am to be employed here some months projecting military roads and

---

120 E. Thornton, *Gazetteer of the Territories under the Government of the East India Company.* Chittoor, in the northern district of Madras. A judicial establishment, 80 miles west of Madras.

making a military survey of the country. St. John of whom I have not yet spoken comes on as well as can be hoped. His regiment will shortly go to some station as the encampment is breaking up but where I do not yet know.

Appointments are so scarce now that he has not been able to obtain one yet, although the Commander in Chief has every desire to serve him, the Colonel's health now remains pretty good: he got a few months ago the rank of full Colonel and with it by a new regulation is entitled to £1000 a year even in Europe. The last letter which I have received of yours is dated February 27 1804.

I have not addressed any lines to my mother, I could give no further account of myself that I could dare to hope would interest more than the foregoing with regard to my anxiety and interest upon her account. I hope she and Mrs Messiter will never entertain of doubt. My connection of them is of such a nature that not to mention the amiableness of their individual characters they must ever come under my warmest regard and esteem.

10 October 1804 (*Received March 25 1805*)
Madras. The last letter I wrote to my dear Father was dated 14 August last when employed with a detachment serving in the Chittoor Pollycues. To give then an account of myself since that period. We made a tour of the disaffected country and destroyed all the strongholds and fastnesses without suffering much loss. Our greatest, though trifling was at the attack of a fortified height called Poloor Droog and as it was ridiculous enough I shall mention a few particulars of it. Droogs are hill forts, this was a very high one and had on the ascent two or three breast works which were carried by the bayonet and there we scrambled on to the top which was at the accessible parts defended by a wall about 8 feet high in which was a small door made of strong planks placed at sufficient distance one from another to fire through. The party storming was 4 flank companies and a party in reserve were advancing in more regular order up the hill. I happened to be the oldest Captain of the former though it was not expected I would have joined it. A few of the foremost among us looked in at the gateway but the enemy could not face us there as our fire was superior to theirs. We were therefore obliged to wait for pioneers with tools to break open the wicket of the gate and we got the men to take shelter close under the wall as they were a little galled by a flanking fire. It would appear that they wished this, for we had no sooner got into this situation than they threw upon us from the top of the wall large stones and fragments of rock which they had collected for the occasion.

This was so unexpected a salutation, that as we could not get the gate broken open, we agreed to fall about 150 yards back to some rocks where we would be unexposed. At this moment a Sepoy standing on a stone a little above me was struck with a large fragment which broke his back and overset him on me. This tumbled me also and as a retreat was made with more velocity than order I was rolled about 100 paces down the hill. On gaining the cover we took up a position and waited patiently for a gun which we sent down for and was carried up piecemeal with much labour on men's shoulders. It was opened before sunset and had so nearly destroyed the gateway before dark that the enemy did not think proper to wait a storm but evacuated it during the night. The detachment having been broken into small posts at the end of last month I came down to the Presidency on some business and to be present at the departure of my good patron General Stewart who goes home in the fleet now about to sail. As soon as matters are arranged I shall return to make a military survey of the country.

The late unfortunate business on the Bengal side in the total destruction of Brigadier General Monson's detachment renders it necessary that a new campaign should be opened with vigour on this side of Holkars dominions,[121] and as General Wellesley is coming round to command it from Calcutta, I have written to request he will desire me from Headquarters to take charge of the Quartermaster Generals' Department. I fear I shall not succeed; however as it is merely to have the honour of serving under so distinguished a General there is no indelicacy in making the request. Should this fail there is another plan on the tapis but not of my own a suggestion.[122] Lord William Bentinck has taken into consideration the necessity which exists here of a military seminary in imitation of that lately instituted in England at High Wycombe for the instruction of officers in staff duties.[123, 124] He has paid me the compliment to discuss the subject with me and told me he was desirous of placing me in the superintendence of it with the assistance of some other intelligent officers. He has had so much business since on account of the despatches preparing for the fleet under orders to sail that nothing further has taken place and perhaps never may and I have been induced to mention so much of the business to you by (I suppose) a ridiculous vanity of shewing the light in which the Governor looks upon my professional accomplishments. St. John has arrived by this time I presume at Poonah as I had a letter from him some time since dated at Hyderabad. I am happy to observe that his regiment is ordered for the approaching campaign which, as it has all the appearance of becoming an active one, will be much for his advantage. Webb, now Resident at Burhampoor,[125]

121 C.E. Buckland, *Dictionary of Indian Biography* Colonel William Monson, 1760–1807 arrived in India with 52nd Regiment. During 2nd Maratha War was severely wounded storming Alighar 1803. Made a disastrous retreat before Rao Holkar in 1804 when his loss of ordnance, supplies and the desertion of British Officers was called a 'disgraceful and disastrous event.' His last action was in one of the failed assaults against Bharatpur 1805 after which he returned to the UK.
122 'Tapis' a textile worked with artistic design such as a carpet or more likely in this context a tablecloth <www.collinsdictionary.com> (accessed August 2017).
123 'Necessity which exists here' suggests that the Military Seminary or Cadet Company at Chinglepat had moved, see fn 231.
124 Royal Military Academy founded in 1799, moved in 1813, then became a senior part of the Royal Military College Sandhurst in 1820. In 1858 became The Staff College, Camberley. The East India Military Seminary at Addiscombe was not founded until 1809.
125 E. Thornton, *Gazetteer of the Territories under the Government of the East India Company,* Burhampoor now Burhanpur. Held by the Marathas from 1681 but after the 3rd Maratha War annexed by the British in 1818. Webb(e) was the civil servant who was Secretary to Colonel B. Close in 1798.

has applied to have St. John appointed to the command of his escort: it will probably take place after the campaign. Robert is remarkably well now, though he was lately otherwise. The Colonel also enjoys good health as has without the least interruption, dear Father your most affectionate son V B.

You must not omit (though I have scarcely paper enough left to request it) to remember me in the most affectionate manner to my mother and sisters.

1805

25 February 1805 (*Received 17 September 1805*)
Camp Chittoor. My dear Father, I have this moment intelligence of the arrival of six Indiamen at Madras and my expectations are sanguine to receive some pleasing news tomorrow, I haste therefore to give you some account of myself before I am so much overwhelmed by the expected tidings as to throw all order and regularity out of my head. I wrote last to you from Madras having gone there on some business from the field and attempts were made to bring the rebels I had been serving against to some sort of reason by conciliatory measures. They failed and a strong force was sent against them under a new officer to crush that obstinate spirit at once. I was again directed to proceed there when General Wellesley arrived from Calcutta with the intention of commanding an army on the Bombay side in cooperation with General Lake against Holkar, the hostile Maratha chief. He was good enough to say he would be glad to have me with him and applied to the Commander in Chief who refused on the plea that, as he only commanded in chief by seniority until Sir John Raddock should arrive,[126] he would not be excusable in detaching any of the General staff from the Carnatic as Sir John might wish to have them at Headquarters on his arrival. This having failed, he applied to the Governor who said that it would be 'prejudicial to the service if Captain Blacker who had much local knowledge of the country possessed by the rebels and was called away from the service to any other.' Thus ended my hopes of accompanying General Wellesley on an expedition which in the end never took place, for General Lake, having obtained some decisive successes, the war was put an end to on this side of India and the Captain went to the rebels.[127] The only business of any consequence was the attack of a fortified hill where I had the honour of conducting a party by pathway through a thick wood and circuitous route to the top in hopes of surprising the party. I had arrived with a few Grenadiers covering my reconnoitring within a few paces of the top under shelter of the wood and some rocks when I could distinctly overhear the enemy expressing their suppositions to one another respecting where we might be. We lay there snug until the attack might be brought up but the place was so confined that but few could be brought to act at once and those that did

126 A mis-naming. Major General John Francis Cradock, later 1st Baron Howden. See previous fns.
127 Blacker, refering to himself in the third person.

make the attempt were obliged to give it up after upwards of one third of the men and officers being killed and wounded. The enemy evacuated the hill during the night fearing a more regular attack in the morning as this had been a 'coup de main.'[128]

Any further operations consisted of petty skirmishes in the woods to which we confined them until they were starved into the pleasure of Government and some who have remained obstinate have been taken and hung. Such has been the termination of our three months rebel campaign and I look out in the course of a very few days for orders to proceed to Madras.

The Colonel enjoys now very good health and has been lately removed from the court of Poonah to that of Burhampoor.

Poor Mr Webb was Resident at the latter place, where he died of a fever. He might most probably have saved his life had he early changed air but he was so zealous to discharge the trust reposed in him, at that period a most heavy one, that he refused to abandon his post whilst he could possibly remain in it, and thus fell one of the first men in India in point of character for abilities and public honesty. The Colonel sincerely laments the loss of his sincerest and most intimate friend with whom he had risen in life to high situation.

St. John has had a most severe attack of illness which was likely to have proved dangerous to him. He took one of the most extraordinary rides I have heard of from Hyderabad to Poonah to pay a visit to the Colonel. The consequence of which was that an abscess was formed in his liver and luckily for him broke downwards, had it broke in the contrary direction it must have proved fatal to him I am told: he was much recovered by my last letter from him but was not sufficiently well to accompany the Colonel immediately to Burhampoor in charge of his escort. He spoke of a trip to sea for the recovery of health. Robert Close has been much troubled by a fever which he has not been able entirely to shake off for a considerable time past, he still continues in charge of the Resident's escort there and writes to me about once a month.[129] I have received a letter from Mrs Vereker by a Mr Byan who has come out in the military line, it was with some difficulty I could find him out as the letter came to me by itself without any line from him.[130] I wrote to a person however of that name and it proved to be the right one, I have had an answer from him saying he is in the 1st Battn. 6th Regiment of Infantry and preparing to join his regiment now in the field.

I now desist until I hear whether or not the fleet arrived has brought any letters for me. Agreeably to my expectation your letter of the 4th August last has arrived and brings me the pleasing intelligence of the health and happiness of all the family. The

128 French expression meaning 'a sudden attack.'
129 W. Dalrymple, *White Mughals* (London: HarperCollins, 2002) pp. 123–8. The Resident Agent at Hyderabad was Major James Achilles Kirkpatrick, 1764–1805.
130 E. Dodswell, & J. Miles, *Alphabetical List of the Officers of the Indian Army 1760–1834*, Martin William Byam. Joined HEIC army 1803, Ensign 1803, Lieutenant, 1804. 'Struck off' 1809.

letters you allude to of February 27th and April 17th have also been received. The perpetual almanac you entrusted to St. John met with some accident I believe on board ship for he never produced it. I am glad to hear Mr Knowles has contrived to send you the stick even though it had been broken, the care you propose to take of it for my sake is truly flattering. I have been much surprised by the account you give of my grandmother coming to Bath and have sent an extract of that part of your letter to the Colonel notwithstanding he will most probably have had it direct from home himself.

It pleases me much the account you give of Charlotte. I shall not know her when I return three or four years hence and I shall have so many relations to visit who are scattered over England and Ireland that it will be difficult to determine where to go first. Mr and Mrs Noble will become quite Frenchified by such a long residence upon the continent; I owe Mrs Noble a shawl which I have been prevented sending hitherto by the difficulty attending any such exportation: there are now some new regulations made on that subject so that I hope to get it accomplished by the next fleet. You will recollect what happened to the chains, I am not sure whether or not I mentioned in my last letter the steps my agents are directed to take concerning them but I think I have. They have been desired to correspond with you concerning them. St. John has no situation which gives him any advantages besides his regimental pay; if he accompanies the Colonel in charge of his escort it will relieve him from the expense of keeping his own table. You must be well convinced that I shall lose no opportunity which may offer of serving him but the opportunities I must say are becoming very few and orders from home every year render them still fewer. And in short time they will soon place the military establishment on such a footing that persons will come into it because they may not be able to exist at home and thus deter all young of education from entering it. I have heard from no other member of the family but yourself which I am at a loss to account for and William has dropped me entirely, indeed it is in general about the month of August that I receive the greatest number of letters. Make my love to my Mother and Sisters and assure yourself my dear Father that I remain your ever affectionate son V. Blacker.

9 September 1805 (*Rec'd 14 June 1806*)
Madras. I have received, my dear Father, all the letters of 1804 which you enumerate in yours of February 18th 1805. The latter I have had but short time in my possession so that the present will have a speedy reply to it. I have mislaid the memorandum of the date of my last to you but of one thing I am perfectly satisfied, that no occasion of writing has escaped me. I wish Grace's marriage was concluded I long to see my sisters settled in to their liking and 1½ years is a time so long that many unforeseen circumstances may occur before its expiration. St. John passed some three months with me after his trip to sea for the recovery of his health. He had become quite stout when he left me to travel overland to Goa and there to take his passage for Bombay. The last letter I received from him was dated at Seringapatam and he mentioned having found some friends of the name of Young there related to Lough Cask family.

I saw the outside of your letters to him and sent them forward with a new direction, they're all directed to the care of Messrs. Hope and Co, I think it would be better to omit that part of the address in future as the letters will always find him and Hope and Co. are only shopkeepers. The report had no foundation that I was appointed to the division of the Quartermaster Generals' Department with the Hyderabad subsidiary force. I should be sorry to exchange my present situation for it, the emoluments are not greater a year each (about £1500) and certainly my present one is the most pleasant and also has claims which the other does not possess. I hear more frequently from the Colonel now than ever I did before, he retains excellent health but you will not see him I fancy so soon as you expect. My dear Father must be well convinced that I can have no pleasure equal to that of gratifying him. I have not since the first two or three letters after his marriage addressed a separate part to Mrs B which has really proceeded from an entire dearth of any subject more appropriate than another and I am reduced to the necessity of a most particular account of myself which I no doubt suppose is communicated to her and I never fail to express my regard and affection for the wife of a beloved and esteemed parent.

I have received a letter from Sam lately who seems to enjoy much happiness and I am sure he well deserves it. I lead a very different life from his but I suppose there is not one who can appreciate in a higher degree the comforts and pleasures over altered life than myself, pleasures however that I am likely never to enjoy.[131] Maxwell has not written to me for an age and as I hear so pleasant an account of him I am pretty well satisfied. William also has been rather negligent of late, the accession of the £5000 should assist him very much. From Catherine I have heard an account of her trip to town to see her new connections, I write to her by this fleet. I made quite happy by the description I hear of Charlotte and I trust by her own application she will make the most advantage of the opportunities afforded her by her friends. I hope no preventative will be omitted by my father to the gout, I am truly happy you have escaped it last winter notwithstanding its threats.

If Bonaparte attempts the invasion it will be of desperate consequences in any event but he must have too much prudence surely to think seriously of it. He certainly, I should hope, would be repulsed but it would be more by the native valour of the nation than the discipline of the mass.[132]

I observe you still remain persuaded that I am only a lieutenant. I have been some years now above that Honourable rank and independent of my situation in the General Staff of the Army having only one Captain above me in my Regiment; however I must also observe that there is only one below me. I have received my encyclopedia from home, elegantly bound in Russian leather which is never

---

131 A reference to his bachelor state. He married in 1813.
132 A perceived invasion of the UK. Napoleon amassed an army and barges in 1804 to invade Britain. After the Battle of Trafalgar in October 1805 British Naval power was dominant, Napoleon could not secure the Channel and the threat diminished.

attacked by insects in this country like every other, it is the latest edition with the supplementary two volumes and has cost me about £50 when landed here. You will not be surprised that the instruments I got out should have cost me £150 when one alone (a grand theodolite) stands me £50. I have however parted with most of them again as my appointment in the Quartermaster Generals' Department relieves me of the survey duty. Before however I was placed on this footing I had written home for some more instruments which will amount to a £100 but I shall not lose by them as I can part with them upon their arrival for at least what they will have cost me. It will be difficult to give you a distinct idea of my duty as Assistant Quartermaster General. In many respects it is the same as my superiors except that he has the responsibility and he has more to plan and myself more to execute. My uncle's going home would certainly in some degree affect our interest in this country but not so much as it would have done two or three years ago. Changes in ministry take place in India as well as in England and some very great ones have ocurred within the period I allude to. For my own part I am settled in a manner which gives me some opportunity of recommending myself and of occasionally assisting a friend, so that if I do not think myself fortunate, I must be a discontented fellow. Robert Close is a most promising young fellow with a degree of prudence and a steadiness that are seldom found in one of his years, I really believe that his income is nearly, if not entirely equal to my own with this very great difference, that he lives at no expense and I at very great. Present my dear Father my sincere love and affection to my sisters, with Mrs B and you and believe me your truly dutiful son, V Blacker.

NB fail not to return my remembrance to Miss Messiter and say how much I am gratified by her and Mrs B's flattering recollection of me.

1806

11 February 1806 (*Rec'd 20 July 1806*)
Madras. It is now a considerable period and my dear Father since I have had any letters from England so that I may add that of novelty to the many other pleasures I shall receive from news by the next fleet. I have been stationary at Madras since my last letter to you the date of which I cannot exactly command at present but it must have been by what is termed the October Fleet. I have therefore have very little new account to give of myself, my abode here not being productive of so much variety as my former peregrinations through the country. We are anxiously looking out for the arrival of the fleet which sailed from Cork on the 31st August and can form no decided opinion respecting the destination of the expedition it accompanied. My friend General Baird I perceive is in command of it which induces me to suppose that more is to be done by fighting than by negotiation.

Since St. John has left me I have given up the house I live in and pitched my tent on the first day of the year, I propose continuing in it until a small box which I am a erecting for my own accommodation shall have been finished.[133] I found I was not equal to the payment of house rent in the genteel part of the settlement and in the vulgar part I was resolved not to know of. I therefore fixed on the plan of building for myself in the former situation a house equal to my wants which I can do by expending on it a sum of money, which would have produced less interest than I should have to pay in house rent for the same quantity of accommodation. The situation of my estate is adjoining the gardens of the Quartermaster General and with him I live whilst my house is building,[134] but I am so continually engaged out that it is a difficult matter to say where I live most and when I am not particularly invited I have still my choice out of two or three general invitations. Our present Commander in Chief as well as his Lady by no means enjoy good health;[135] they are therefore going to the Mysore country next month in order to avoid the hot land winds which blow during the summer. I go with them as far as Arcot and then return to Madras. They are extremely pleasant people and make it quite a study to behave in the most affable manner to all ranks. My latest letters from Colonel Close inform me that St. John had left him in order to join his regiment, whence he was to proceed with a detachment of cavalry as an escort to the Resident at Hyderabad.[136] I do not find that St. John becomes given to study more now than formerly and indeed without it is in some measure the natural bent, it is seldom or ever to be acquired: however in general such disadvantage has something to balance it and those who are not studiously given have often great animal spirits, than which nothing is more necessary to carry an individual through the labours of this country. As well as I can recollect I possessed a tolerable good share of that article formerly, but now I am sorry to say it is in great measure evaporated and I am obliged to have recourse to all sorts of varieties to keep myself interested. You will be surprised at the direction of my pursuits when I tell you that I set up for an architect, an anatomist and painter besides assuming some little proficiency in the several studies more intimately connected with my profession. It is difficult to say what will be the termination of the Maratha affair, the last we have been at war with sent an Ambassador to make peace, the preliminaries of which were signed but now the chieftain himself refuses to ratify them. So much for the Bengal side. On the Coast side everything looks like peace but here there is no dependence ever to be placed on appearance.

133 H.D. Love, *Vestiges of Old Madras.1640–1800.* (London: John Murray, 1913) vol. III. A nine acre plot known as Blackers Gardens,' Mount Road, Teynampett, Madras. In 1893 the residence was the clubhouse of the Madras Boat Club.

134 A. Mackenzie, *History of the Munros of Fowlis.* (Inverness: Mackenzie 1898) Quartermaster General Captain John Munro, b.1778 joined HEIC 1791 Lieutenant, 1794, Captain 1800, Major 1811 Lt. Colonel 1818, retired 1837, d.1858. During his later service appointed as Resident to several Native States. He married Valentine's sister Charlotte in 1808.

135 Major General Sir John Cradock, later 1st Baron Howden. See previous fn.

136 C.E. Buckland, *Dictionary of Indian Biography*, Captain Thomas Sydenham, 1780–1816, the Resident at Hyderabad in 1806 appointed after death of James Kirkpatrick. Previously, Valentine had reported that Robert Close was the officer in command of the escort. (See letters 9 September 1805 and 8 July 1806.)

A Mr Yates who arrived here on some trading speculation brought with him last year a letter from one of my aunts to the Colonel: his speculation has not succeeded and he goes home in the present fleet having in charge from me a bundle of Argus feathers for my sisters,[137] I am told they bear a high price at home and they must be hereafter still more dear as we have no longer possession of the Island the bird inhabits; a friend of mine last fleet sent home a similar parcel of by no means so good ones to the Princess Amelia.[138] Notwithstanding this I have desired Mr Yates [who has got some also] to let them go if he cannot bring them clear without expense. I do not write to the rest of the family by the ships as all their letters have formerly been replied to and my stupid abode at this place affords me nothing to communicate. Pray therefore make my most affectionate love to my brothers and sisters and believe me to be, yours of the most faithfully and sincerely V. Blacker

9 July 1806 (*Rec'd 9 April 1807*)

Madras. I wrote to you my dear Father about a month since a letter which you will never receive, as the fleet which was to have carried it sailed from Bengal, and the Government there would not detain it for the arrival of the packet of letters from Madras. My former therefore was left behind with other Madras letters and lest you should be surprised at a long silence upon my part I thought proper to write to you over.

Since my last I have received your favour of the 19th December by a fleet which sailed in March but have not heard from any of the rest of the family except Mrs B. You will have been happy to hear ere long that St. John has quite recovered and becomes as handsome as ever, that he is now attached to the escort of the Resident at Hyderabad;[139] the line in which I formerly commenced and that Robert Close has followed my example in. I entirely concede in your sentiments regarding the continental politics, but I observe you think the progress of our information more tardy than it really is. We had almost every week an account of the progress of operations of the Army by way of Constantinople and Bussara within two months of that actual occurrence, nor are we always indebted to the English papers for our information respecting our own country as the Hamburg news is frequently before it. Your favour of the 30th of September I never expect to receive, as I conclude it to have been in the *Belle* packet and taken. I rejoice at the pleasant intelligence regarding the family in general but must regret there being any appearance of uncertainty in what relates to the termination of Grace's affair. I must have a picture of Charlotte to see what she has grown up to and only wait to hear the results of a letter of credit I sent home with some commendations in order to arrange for defraying the expense of it. The Colonel

---

137 Great Argus, a species of Pheasant.
138 Amelia, 1783–1810. Sixth Daughter of George III <www.regencyhistory.net> (accessed August 2017).
139 See letter 25 February 1805.

I presume will leave India about the beginning of next year, and however I must regret his loss, I must rejoice at his leaving this country on his own account, but cannot in the most distant manner speculate on the mode of life he will adopt in England. Robert Close gets on remarkably well and will be a man of fortune long before I shall, if such a thing shall ever happen. St. John's prospects are by no means so good as his Cousin's but I trust he will get on in time.

The regulations of the overland packet are so strict that I must confine myself to this small compass and weight of paper. Believe me Dear Father to remain your ever affectionate son Val: Blacker.

To Mrs Blacker[140]

My dear madam, I am happy even on this small remains of paper to have an opportunity of thanking you for the share you have taken in my father's last letter and hope the obligation will be frequently repeated. It is to me very interesting news that I have occupied any part of Lady Powis's recollections, as I am sure her kindness to me will never be effaced from mine. I cannot say much of Mr Dodswell's success in India but hope he will do better in England for which he sailed a year since.

With best regards to Miss Messiter, I remain my dear Madam, yours faithfully VB.

12 October 1806 (*Mr Linley delivered it July 26 1807*)
Madras. My dear Father, this will be delivered to you by a very old friend of mine (Mr Linley) who is about to leave India for ever and expressed a wish to meet the friends at home of one he knew so well here. My father will find in him a very sensible, unaffected acquaintance, and my sisters an excellent connoisseur in music. Wells or its neighborhood is his native place, a circumstance which makes him more anxious to be acquainted with its present inhabitants. He returns home with a very moderate fortune, but the springs of life being gone and his disposition being easily contented he considers it better to return to his nature and enjoy the rest of his life. Ever my dear Father your most affectionate son, V Blacker.

18 October 1806 (*Rec'd 16 April 1807*)
Madras. My dear Father, the last letter I have had the pleasure to receive from you and was answered by mine 9th ultimo which went by the overland packet. I wrote to you also on the 9th July also by the overland dispatch both which I hope you have received, the latter of which was to give the Earliest intelligence of my good fortune in having been appointed Deputy Quartermaster-General of the Army. I have delayed until nearly the last writing to you in hopes of the arrival of the fleet which sailed from England on the 1st of June that I might have some letter of a late date to reply to, but there are now little hopes of its appearance until next year, for all the fleets which arrive in the Bay of Bengal, after the 15th of October keep clear of the Western coast

140 Valentine's step mother. His father had married Susan Messiter in 1801.

and either pass the monsoon in Calcutta or our Eastern settlements. It is not necessary that I should adopt your plan with regard to regularity in writing as I am almost entirely at the Presidency I am well acquainted with the time at which the ships sail and consequently am enabled to write on the last day. I hear frequently from the Colonel and in his last letter he informed me that he hoped to leave India before the end of this season which in Bombay means of December and January. My intention is to leave Madras early in November and proceed across the country to the opposite coast and get a passage up to Bombay at which place or at Poonah I shall find the Colonel preparing for his departure from India. What an era in the life of one who has spent so many years in it and with so much eclat. What his plans of life will be on his arrival in England I cannot guess and I really fancy he has not formed any for himself. So unacquainted must he be with life and manners in England, having no means of judging except by his recollection of what they were between 30 and 40 years ago and from the partial accounts given by later arrivals, that he will no doubt be suspicious of the grounds on which he would now attempt to make any arrangement for the remaining years of his life. He has risen to the highest situation that it is possible for a Company's military servant to hold and most probably he will have attained the rank of a General officer before the expiration of three years furlough to which he is entitled before he is called upon to resign.

You will hear extraordinary accounts of the late mutiny of the troops (a part of them) and of a spirit of disaffection to our service which suddenly showed itself to a very alarming degree,[141] owing to the intrigues of the sons of Tippoo Sultaun, a dislike to our judicial arrangements which obtained among the inhabitants at large; and a dread they entertained we have the intention of converting our Indian subjects to our own religion induced several battalions to refuse wearing their customary bonnet with a small alteration directed by the Commander in Chief, considering that it was our intention to attack their principles through the medium of their dress. This will appear strange to a European who has not resided in India, but their excessive ignorance is such and their detestation of any change in custom so rooted as to render them easy dupes of any designing persons who can seize a pretext to work on their passions. It might be urged that all authorities here should have been aware of their antipathy to innovation but this was to a certain degree necessary and that many other innovations have been made of much more real consequence, but they were not ushered in by a combination of adverse circumstances which afterwards appeared to be the case

---

141 P. Mason, *A Matter of Honour.* The Mutiny at Vellore July 1806. Three Madras Native Infantry battalions, 1st/1st, 2nd/1st and 2nd//23rd, possibly encouraged by feelings of sympathy for the relatives of Tippoo Sultan held at Vellore, mutinied after their grievances over pay, uniform, the wearing of 'joys', (earrings) moustaches and beards were ignored. 14 Officers were murdered by mutineers from their own regiments and they killed or wounded 115 troops and officers from HM. 69th Regiment. The mutiny was brief and ruthlessly suppressed within 24 hrs by 19th Dragoons from Arcot led by Lieutenant Colonel Rollo Gillespie. pp. 237–242.

in this instance. The catastrophe you will have heard of before the arrival of this letter and therefore I omit describing the horrid massacre of the European officers (both men and officers) by the 2nd native battalion at Vellore.

I send home in charge of Lady Georgia Stewart proceeding from this country three Cornelian necklaces directed to you, but who these are for is more than I can tell, as St. John (whose property they are) has not informed me. I have also given a letter of introduction to you a Mr Linley[142] who is going home and as he considers Wells his native place he has begged me to present him to your acquaintance. You will find him a worthy sort of man and a great musician, and the last situation which he has held here is that of Sub-Treasurer, and though it is a tolerably good appointment he relinquishes it to return home with what he has.

I was surprised a few days since by the familiar address of someone whose face I perfectly recollected and found out to be a Mr Pepper who came out in the same ship with me and spent a day with us at Chester: he is going home on leave, the same silly sort of fellow he was then. Robert Close and St. John are in very good health and spirits, the former getting on very fortunately and the latter very pleasantly. Present my best love to my sisters and to Mrs B. to whom I wrote a few lines by the overland dispatch, make my remembrance to Miss Messiter and believe me dear Father your most affectionate son, V. Blacker.

1807

July 1807
My dear Father this letter was written in July 1807. The last letter I have had the pleasure of receiving from you was dated in December, the last I have written was from Poonah. I have not *(illegible)* enough to reply particularly to the former or to give an account of myself since the latter. I have had a letter from Grace mentioning her disappointment with regard to her matrimonial speculation and have by this opportunity written to invite her and Charlotte to visit me in India and have provided them an introduction to the first society and a most brotherly reception. I now my dear Father address you on the subject as the person whose consent and interest is most deeply concerned. If you see the plan in the advantage point of view you will give your consent to it and send them out in the most handsome style. I suggest your remitting to me their small fortune as a standby for them against the worst that may happen which shall be placed at high interest on Government security and hope that

142 *Oxford Dictionary of National Biography*, William Linley, 1771–1835 Author and Musician entered the East India Company's service as a writer in 1790. In 1791 he was appointed assistant to the Collector at Madura and Dindigal. By 1793 he was deputy secretary to the military board but returned to England in 1796 on grounds of health. In 1800 Linley returned to his duties at Madras, was appointed paymaster at Nellore in 1801, followed by appointment in 1805 as sub-treasurer and mint-master to the Presidency, Fort St. George. He finally left India in 1806, devoting his time to composing music.

my brothers' will contribute to the passage, money and equipment, that their fortunes may remain untouched. Any expense this will cause them will be a drop of water compared to the additional housekeeping I shall experience and I would not presume to take myself a greater share of brotherly affection than they possess. Forgive, my dear Father the haste of this, I have not a moment to spare and delay not writing to me by the Earliest opportunity both overland and by sea. I have heard from William at Buenos Ayres and am anxious to the last degree to hear again. My love to Mrs B and Miss Messiter.

My dear Father
   Ever yours affectionately
   V. Blacker
   The Colonel says he will soon take you by the hand.

Undated (*Received 15 April 1808*)
My dear Father, since the 22nd of last month, the date of my last letter to you nothing has occurred to me worthy to be made the subject of a letter, but as I have always hitherto made up a letter whether I had a subject or not, I have not thought it necessary to break through my continued habit. What with business and amusements I have never known so restless a month as this last and I have some pleasure in supposing that after the fleet sails we shall have a little quiet: the quiet will soon degenerate into stupidity and we shall wish them all back again.

My library ensures one a resource and indeed without it, although possessing everything else, I know not how I should get along. In composing of the plan of my house I did not forget to set apart a particular portion to be fitted up solely as a study and my library though not very extensive, contains all the principle English, Latin and French authors to which I mean to add some Italian, as I am already provided with the dictionary and grammar of that language. Perhaps I have altogether about 700 vols. and there yet remain a few spare shelves. Beside my library I have a further fund of amusement and that is in my garden. The vegetation is so quick in this country that young orchard trees which I planted two years ago in commencing my house will produce fruit next season and some particular kinds have already borne. My flute is not entirely given up as you seem to suppose, and it is not long since I had a grand concert at my own house, which contains an apartment well calculated for that purpose. However to give you a better idea of my edifice I shall have a drawing made of it and perhaps be able to send it by the next fleet. I beg dear Father that you will present my affectionate regards to Mrs B and Miss Messiter I remain most faithfully yours.V Blacker

St. John writes to me frequently and continues well employed at Hyderabad. I shall procure for him and shortly, permission to visit Poonah, as the Colonel has sent intimation to the Supreme Government that he intends applying for permission to resign his situation.

29 February 1808 (*Received 20 August 1808*)

My dear Father, the last letter I have received from you was dated 31 July, two of the ships coming here it is feared have been taken, and which had most of the letters for this place. The Colonel still remains in India, and without he pays a little more respect to his private views than to public ones, he will never get out of it. Every Governor General finds himself so confident in having him at the head of the Maratha concerns that he wishes to detain him during his own Government. And yet there is not an individual in India who sighs more ardently after his native country than he does, and nothing but his devotion to the public service could have prevailed on him to acquiesce in Lord Minto's late request.[143] Sir G. Barlow upon landing at Madras observed that Colonel Close's character was as strongly expressed by his consenting to remain in India as if by any other act he had performed.[144]

This is the worst country for an older man, he has no person to administer to his comforts or to pay him the least deference. He is considered as a burthen to society by preventing the rise of others possessing more activity, for every person here is the votary of ambition or money. Sooner than remain in India to be overtaken by any of the infirmities of age I would retire on the pittance of 350 a year which I shall most probably be entitled to when my periods of service shall have expired.

As to accumulating a fortune it is entirely out of the question; it is never done on a salary except in that of a Resident who has all his expenses paid. Fortunes are made by forswearing oneself once a month at least as far as a solemn declaration in honour goes.

My friends therefore may expect to see me return a poor man but I hope untainted by the smallest imputation against my conduct in the public service of this country. During Lord Cornwallis's war[145] in this country any number of the Colonel's friends got round him to persuade him that, provided he would accept of the prize agency of the Army,[146] they had no doubt to be able to collect for him a sufficient number of votes and the report is that he flew off from them terrified at the mention of a proposal, which, was he to accept, the most upright conduct could not save him from the aspersion of peculation. Show me his equal among all your public characters who are contending about places and pensions to the ruin of the country. By stinting myself of my present enjoyments I might be able to save something out of my salary, but to

143 C.E. Buckland, *Dictionary of Indian Biography*, Gilbert Elliot 1751–1814, created Lord Minto, 1797 appointed Governor General, July 1807.
144 C.E. Buckland, *Dictionary of Indian Biography*, Sir George Hilaro Barlow, 1763–1846 appointed Governor of Madras 1807–13 in place of Lord Bentinck who had been recalled.
145 The Third Anglo-Mysore War, 1790–92. See entry under Background.
146 Prize Agents. Usually Officers officially appointed and responsible for the disbursement of the proceeds of plunder 'the spoils of war' amongst victorious officers and ranks on a pro rata basis. Later conventions on the laws and usages of war declared looting etc a war crime.

what purpose, I have none depending upon me and never expect to have and the expectation of enjoying it hereafter is too uncertain to operate upon me.

It will be very difficult, it is apprehended, to either keep or lose any of our present possessions, a French Force is collecting in Persia: there is also a disaffection in the native powers to us, united to the system of Government which prevails here and at home conspired to make the continuance of our authority very problematical.

I suppose Grace and Charlotte, if they accept my invitation, will sail about this time and I will expect much pleasure in July. I have made some alterations and additions to my house for their better accommodation. Since my last I have lived quietly at Madras; this therefore is a letter of reflections. In a letter I have lately from Robert Close he seems to lament the suspicion you entertain of our not being upon as friendly a footing as we ought to be. Our correspondence is not very regular, yet we have the strongest confidence in each other's friendship I have the best accounts both from him and of St.John. He still lives at the Residency at Hyderabad but I presume he will by this time have joined his Regiment which has been ordered with some others on an unexpected service. Present my affectionate regards to Mrs B. to Mary and Cath, the latter of whom has given over writing to me. Yours my dear Father most affectionately V. Blacker

27 July 1808 (*Received 15 May 1809*)
My dear Father, yours of the 9th of January gave me more pleasure than any letter I have ever received, although a bold expression. My invitation to my sisters has been accepted with your entire approbation and so many of their friends, and has added to my prospect of happiness. I immediately communicated this intelligence to the Colonel who by return of post begged permission to present his nieces with the handsomest carriage and horses to be procured, and I have accordingly transferred to him the honour of paying for a fashionable Barouche and a pair of the best blooded Arabs to be had:[147] the whole equipage is prepared for their reception. My house is prepared for their reception but I do not intend to bring them to it in the first instance being desirous they should have the introduction of a female friend regarding 50 circumstances a bachelor is quite ignorant of. They will therefore spend a week or two with Lady Strange, by whom I will have the introduction of the lady of the first rank in this place, as her husband Sir Thomas Strange is His Majesty's Chief Justice at this Presidency, next in situation to the Governor whose lady is not arrived. Your explanation My dear Father respecting money arrangements is perfectly satisfactory and I hope you will have understood by my after letters that I did not calculate on the circumstance of my sisters having a £1000 each being the means of procuring them a handsomer establishment in life than if they had it not. You will be surprised to hear

---

147 A four wheeled horse drawn carriage with two double seats, collapsible hood and separate driver's seat.

that St. John is gone to Persia after our Envoy in command of a troop of volunteers.[148] I wrote to him immediately upon receiving your last letter, but had no opportunity of hearing from him since. I mentioned to you in a former letter that my friend the Resident of Hyderabad took much interest in superintending the improvement of his mind and I cannot deny myself the pleasure of giving you an extract from a letter of the Colonel's after he had seen St. John on his way to Persia. I wish you could have seen him as I did when he passed to Bombay; I never saw a young man so much improved. At the recommendation of Captain Sydenham he went through a course of historical reading which has enlarged his views, given a taste for new objects and had a wonderful effect on his conversation.

Two of the ships which sailed early in March arrived here five weeks ago, although the remainder has not yet come in. I have been told by a passenger that two Miss Blackers had engaged a servant taken hence by a Mrs Cramer and were to sail in the April fleet, I therefore look to the 15th of August as a day of happiness. I write this letter in hope of it going in the packet to be dispatched from Calcutta to which place it goes inclosed. I remain my dear Father with love to all friends at home most faithfully yours V. Blacker

23 October 1808 (*Received 3 June 1809*)

Oh my dear Father, I never had so many letters from you before me unanswered on any former occasion. The interesting event of my sisters of leaving England and their friends called forth all your attention and the habit of reflecting upon it produced a great deal of writing. Most worthy they are of every solicitude and I am sure my father has every reliance on the care and anxiety for their welfare they will experience on my part. I have no tie so near me as they are and should I be so fortunate as to the means of making them happy I shall feel satisfied with regard to the social duties here.

My own experience of the world has convinced me that professions do not always imply the certainty of performance, but I would not on account of this consideration refrain from expressing what I really feel, as it is satisfactory to myself, and maybe consolatory to a parent solicitous about the happiness and prosperity of his children. They are dear girls and their own good conduct disarms me of all authority. I will not attempt to describe what were my feelings on going on board for them. They were the most overpowering I had ever experienced or perhaps ever shall, but enough on this subject, and I shall weary you and I doubt not you will have a great deal more from my sisters. I wrote to you on July 29. Since then Robert Close has put in his claim for permission to contribute a curricle and a pair of horses, saddle horses or whatever should be most acceptable. You will observe from St. John's letter to me from Busrah which I have put under cover and sent to you,[149] that he has picked up a horse for Charlotte so that we shall be, at all events I hope, well mounted. You have

---

148 Sir John Malcolm, 1769–1833 see previous fn.
149 Busrah now Basra, Iraq. Ed.

done wonders my dear Father in regard to getting together the money for my sisters, William has furnished them with a letter of credit on Greg in London for £2000 and I have negotiated their bills to that amount and it is now vested in Company paper. The £460 British which remains your property shall be held ready to be remitted to you so soon as either of the events you mention shall occur in the meantime the interest I trust will prove fully adequate to the object of dressing them without having recourse to my brothers' generous offers of assistance. Your letter to Grace and Charlotte on their leaving you is just what I would have expected from you on the occasion and gave them a fair opportunity of judging of the expediency of refusing or accepting of my invitation than they could have deduced from their own consideration of the subject. Your letter to them also on the subject of any connection they might form in this country must have the beneficial effect of giving them settled opinions on the subject which is peculiarly desirable to have prepared on every occasion wherein reason is liable to be warped by passion.[150]

Many thanks for the almanac, it hangs in my room immediately over my writing table and frequently catches my eye. I have already commenced on a view of the house before receiving yours but have not been able to finish it in time. I must therefore postpone it until the next fleet. I know nothing of the probable period of the Colonel's departure from India but hope for his own sake that it may not be very distant; he always mentions my sisters with much affection and I'm sure that a former surmise of yours regarding his sentiments towards yourself must have been entirely unfounded. I look upon myself as his most intimate last remaining friend in India, since Colonel Wilkes will proceed to England by this fleet.[151] I have entrusted him with a seal set according to the Indian fashion for Mary with her name engraved in Arabic. I shall write to her about it myself however, and now that I am upon the subject of seals might I request to have a sketch of your coat of arms. I know nothing of it but the motto and crest and the panels of our barouche look quite bare without something of the kind.

With most affectionate wishes to Mrs B and Mrs Messiter I remain my dear Father your most sincerely and faithfully V. Blacker

29 December 1808 (*Received 28 April 1809*)
Madras. My dear Father, my last letter was dated October 23rd. I begin my letter very near the top of the paper, although I am by no means sure that I shall have leisure to write to the bottom. *The Georgiana* packet has just come in from Bengal on her way to

---

150 Eligible females from Britain visiting India ostensibly known as 'The Fishing Fleet.'
151 E. Dodswell & J. Miles, *Alphabetical List of the Officers of the Indian Army 1760–1834,* Lieutenant Colonel Mark Wilks, joined HEIC 1781, Ensign 1782, Lieutenant, 1789. Captain 1798, Major 1804, Lt. Colonel 1808. Retired 1818, died 1831. Author of Historical Sketches of Southern India, 1810 3 vols. which Wilks dedicated to his great friend Colonel Barry Close.

England and is to delay a few hours here.[152] The last letter I have received from home is written by Sam and dated of the 1st May at Portsmouth: I shall reply to him by the regular fleet which will sail a month or six weeks hence but the present the most I shall be able to perform is a letter to you and Mrs Noble.

I hope by the regular fleet dispatch to send you Government bills for the amount you advanced Charlotte, as she forsook my protection on the 8th of this month for that of my most intimate friend-Lieutenant Colonel Munro, the Quartermaster General of the Army, who was the deputy of the office when I was the assistant and, on his promotion, I succeeded him. In some degrees our interests have been generally connected, and a friendship for the last six years has been uninterrupted. His character as a man of talents stands in the highest rank and he has played a conspicuous part in the public affairs of this place for some years. Any of the authorities who have lately gone home will bear testimony to this, perhaps some to their cost. His distinguished character is a topic most fully dwelt on in all the notes of congratulation I have received on the occasion of my sister's marriage to him. He is not a man of fortune now, but looks to go home in the course of some five years when he will still be only about 37 years of age. His constitution is completely unimpaired and I am sure my Father will place a just value on all the circumstances when compared with their contraries however great a fortune might accompany the latter. We have adopted a plan which promises comfort and economy to all parties, it keeps my sisters together without leaving me by myself.

The new married couple have taken my house (the contribution upon my part) and they keep the table as theirs. This arrangement at the same time that it affords the most happy society considerably reduces of the expenses of both parties. I am convinced you will approve of it and could you but see us would think us very enviable. Mrs Munro will have her chariot and pair, they each have their respective riding horses independent of the conveyances and horses required by Colonel Munro and myself, so that we consider ourselves equal to any undertaking. We still however intend to be very frugal as we acknowledge that one party will have little pleasure in India when the other leaves it.

There has been no opportunity of hearing from St. John lately but I have heard of his having gone on a tour on the Euphrates and Tigris: I look for letters from him daily and trust that his expedition up the Gulf of Persia will ultimately be of much use to him.

I have received a letter from the Colonel a few days since but he says nothing of going home. He will no doubt let you know his sentiments regarding the match of his niece, to me he says it is most desirable in every point of view. I should like to read over what I have written but really have not the leisure to do so. Believe me to remain, my dear Father your ever affectionate son,
    V Blacker

152 'Georgiana,' an HEIC packet built 1796 and 350 tons made several journey's to Bengal and India.

1809

Colonel B. Close to Rev. St. John Blacker.

20 January 1809 (*Received 24 July 1809*)
Poonah. My dear St. John, you complain of my silence and with so much justice that I am afraid to attempt an apology for it. Perhaps I went too far in conceiving that the fullness of my friend Valentine's correspondence would be received as compensating for the deficiency of mine. If this has brought blame upon me it is at least flattering to me to find that you continue to take an unabated interest in hearing from me. The disappointment which my detention in this country occasioned to all the family could not but give me great anxiety and in such a state of mind the kind expressions you conveyed to me on finding that I had judged it my duty to acquiesce in the suggestions of the Governor General did not fail to bring me proportionable consolation. The subsequent appearance of the French in Persia excited fresh apprehensions in the breast of the Bengal Government and Lord Minto's recommendation to me not to quit India at such a conjuncture referred to stronger grounds than that which I had before received from Sir George Barlow. The late favourable change in Europe however will I hope release us all from anxiety of French influence at the Persian court and if the political course we have taken at home succeeds, the period cannot be far distant when circumstances will be such in India as to set me free.

Situated so remotely from Madras, I have not yet had an opportunity of meeting my nieces. Miss Charlotte, as you will hear probably before you read this was married a short time ago to Lieutenant Colonel Munro, Quartermaster General on the coast, a very distinguished young man and an intimate friend of Valentine who is his deputy in office. Such a union cannot fail of being happy. St. John proceeded with his troops last year to the Gulf of Persia as part of the escort of General Malcolm who was at that time apparently destined for the Persian court. The General arrived at Bushire and returned shortly after to Bengal leaving St. John and his party at the former and from thence the escort was ordered to Bussorah and soon after his arrival there St. John proceeded on a visit to Baghdad returning in October last to Bussorah where he now is. General Malcom is at present at Bombay destined to return to the Gulf where St. John will again join him. The climate of Bussora, which in the winter is rather sharp, has contributed to the improvement of his health. In his last letter one dated December 4th he speaks of himself as being stout and robust. I made a direct push last year to get him appointed as an assistant to this Residency but was told with civility that the late orders of the Court of Directors prohibiting the appointment of any military man in future to a Residency at a native court were so strict as not to admit of being disobeyed, thus you see fortune has not begun to smile upon him. While at Hyderabad with my friend Captain Sydenham he went through a course of reading which improved him beyond description;[153] with this accession of knowledge and the addition of a few years to his age he is become steady, reflecting and very respectable in conversation.

With me he would have had the leisure for further study and improvement and I shall ever regret that my application to fix him here did not succeed. General Malcom is his friend and I hope to see his prospects brighten ere long. I have been highly gratified of late by receiving a kind visit from General Champagne whom I hope will succeed to the command at Bombay.[154] If you continue to communicate with Colonel Massey you must make my cordial remembrance to him. I give this letter to Mr Gowan of the Madras Civil Establishment who has resided with us for some time and is about to embark for England, his father is from the North of Ireland but settled in England many years ago and passes much of his time at Bath. I rather think you must be acquainted with the family, he is a very fine young man and I hope he may have an opportunity of meeting you as he knows as much about me as I can well describe myself. Though unknown to (Mrs I should say) my sister Blacker from being so long detained in this region you must convey my best wishes to her.

Yours my dear St. John most affectionately,

B. Close

10 March 1809 (*Received 9 December 1809*)
Camp in Travancore. My dear Father, I have received your letter of the 6th of September and at the same time one dated three months before it. It is very true we had a severe storm the 10th of December 1807 and my house suffered much like my neighbours. Your account of Mrs Agnew pleased me much, I hope to see her return here having no doubt that her husband Colonel Agnew will be reinstated in his situation of Adjutant General. This will make his victory complete as he has been certainly ill used.[155]

William's conduct has been very satisfactory and what I would have expected from him. He seems scarcely to have overdone the rage of wandering and I dare say will be prompted again to leave Belfast.

My letters of I know not what date, having nothing but my bureau de la guerre, will have given a full account of all from the arrival of Grace and Charlotte. I sent the bill for the £464 from Charlotte, and a large a bundle of papers relative to the business between the Commander in Chief and the Quartermaster General explaining everything until his sailing. The Governor here resented his publishing the paper he did

---

153 Captain Thomas Sydenham, 1780–1816. see previous fn.
154 Not indentified. There were two brothers Champagne. Josiah b.1753 and Forbes b.1764. Both served in India for periods c.1800–1810, always in Kings Regiments and both rose to Lieutenant General. Neither served as C–in–C Bombay.
155 E. Dodswell & J. Miles, *Alphabetical List of the Officers of the Indian Army 1760–1834,* Patrick Vans Agnew, Ensign 1774, Lieutenant, 1780, Captain 1785, Major 1796 Lieutenant Colonel 1798, Colonel 1804, Major General 1814. I have been unable to discover the reason for Blacker's comment of 'ill used.'

so much that, not being able to recall the fleet, a fast sailing vessel was dispatched to Ceylon where he was dismissed from the command.[156] I proceeded on field service the 31st of January, travelled across the peninsula to Tellicherry, went by sea to Quelon in Travancore on the 15th of February. So many troops had been poured in that after a short resistance, the contest was given up. I now write within 5 miles of the capital Trivandrum. I hope to be at Madras in about six weeks via Ceylon which I have not yet seen. My preparations for my expedition prevented my sending you the plan and elevation of the house, which I will send you by the first opportunity. I have to express my deep regrets for the attacks from the gout you have had, guard my dear Father every avenue from such a foe. I agree with you that all apprehensions from the French are for some time done away. How conspicuous a situation is England in at present, and how much so Sir Arthur Wellesley whom I esteem my friend, I should give anything to be with him in Portugal. The company's service is a place of obscurity and should their troops be transferred to the Crown I shall seize the first opportunity to change to a more extensive theatre of arms.[157]

St. John is gone in quest of Sir John Malcolm to accompany him through the northern provinces of Persia, he appears in good spirits. The communication between this and Madras has been interrupted so that I have heard but little of Grace and Charlotte, the latter and her husband promise to enjoy every happiness which mutual affection can promise.

Love and affectionate remembrances to all friends. I remain my dear Father, yours most faithfully V Blacker

9 May 1809 (*Received 21 Sept 1809*)

Madras. My Dear Father, I don't know what was the precise time of my last letter to you nor is it perhaps of much consequence as I think it likely that you will not receive it, as it was dispatched through an uncertain kind of channel. I wrote in March during my abode in Travancore giving an account of my progress to that place and sent my letter to Columbo,[158] having heard of a vessel to sail from that place to the Cape.

156 This appears to be a reference to part of the major disagreement between McDowall and Munro over the Tent Contracts which resulted in Munro being arrested. McDowall was later dismissed as C-in-C. See letter 4 September 1809.
157 A reference to The Peninsula War 1807–14.
158 *Edinburgh Annual Register* July 1811 p. 193. Travancore, a native state ruled by a Rajah within Madras Presidency. A rebellion in Travancore, Quilon and Cochin in December 1808 instigated by Ministers of the Diwan where native troops had attacked British forces and the Resident with 145 casualties. The rebellion was finally suppressed in February 1809 with troops from HMs.12th and 17th Regiments. The Rajah who had initially joined the rebels defected to the Company. The Rajah had been in debt to the Company and the Resident recommended the dismissal of his troops. During the conflict on 28 Dec 1808 an atrocity occurred when 30 British soldiers were drowned. The new Resident was John Munro.

I believe you will think one of the most material incidents of this letter to be my dear Grace's marriage which took place on the 6th Inst to the great satisfaction of us all and I may say of the society in general, with the exception of one young lady who was very desirous of occupying Grace's place. Mr Robert Alexander,[159] your new son in law, is a gentleman of the most respectable character and of good connections, the Cousin German of the present Lord Caledon. He is about 37 years of age and holds one of the most desirable civil situations at Madras, being a second member of the Board of Revenue with a salary of £4500 per annum. Mr Alexander has been a widower for 4 years and has a son by his first wife at school in England. I knew nothing of his having paid his addresses until my arrival here from Travancore, for having found some difficulty in proceeding from thence by land, I took my passage in a small vessel and I thus missed all the letters which were intended to inform me of the event. I found that he had already solicited her hand and that all required was my consent and presence. They are living in a house within a few 100 yards of mine so that there is not much likelihood of the intercourse being prevented by our separation. Charlotte continues to be very industrious at her pencil, improves daily, and has contributed to the adornment of my pavilion by some quite masterly landscapes. The present opportunity of writing is in consequence of a vessel being taken up as an extraordinary packet to carry home dispatches respecting the state of the Army. The Government have been drawn into some strong measures by their proceedings and perhaps the enclosed printed General Order may give you the best idea of the business which the contents of a letter may admit of. It may be further satisfactory for you to see it as it is the production of Munro. I could wish you would take an opportunity of sending it and other enclosures to Maxwell who I presume feels interested in all circumstances involving points of law. By the last accounts we have received of St. John, he was on his way in pursuit of Sir Harford Jones,[160] the Ambassador to Persia, and I suppose he may now be somewhere near the borders of the Caspian Sea. This trip will no doubt prove highly beneficial to his constitution and equal to a trip to England and I entertain little doubt of having him employed on the staff as soon as we can get him back. Robert still continues an Acting Resident and likely to remain so as his conduct in that confidential situation has received the most decided approbation of the Bengal Government. Grace can scarcely bring herself to suppose that the little chubby fellow she saw a few years ago in England should now be the man of consequence he is. I have not heard from the Colonel for some time, but believe he is well, without having been able to fix on the period of his departure, how melancholy sometimes to be so useful. I shall write to Mary by this opportunity and also to Mrs

159 T.H. Beaglehole, *Thomas Munro and the Development of Administrative Policy in Madras.* p. 112. Robert Alexander, civil servant is now recorded as President of the Board of Revenue 1816.

160 *Oxford Dictionary of National Biography*, Sir Harford Jones, 1764–1847. 1st Baronet. Diplomat and Plenipotentiary at the Persian Court 1807–11. Assumed surname of Brydges 1826.

Noble and beg my dear Father that you will present my affectionate remembrances is to all relatives, believing me yours faithfully V. Blacker.

4 September 1809 (*Received 23 January 1810*)
My dear Father, I am now 120 miles from Madras, and have just heard a ship is to sail immediately to England. The proceedings of this army has at length broke out into open rebellion, have seized the treasures at different stations, abandoned their posts contrary to orders and occupied positions of defence.[161] One recontre has happened between the Government troops and the rebels in which they were routed and dispersed and it was followed by the good effect that all the party within our own territories shortly surrendered, but the Army of Observation on the frontier of our Allies and 800 miles from Madras hold out and threaten to involve the fate of British India in their own fall should such happen. Their threat is vainglorious and I am now attached to that force ordered against them. Before coming to extremities with them, the Government requested the Colonel to leave his Residency and proceed to Hyderabad, the headquarters of the rebels and to assume there the military command and political charge hoping that his influence and popularity would bring the rebels to their senses. He travelled a day and night; on his arrival he adopted his measures but they were unsuccessful and to avoid being taken prisoner he was obliged to move off. Upon cold reflection some of them have come round but the advanced army still hold out demanding what they call honourable terms. If they continue in this mind they must either fall or abandon their native country and join our enemies whom they were placed to watch. A respectable Army of the King's Troops is collecting against them brought from Bombay and Ceylon. Colonel Close is in orders for the command of it with all the political powers of Government.[162] I am sent as his Quartermaster

161 Malcolm, J. *Observations on the Disturbances in the Madras Army 1809.* (London: W. Miller & J. Murray, 1812) Serious indiscipline and disturbances by 100 Officers of The Madras Army over the abolition of the 'Tent Contract System' in 1808 caused a tremor throughout the Madras Presidency. The system had provided officers with lucrative contracts with local bazaars and, enraged by the loss, Officers abandoned their posts, seized treasure to pay their troops and refused the orders of the Governor General.
The Commander in Chief of Madras Lt. General H. MacDowall supported his officers and had the Quartermaster General John Munro arrested for publishing a document which disagreed with his view as the C-in-C. Munro supporting instead the Government stance. McDowall was eventually relieved of his command. Looting took place and loyal Company troops and Kings Regiments confronted the 'rebels' some of whom were arrested. 3 Lieutenant Colonels, 3 Majors and 16 Captains were suspended or court martialled but leniently punished. Lieutenant General H. Mc Dowall had already left for England but drowned when his vessel *'Lady Jane Dundas'* sank near the Cape of Good Hope. Wellington took the view that 'the affairs of the Presidency had been much mismanaged.'
162 A & H Tayler, (ed.) *Letters of John Orrok* (Aberdeen: Milne and Hutchinson, 1927) p. 108–113. Orrok 1779–1828 was a Captain in HM 33rd Regiment stationed at Hyderabad and a witness to the events. He described it as 'The Madras Mutiny.'

General and I hope St. John will be appointed his aide de camp, he is now on his way from Bombay to Madras. He was appointed by Sir Harford Jones Secretary to the Persian Embassy but has been recalled by this Government. He has been engaged in action in the Persian Gulf and he has received the thanks of Government for his and another officer's behaviour to which is attributed the conduct of the men. Charlotte's letters to me are in Italian, she has a great capacity in learning languages.

Yours my dear Father ever affectionately V. Blacker.

1810

5 April 1810 (*Received 1 October 1810*)
My dear Father, I arrived in consequence of an order to repair to Headquarters from the Army under Colonel Close two days since, my route

Lieutenant-General Hay McDowall, C-in-C Madras 1807-1810.

through a barbarous country and therefore had an escort for 600 miles, which took me up to 20 days with my horses and camels: I then dismissed my escort and for the last 500 miles travelled post. On my arrival at Madras I found Grace and Charlotte well, Munro made Resident at Travancore and yesterday I was appointed Quartermaster General of the Army with the rank of Lieutenant Colonel.[163] The Munro's will not leave this place for some months, and their salary which amounts to from 1000 to 1100 pagodas per month (£4404 p.a) will accumulate. We shall suffer great loss by their departure, yet their situation will be much improved and I have thereby obtained the great object of my ambition. Our next great object will be to provide for St. John some permanent situation. He is at present pleasantly enough situated as political assistant to the Colonel and his aide de camp, but these depend upon the Colonel's movements and the service upon which he has been, is effected. Here then the Colonel's general military and political authority end and he intends to visit Madras in hope to return. He will bring St. John with him and they will see Grace and perhaps, Charlotte, who is to continue until she recovers after her confinement. It will gratify you that St. John has returned from Persia, a very intelligent young man of business and has given the Colonel much satisfaction as a Political Assistant. He (St. John) lost his horses in the Persian Gulf, no doubt they were insured but were to him invaluable. You have

163 E. Dodswell, & J. Miles, *Alphabetical List of the Officers of the Indian Army 1760–1834.*
This was likely to have been a brevet rank as official records show that Valentine was not promoted Major until 1818 and Lt. Colonel 1823.

no doubt heard of the desperate engagement he was in and his being thanked by Government V.

All my papers and memorandums (sic) are many hundreds of miles from me, the plan of my house has not from the confusion of affairs been sent. What a noise your son in law Munro has made, the subject of repeated encomiums (sic) recorded by all the authorities in this country and at home, but I dare say abused by his enemies and invectives have been prepared here for publication at home. I sent you many papers upon the subject which I fear have been lost. The Governor General thinks so highly of him (Munro) that, not withstanding the repeated orders of the Directors that no military man should be made, he has been appointed.

I have no account of the bills sent home in January 1809.

Remember me most affectionately to all friends under roof and believe me and C & c. Finished 7th of May 1810 Blacker.

13 July 1810 (*Received November 1810*)
Madras. My dear Father, I have an immediate opportunity of answering yours of the 30th of January. The Colonel is now within 200 miles and expected here the 25th. Having a friend that lives with me I have been obliged to take a house convenient to my own. Mr Pule, the Secretary of Government in the Military Department, is my chum, but independent of that I should not have been able to provide for my uncle's long retinue, I will however see more of him than my chum as we are sometimes three or four days without meeting. When he is at breakfast I attend the Commander in Chief, when I return he is at his office. I dine at home, he out, by which means you will see we cannot well quarrel. The Colonel before he left the Army, sent St. John to Poonah for his papers, after which he went to Bombay where he is kept by the monsoon having set in so violently that he must return to the Colonel by sea.

We are now expecting our new Commander in Chief Sir Samuel Auchmuty.[164] His appointment has given great satisfaction, he knows India well and is well acquainted with Sir G. Barlow, the former was the Adjutant General when the latter was Chief Secretary to the supreme Government. I have not yet taken the Colonel's passage and, except that a ship comes from Calcutta, I will take accommodation for him in the October Fleet and you may expect him in April. You will receive satisfactory accounts of the suppression of the late disturbances and they are considerably worn away but it will require a transfer to the King's Army of ours;[165] what the effects that may have upon staff officers is hard to say; it will probably be prejudicial to us. I now

---

164 C.E. Buckland, *Dictionary of Indian Biography*, Sir Samuel Auchmuty, 1756–1823. A volunteer in the British Army in 1777 during the American War of Independence. Served with the 52nd Regiment in India from 1783 t0 1797. Promoted Major General 1808 and Commander in Chief Madras 1810. Returned to UK in 1813. Lt. General 1815. Died 1822.

165 The HEIC Army was incorporated into the Crown forces in 1860. There had been eight separate Acts of Parliament up to 1853 trying to regulate the conflict of interest between

intend whether rich or poor to return in 1820. My brothers will be then very rich, this I cannot be except by legacy or lottery. Poverty annoys me not. Few in the character of gentlemen are more moderate than I am, a happy circumstance considering my prospects: my friends will however receive me kindly, or poverty would be a great misfortune. I have much business in my office, as soon as the Colonel arrives, the Munro's set out immediately. I have nothing more to add but the best remembrances to all friends and am most affectionately yours, V. Blacker

10 September 1810 (*Received 24 February 1811*)
My dear Father, the last ships to all great annoyance brought not a letter from you to any one of us, which we attributed to your not knowing the time of the fleet sailing. The last letters were satisfactory in every respect but one, your being tormented with the gout. It is relief the knowledge of the occupation you can find and the resources of your mind. I have long been desirous of having your portrait and had come to the resolution of requesting it, but it would be more satisfactory to have your bust in marble. I only fear my gratification in this point might put you to inconvenience, sooner than which I would forgo the desire. I wish you to attack the Colonel also for his bust, I may perhaps mention the subject before he leaves me.

I am not willing to put any limits to the expense and the Colonel will answer the demands of my numerous communications. My whole occupation and pleasure consists in my official duties and my library and if I can accomplish my object of placing in the latter the busts of two whom I hold so dear I will be happy.

The Colonel has arrived at the term of his service in India and has I think every prospect of happiness in England. He is well calculated to conform to the manners of society he will fall into, notwithstanding his pursuits will now be so different from what they have hitherto been. People here were much disppointed having expected to find him very reserved in his manner from his highest situation, in place of which he mixed with the greatest freedom and in every plan of sociability.

I send you by him the ground plans of two storeys and the front elevation of the chateau, the others will be sent by the next opportunity. The Munros left us about a fortnight after the Colonel's arrival and are by this time nearly half over the journey they were at Pondicherry. Grace I suppose is writing fully concerning our dispersal. St. John embarks with the expedition against the French islands, he is very lucky in being appointed ADC to General Abercrombie.[166] My love to Mary and best remembrances to Mrs B and I remain my dear Father ever most affectionately yours V. Blacker

political and military government of the HEIC, the duty owed to a vast population, its commercial interests and responsibility to shareholders.

166 C.E. Buckland, *Dictionary of Indian Biography*, John Abercrombie, 1772–1817 joined regular army 1786 and fought in Europe and Egypt. A prisoner of the French 1803–1808 he was promoted to C-in-C Bombay in 1809 and temporary Governor of Madras 1813–14. Lt. General 1812. KCB 1814, Died 1817.

20 October 1810 (*Received 9 March 1811*)
Madras. My dear Father, I have received yours of April 17th which arrived in the same ship with a new Commander in Chief Sir Samuel Auchmuty. Colonel Agnew has likewise arrived and brought with him the appointment of Adjutant General from the Court of Directors, requiring however the approbation of this Government. The latter was impossible on many accounts and as Colonel Agnew from his rank cannot take command of a battalion and no greater command being vacant for him he has been appointed the Secretary of the Commander in Chief which is a place requiring much information of this service. He speaks however of going home shortly having accomplished one of his objects that of being appointed to his old situation of Adjutant General by the same authority which removed him.[167] My last news from the Munro's was dated from Cortallum on the borders of Travancore and described as one of the most romantic spots in the world. Charlotte writes quite in raptures of it and says that all the accounts she had of its beauty fell far short of the reality. I believe they propose spending some time there every year and have a house at it. They have indeed different houses in the Travancore and Cochin territories and I believe mean to beguile their time by excursions from one to the other. Charlotte was rather weak leaving us but the journey appears later to have done her a great deal of good. I believe Grace will endeavour to pay them a visit sometime hence and as she suffered during the last of the hot weather I am in hopes she will endeavour to escape the next. St. John has proceeded under very favourable auspices on the expedition. I have prepared all the remaining drawings of my chateau and hope to have sent them home by a passenger who was to have sailed this month, but unfortunately the ships taking passengers has been countermanded and a vessel by which this will be sent is only a packet. My plans must therefore remain with me until an opportunity offers. The loss in the Barker family is very unfortunate but they may probably receive a future cause of consolation.[168] Scarcely anything has occurred since I last wrote to afford subjects for a letter, we are all well, rejoicing at the success of friends at home. With my best remembrances to Mrs B and Mrs M, I remain my dear Father ever faithfully yours,
    V.Blacker
    I have made no mention of Mary, not knowing whether this will find her with you.

1811

10 March 1811 (*Received 22 September 1811*)
My dear Father, six days ago I wrote to you by the '*Sylvia*,' St. John's fate is now decided, who is now directed to proceed to Bombay to await their his final instructions for the purchase of horses up the Persian Gulf for the Cavalry. If this plan

167 See letter dated 10 March 1809.
168 The death of his brother-in-law, Charles Barker had married Valentine's older sister Catharine.

succeeds of mounting our Dragoons, St. John will probably be commissioned also by the Bengal Government to perform the same service for them, in which case perhaps the situation may be worthy his holding it during the remainder of his service. At all events the situation in question will occupy him comfortably until he hears from his uncle regarding some other prospects he had. His salary will be 200 pagodas per month (the amount will be £840 p.a.) besides regimental pay and field allowances of his rank whilst employed as an Agent for Horses. I was very long in sending you a plan and elevation of my chateaux owing to various interruptions in the undertaking. I sent you some plans by the General and you will think I mean to deluge you with them when you know that a further collection accompanies this letter to the address of the General at Messrs. Coutts & Co London. I remain my dear Father faithfully yours, V. Blacker

Undated (*Received 28 March 1812*)
My dear Father, we are all in high spirits here, having this day heard of the success of our expedition to Java.[169] Our loss has been great but so has been our conquest and tends to show we can beat the French in any quarter of the globe. Since the departure of Grace I have lived with my old friend, that is, he dines with me or I with him, but the partnership will soon be dissolved as he is appointed a Provincial Judge and must go to his station and I long much for the return of the Alexanders as I shall be lost in the short days if they do not arrive before the monsoon.

Sir Thomas and Lady Strange still continue their friendly attention or I would not pass my time as pleasantly as I did, but I expect the Alexanders soon as I have heard of his arrival at the Isle de France from the Cape. Grace has so well recovered as to open a ball at Port Louis. Your observations as to the transfer of the Army are true, but not insurmountable, an officer who has served in India, provided his health is good is calculated to serve in any part of the world, although an officer unacquainted with the language and customs of this country could not do well here. Yet all these might be got over and the General understands this subject very well and has written upon. The boasted pension given after 25 years residence here is not so great as imagined. I sincerely wish the medicine you mention from which you receive so much benefit in the Gout had been discovered long since: it would have saved you much pain.

The General[170] in his letters expresses very warmly the pleasure he has received in the friends he has met and Maxwell's conversation seems to have pleased him much. Many thanks for the trouble you took as to the busts. The General says you suffered

---

169 British Library, in Autumn 1811 a British expedition with 2 Divisions of troops from
     India defeated and removed the French forces who had occupied and annexed the former
     Dutch island of Java since 1795. Java was restored to the Dutch Republic in 1814. <http://
     blogs.bl.uk/asian-and-african> (accessed August 2017).
170 Major General Sir Barry Close. The former Adjutant General Madras Army.

in the operation, the performances of Flaxman[171] are very great and I only fear he will have no regard to my impatience. My consolation and enjoyments consist in my publick associations and my library, the first gives me much to do and reflect on, yet from the middle of October to the same time in December I have respite, reading by candlelight is too severe to be practised here and the evenings are passed in company.

The absence of the Alexanders have occasioned me to see a good deal more company than when they were here. A single man is obliged to be at more expense here than in any other half of the world where in the country he meets companions and in the town's places of entertainment, India furnishes none of these, and you have scarce a piece of marble or painting to look at. A man holding a superior situation, must comply with the custom of hospitality, or scarcely anything would be said in his favour as a member of society. In a subordinate situation a young man is not expected to return civilities, only to make himself agreeable. I shall hold in recollection of your introduction of Lieutenant Bridges but the 'Hussar' frigate not yet come upon the coast from Bombay.Munro's direction is: Major Munro in Travancore, he is extremely occupied at present and his luminous dispatches with respect to Travancore have given the greatest satisfaction to Government. The most extensive confidence is placed in his abilities and judgment and he has the entire control over the country. Since his arrival the Rajah has died and a Queen has been placed upon the throne according to their laws until a male of the blood royal shall be borne. The minister has been turned so that Munro is now Rajah, Minister and British Resident.

Charlotte expects to be confined in November and a boy is confidently expected to keep little Charlotte company, her progress in painting in oil is astonishing and meets much applause. I send her supplies of materials and it is happy for her to have such a resource whilst Munro is occupied.

St. John is now upon his passage from Bombay to Persia to purchase Arab horses. As I before mentioned, he was in very good health when I last heard from him. Robert Close expects to be removed to the Poonah Residency where his friend Mr Elphinstone succeeded the General.[172]

I should like to engage extensively in any favourable annuity on good security in England. All those plans in this country have failed. Money now gives but 6 p.c. and there is no means of sending it home but at considerable discount. I beg you will present my most affectionate remembrance to Mrs B and all my friends, I am my dear Father most faithfully yours whilst, V. Blacker

---

171 *Oxford Dictionary of National Biography*, John Flaxman, 1755–1826 a leading British Sculptor.

172 C.E. Buckland, *Dictionary of Indian Biography*, Mounstuart Elphinstone, 1779–1859 British Administrator in India, later Governor of Bombay until 1829 when he returned to the UK.

29 February 1812 (*Received 24 July 1812*)

Madras. My dearest Father, I returned here yesterday, after an extensive tour with the Commander in Chief. During my absence the Alexanders returned from the Isle de France, and Grace has not profited as much as she could have wished from the voyage: she is now better than when she landed and I hope she will be more fortunate than upon former occasion. They were quite surprised by the former library being enlarged into a dining room, and you shall have a new plan of the alteration. The Alexanders were afraid, as Grace was to be kept quiet and not see company, that our continuing to live together might be inconvenient and it required some letters before this point could be fully explained. My Dearest Father I am distressed for all the pain you have suffered under Flaxman's hands and to no purpose. I shall be entirely satisfied with the portrait, and more especially as I shall have it so much sooner than the bust. Poor Charlotte has had a severe fever but is now well and writes in good spirits. Travelling agrees with her and St. John she thinks surpasses even Charlotte if possible. I apply myself at present to much gardening, it has been attended with some pains and expense but am amply repaid, our only difficulty is to procure seeds as many vegetables only succeed here from seeds produced in a cooler climate.

I once met the Mr Maquay an officer in the 4th cavalry, I believe St. John knows him very well.[173] You may depend upon my paying every attention to Mr Bridges should he come to Madras. My last letter from St. John was at the entrance of the Persian Gulf and he must have arrived long since at Persia or Bussorah, he was quite well.

Robert Close has joined his friend Mr Elphinstone at Poonah by effecting an exchange from Nagpoor. The ships are to sail positively tomorrow and I will have some little rest after the bustle we have been in these last three months. Our tour was agreeable and many of the animosities which subsisted in the Army have been ameliorated.

The exercise we were obliged to use prevented any unpleasant effects from the excess which sometimes prevailed but many dinners await us at Madras. I request my dear Father you will present my best regards to Mrs B and Mary and believe ever faithfully and affectionate yours, V Blacker.

29 February 1812

My dear Father, your letter of the 11th of July is just received. William's misfortune is a severe blow upon all his friends, poor fellow,[174] I shall hope for better intelligence of him and not give way to the reflections that present themselves. I am sorry to hear the General's complaint of fever has returned to him at Elm Park. Many thanks my dear

---

173 E. Dodswell & J. Miles, *Alphabetical List of the Officers of the Indian Army*. George Maquay, Madras Cavalry, Cadet 1803, Cornet 1805, Lieutenant 1812, Captain 1819, retired 1823.

174 The reason for this comment is unknown. His brother William 1776–1850 was unmarried. See further reference in letter 19 June.

Father for you're sitting for your picture, I hope the General will soon send it out as I am very impatient to have it. The General will pay for it.

Yours ever VB

19 June 1812 (*Received 20 November 1812*)
My dear Father, yours of the 16 January was delivered by Mr Smith with your picture of which he took a most particular care. It is a most admirable likeness and good painting and will this day be placed over the centre door of my front hall above stairs opposite to the Generals' picture. I have made so many additions to my house since the Alexanders are to occupy that I hope by the next ship in a month to send you the new plans and elevation.

You will think me very wrong in expending so much upon my chateau in a country where every person wishes to remain as short a time as possible and I am a little of the same opinion myself. However the fact is that every person agrees with me that the house is more valuable now by more than the additional money I have laid out upon it. I have now done with brick and mortar. My garden has been also a serious expense to me but it is the envy of many and I am sorry to say induces many to take from it such things as are not be had elsewhere for money. I am very glad you have engaged with a painter for two miniature paintings of the portrait as I could not do justice to it. When in the Quartermaster's office as Assistant I pursued the study of painting but I have got so much to do that I was obliged to drop it all together. The same disadvantage attends reading but not to so great an extent: I get up at daybreak except when the press of business calls me to other employments. After breakfast my official duties require me and, if the post does not bring me much business, I perhaps get back to the garden in time for an hour to myself before dressing for dinner at half past eight o'clock. I have received from the General a very handsome gold watch and some recent publications; he has not however sent a seal with the coat of arms. Will you execute this commission for me as you are so near the Metropolis? The General does not mention Mr Flaxman in his letters or the bust. Your change of residence will give you many commns (sic). The following I wish not to be mentioned, busts in plaister of Paris I know are cheap, I have one of Caesar and one of Cicero and wish to have of the same material Homer and Demosthenes, a Shakespeare, Milton, Newton, Lock and Virgil. All as large as life or very near and draw upon me for the amount. They will require the utmost care in packing, which would be best done in bran or they will be ruined before they arrive here. I admire very much your residence on the banks of the Thames, but I hope to see many parts of Europe before I see it. Sam and I had a friend near Richmond. I am not a quite unacquainted with Twickenham, Goldsmith has celebrated it.

Our sandy and a stiff clay soils affords no such scenes as you have. On the Western Coast of the Peninsula the scenery is delightful from the variety of the grounds and numerous rivers, produced by the great chain of ghauts being within about 50 miles distance. My letter from the General is not long yet touches upon many interesting points except his not mentioning the expectations St. John had formed from his interest in the diplomatic line. I have written to St. John to this purpose who I suppose is now wandering in Persia investigating the different sources for the supply of horses and will return to the coast of the gulf before the time of dispatching horses for India which takes place in September and October. Poor Charlotte has had very bad health having been tormented by a fever which hangs on her for many months. Nor was that her only misfortune, as she was lately exposed to the risk with all the other Europeans at Quilon of being massacred.[175] A state prisoner there confined found a means to tamper with the native troops viz: Charlotte's letter page and her letters upon that occasion do her great credit. Munro tells me she was acquainted with everything whilst the danger was yet hanging over their heads and that she behaved like a heroine throughout. They are now preparing for their delightful residence at Cortallum where there is a splendid waterfall and excellent climate. Should she not be restored in three months it is not improbable but she may return to England and take Grace with her, who poor creature has been again disappointed and requires a change of climate very much. Mr Carter whom you mention has not as yet appeared, when he does he shall be received as you wish. Lieutenant Bridges of the Hussars arrived in these roads a few weeks since but has not yet been able to come on shore. I have exchanged some small notes with him and he hopes to come to us shortly. He expects to be promoted shortly. Poor William I hope has separated from Greg, it is melancholy to begin life again, but I hope it will be under more favorable auspices as I hear from some letters I have received. I had a letter from Sam but not from Maxwell. Robert Close remains at Poonah. Alexander has the prospect of being at the head of the revenue board, Mr Petrie being appointed to the Government of Prince of Wales Island.[176] We are all very anxious concerning the debates that will be upon India affairs of this session. I hope they will transfer the Army to the Crown for all prospect of general service in this country is closed and no army is respectable as long only as it has an enemy it falls in its own esteem and that of others and loses its military virtues. My situation is very favourable in this country I enjoy excellent health, and am the first officer who arrived at the Head of Staff after 12 years' service, the more gratifying as I had many opponents. I have now to beg my dear Father you will give my best wishes to Mrs B and Mrs M, assure Mary of my love and believe me to be most faithfully and affectionately yours whilst V. Blacker

175 BL. Africa and Asia Collection IOR/Z/E/4/40/E362: 1813–1818, *East India Affairs* July 1812 Vol. 13 'that the conspiracy at Quilon will ultimately appear to be confined to a few bad characters in the army.' 4 Companys from HM's Royal Regiment were sent to restore order and re-establish confidence. The residents were not connected to the conspiracy.

176 C.E. Buckland, *Dictionary of Indian Biography*. William Petrie, 1747–1816, appointed Writer, East India Company 1765. Paymaster to army 1772; Secretary in military dept. and translator 1773. President, Board of Revenue 1800. Dismissed from Madras Council for opposition to Sir G. Barlow 1810. Appointed Governor of Prince of Wales Island 1811. Died at Penang.

8 July 1812 (*Received 9 November 1812*)

Madras. My dear Father, I wrote to you very fully the 19th ultimo and only take up my pen that no ship may leave this place without your hearing from me. Grace is gaining ground and even returns visits and speaks of a Ball when the fleet arrives in complt.(sic) to a Miss Chase going to Bengal who is to remain two or three weeks. We have not heard from St. John lately, but from Robert many who is happy in his sister's establishment. He has required a copy from me of yours and the General's pictures. Charlotte is to remain two months more at Cortallum water fall.[177] Munro is detained by business from her at present but hopes to join her soon as his own health is in want of all the salubrity of Cortallum. The affairs of that country are composed and they are no longer in apprehension of personal danger. If the fleet had arrived I should have more scope to write of home and yours my dear Father most affectionately whilst V.B

17 October 1812 (*Received 20 May 1813*)

Madras. My dear Father, since my last of June 19, I have received yours of 2 September by Mr Carter,[178] a smart young man whom we have frequently with us, he is now with his Corps. We have seen as much of Mr Bridges as he could spare from his ship. He is a fine young man and I hope he will not be disappointed in his expectations of soon getting a ship. How great will be your astonishment at finding that Charlotte and her two children are on board this fleet. As Travancore did not agree with the children, the best plan was to place them at home without farther delay and as a long sea voyage was recommended for Charlotte, she thought it best to take them herself. Poor Munro's struggles upon the occasion were very great; before she left him I had every day a letter but since Charlotte left him, not one. Charlotte will fully explain our affairs. About us at present we have a very full house, I scarce ever go out except to an official dinner when I attend on duty. Before breakfast I have society in my library, after breakfast I am fully occupied at my office and in the evening I have the Alexanders, as Grace is not a greater advocate of going out than myself. I am in inabled to rise every morning at break of day, as we say here at gunfire.[179] This is the most delightful season here and yet but a few enjoy it, how long I may be able to keep to this plan I cannot say, but I am sure I shall abandon it with reluctance. Yet public opinion must not be set at nought and I have Charlotte to bring out various things for my table. My house is entirely finished and without injuring the symmetry of it could not add another brick. This you will say is fortunate, and I will agree, I send you a new plan and Charlotte will be the expositor. She will also tell you of my

177 E. Thornton, *Gazetteer of the Territories under the Government of the East India Company*, Courtallum, nr Tinevelly, Travancore, and 'much frequented by invalids.' Noted for the waterfalls 200 ft in height.

178 E. Dodswell & J. Miles, *Alphabetical List of the Officers of the Indian Army 1760–1834*, R. Thomas Hannah Carter, Joined HEIC 1811, Ensign 1812, died Madras Sept. 1813.

179 J. Goldingham, *Madras Observatory Papers 1827*. (Madras: College Press, 1827). The cannon fired from the ramparts of Fort St. George at daybreak and dusk.

garden, orchard and vineyards, in all of which I excel. And I have heard lately from St. John, still in Persia but proposing to visit Bombay shortly; he was in good health travelling much about. Robert still at Poonah passing his time very happily. Pray tell my uncle Sam I received his letter introducing Mr Deveux[180] but as he is for the Bengal establishment and remained but a few days I had but little opportunity of obeying the wishes of his letter. I remain my dear Father always your most faithfully and affectionately, Blacker

12 November 1812 (*Received 9 June 1813*)
Madras. My dear Father, you will be surprised at receiving a letter so soon after my last of the 17th October, the truth is I had not made up my mind to my present resolution, though it has been constantly in my mind since your going to Twickenham. I was very much delighted with the country from Kew to Hampton Court and have often expressed that situation pleases me more than any other, and that it was my intention to establish myself there if I ever had it in my power so to do. My means will probably never be ample and I must limit my desires to my means. I wish my dear Father to expend a sum not exceeding £10,000 in the purchase of a house and land on the bank of the Thames. In case you can find it convenient to become the occupier of it and to effect this object I will subscribe with gratitude to any terms that will make the arrangement agreeable to you. I am not attached to any place in particular. Before I left Europe I was in different places, but have no friends and all of them are too distant from the centre of politicks and the polite arts for my taste. Therefore I wish to be near the Metropolis and according to my former wishes on the banks of the Thames, and I have a predilection for my scheme as the place would descend to me from my Father and which I should always consider with the partiality of an hereditary property. I have been full in my description of this motive and placed it prior to all others, because unless my dear Father it be agreeable to you to occupy the proposed concern my scheme falls to the ground. I may also add I should not feel secure and comfortable in the idea of a property so liable to fraud and mismanagement being in the hands of a stranger but this I adduce more with the intent of showing some worldly argument, than as containing my real motives. Had I some object in England of the nature I have described I should hold my future return there more frequently than I have hitherto done and consequently promote its earlier accomplishment.

As you will perceive my dear Father that my bent it is to induce you to occupy my proposed Chateau. You will consider a reference to your own convenience to be one of your primary guides in the eventual selection of it and therefore whatever choice I may express will be held entirely subordinate to that consideration. Indeed

---

180 E. Dodswell & J. Miles, *Alphabetical List of the Officers of the Indian Army 1760–1834,* Thomas Des Voeux, Bengal Establishment. Cadet 1810, Ensign 1814, Lieutenant, 1815, Captain 1833. Left India vide Asiatic Journal & Monthly Miscellany 1837.

from what I can collect from your letters I think our tastes would very much agree, as you think the situation of Twickenham desirable for the beauty of its scenery, it's convenient distance from town and a suitableness to a small or large fortune. This description suits my ideas and the only apprehension I have is that the object in question will be difficult, tedious or perhaps impossible to accomplish, as situations upon the banks of the Thames are much sought after. I would not wish to be more removed from town than Windsor except necessity brought one to it. A larger house than you inhabit would be unnecessary and burthensome on account of the taxes, should any alteration be necessary, that would be best the work of a season. The ground therefore is the chief consideration as it principally constitutes the value of the property, the more of it therefore the better. It should extend to the banks of the Thames and have some wood, a garden and meadow is easily made but the growth of trees requires years. Independent of the motives already expressed which have given rise to the present letter I may add that the disposal of cash in this country has no longer its former advantages and its security is very uncertain. Private houses are continually breaking to the ruin of individuals and the condition of this country is so flourishing that Government security can no longer be had for money on favorable terms and at the same time this has produced a considerable loss on remittances to England where all wish to send their money from India for these reasons. But for this consideration I should have remittted the £10,000 in question to be held in readiness at your call and a possibility that some time might elapse before my wishes could be put in execution. The opening of the trade to and from India may cause a demand for money here in favour of remittances to England and I have therefore come to the resolution of making purchases only of such small bills as may be on advantageous terms until I hear further from you. I shall then be guided by your advice and shall be prepared to send home the remainder even at a loss. I am so ignorant of the subject of land purchase that I can hint at nothing which you all are better acquainted with than me. Any sales will be most probable for ready money, otherways, my pursuing the plan of occasional remittance until the time I might know if it's being absolutely requisite. My last letters from St. John contain a request that I might obtain his permission to go to England on a furlough for three years, being dissatisfied with his present occupation and I have procured permission when his accounts are passed. Charlotte will be in England before you receive this. I have written to her to countermand an order for the purchase of certain articles of table furniture, have the goodness therefore to inpart this circumstance to her as she may not possibly have received my letter. The Alexanders are as usual and Grace is I believe writing to some of the family. Munro has of late been somewhat unwell latterly and been much depressed in spirits in consequence of Charlotte's departure. Give my best remembrance to Mrs B and believe me my dear Father to remain yours most faithfully and affectionately. Blacker

1813

30 January 1813 (*Received 11 June 1813*)

Madras. My dear Father, yours of the 15th of July came most opportune, as the packet will be closed this day. Poor Barker, he died lamented by all who knew him. Your letter to Mr Alexander gave the pleasing account of Mary Close's marriage which I thought doubtful from the great delay. We have a promptitude in these matters in India which the inhabitants of England have not. I am happy my dear Father that your medicine, the 'eau medicinale' continues to remove the Gout: it would be better to eradicate it, but since that cannot be effected, to alleviate the pain is a great blessing. The remainder of the family except poor William appear to enjoy health and prosperity. Your excellent son in law, Munro, has proposed a plan for him in case he should not fix himself eligible in Europe, that of Commercial Agent for the Travancore Government with the facilities of trading on his own account. It is worth £1300 or £1400 per annum. I have written to him upon the subject, I have also written to the General. My letter in November developed a plan which I shall not enlarge upon until I see how it has been received. In the meantime I am a great economist as Grace will testify. I will forward your letter to St. John in a few days and mean to recommend to him to postpone his trip until I hear from the General. Munro is anxious to have St. John with him and I have not yet relinquished my hope of that object and could I once see him Assistant Resident at Travancore I should be quite easy upon his account. I shall pay all the attention to what you mention of Captain Tolfrey of the 2nd battalion 24th Regiment.[181] Robert Close is well and Grace sent off to him the account of his sister's marriage. Grace is not very stout but all your other friends are in good health, my best remembrances to Mrs B and Mary and believe me ever yours most affectionately V. Blacker

19 March 1813 (*Received 19 November 1813*)

My dear Father, I am this time unfortunate, as reference is made to a letter to me in Mr Alexander's letter. From his letter however I receive much pleasure from the slight manner you mention of a fit of the Gout, may I long to receive such accounts. I write at present from a principle of not letting an opportunity pass neglected having nothing to communicate since my January letter. Grace is again in the thriving way but has, poor creature, a great deal of hot weather before her. As she is writing to you no doubt she will tell you how quietly we live together. Alexander always dines at home and I only out at official dinners which I trust will soon be at an end for a long time. Grace

---

181   E. Dodswell & J. Miles, *Alphabetical List of the Officers of the Indian Army 1760–1834*, Charles Frederick Tolfrey, Cadet 1800, Lieutenant, 1800, Captain 1811, Major 1821. Died 1823. W. Wilson, *History of The Madras Army*. Vol. III. The 24th & 25th Regts. were created to replace the 1st and 23rd Native Regts. who were 'struck off the list of the army' 31.12.1806 for their part in the Vellore mutiny. pp. 169–231.

has called for a plan of my domain to answer some queries of yours which shall soon be complied with. I certainly may say that I am the most successful gardener at Madras, the great want here is seed of vegetables from a northern climate, for those foreign to this climate degenerate so much that the seed from the first crop is not good. Cabbage seed is of great want and when we by chance receive any fresh, which we sometimes do from the Cape, its produce has a delicacy unknown in a cold country. The cabbage seeds sent out here are either too old or do not bear the voyage. I should like the experiment of some cabbage seed in a tin wafer box soldered close down, to ascertain the matter. We have heard from Charlotte from the Cape, but she seems so occupied in writing to her husband as to have forgotten us all at Madras. Munro continues enjoying his tour which has been a service of danger. The Cochin country has been overrun by a banditti which the Government has not been able to repel.[182] On Munro's undertaking this desired clearance, they found themselves so close hunted by his and numerous military parties that a plan was laid for his assassination in order to get rid of their greatest enemy. He received information the very morning it was to have taken place, but his escape was owing to his having mounted his horse that morning for the journey instead of going in his barge as he had invariably done for several days before. Had he not providentially, or as it then appeared capriciously, altered his mind and put his foot into the stirrup instead of the boat his destruction appeared inevitable. They have since been apprehended and hanged on the spot and he continues his extirpation of them with more zeal than ever. We are quite anxious to hear of Charlotte's arrival and whether William will be influenced by Munro's proposal. He will be guided by the prospect it affords which is not well defined and the prospects he will have at home. Although all you have sent out to India have escaped, many are the chances in this climate during the first two years against life. Of my fellow passengers, about 45, there are now not more than 10 alive. Many of these however went off by campaigning which William would not be exposed to. Pray let me have some intelligence of the General's bust which has not been mentioned for a great time. As you my dear Father have had the trouble of having your face pasted for me would it not be possible to have a plaster of Paris cast made from the mould as so much delay attends the marble, if so I should like it done but not sent. Your two miniatures have arrived and excellently finished, there is a substance and plenitude of effect which I have not before seen produced by water colours. The one is hung in Grace's room, the other is on the way to Cochin. My best remembrances to Mrs B and all friends, I am my dear Father yours most affectionately, Blacker

182 C.M. Augur, *The Church History of Travancore* (Madras: E. Masallamani, 1902) p. 738. On Munro's arrival "The country was in such a disturbed and unsettled state that the plots of rival factions, the evil effects of the recent war, the heavy debts with which the Sircar was burdened and the inability of the Native Government to cope with them, all this threatened the entire ruination of the country." See also <www.cochinroyalhistory.org> (accessed September 2016).

5 August 1813 (*Received 22 December 1813*)
Madras. My dear Father, by the *'Cumberland* which has just arrived from Bengal and is to sail in a few hours I can acknowledge the receipt of many letters of late,'[183] but as the letters are at the Garden House I cannot send for them. The principle news I have to communicate is the accouchement of Grace early last month and the good health of herself and son, Alexander the little. He certainly is not the Great, having come into the world a couple of weeks before the expected time. St. John has arrived from Persia and arrived at Travancore, where he was first appointed to the charge of Munro's escort, which put him upon field allowances and lately he has been appointed Assistant Resident in Travancore, which gives him an additional 100 pagodas per month. He will be placed under Munro's orders in political charge at Cochin and has at length obtained the object of his desires, employment in the diplomatic department. General Abercrombie, has acted a most friendly part towards him upon this occasion and effected the arrangement in a manner which will not I hope be objected to in Leadenhall St.[184] Should it not, I am in hopes hereafter of St. John succeeding Munro as principal. I will write to Sir Barry fully upon the subject. The *'Rose'* which is to carry out Sir G. Barlow about the middle of the month will not carry out the notification of the Travancore appointment to the Directors, it will form a paragraph in the October Despatches and Sir Barry will be prepared in case he should see any danger. I hope Charlotte will have persuaded you not to wait for the result of your deference to me regarding the busts. I would rather have them in bronze than in plaster of Paris and had thought they could have been with equal facility procured. It is not my dear Father the price which on these occasions at such a distance is of material consequence, it is the delay which prevents most people in India from the commissioning articles from England. At the same time my dear Father I must acknowledge with many thanks the kindness of your great attention to my commission and which is so much evinced in your taking the trouble of making the reference for further directions. Sir G. Barlow receives from his friends here a very handsome present of a service of plate valued £3500 and a public dinner. Lady Barlow receives a Ball and supper so that they will go off in a good style. Charlotte's letter when leaving Saint Helena has been received. Yours my dear Father most affectionately, V. Blacker.

The last letter copied into the letter book

Calendar of significant events
1639   British purchase Madras, India.
1746   French seize Madras.

183 East Indiaman *'Cumberland'* built in London 1802, made 7 voyages to India. Sold 1817.
184 Leadenhall Street was the Headquarters location of The Honourable East India Company. The building was sold and demolished when the Company's assets passed to the Crown in 1860. Lloyds Bank now occupy the site. Ed.

1748	Establishment of HEIC Army.
1756	Siraj-ud-Dowlah seizes Calcutta.
1756	The Black Hole incident.
1761	Hyder Ali seizes Mysore.
1761	Battle of Wandiwash.
1761	French miltary occupation of India ceases.
1767–69	1st Anglo-Mysore War.
1775–82	1st Anglo-Maratha War.
1778	Valentine Blacker born in Armagh.
1780–84	2nd Anglo-Mysore War.
1790–92	3rd Anglo-Mysore War.
1797	Colonel Arthur Wellesley arrives in India.
1798	Richard Wellesley appointed Governor General.
1798	Valentine Blacker arrives in Madras.
1799	4th Anglo-Mysore War.
1799	Death of Tippoo Sultan. Valentine ill with fever.
1799–1804	Poligar Wars. Valentine wounded twice in action.
1801	St. John Blacker and Robert Close arrive in India.
1802–05	2nd Anglo-Maratha War.
1802–05	Valentine mentioned in despatches.
1802–4	Valentine Blacker appointed Assistant QMG.
1805	Both Wellesleys leave India.
1806	Valentine Blacker Deputy QMG.
1806	Mutiny of Madras Native Infantry Regiments at Vellore.
1808	Grace and Charlotte Blacker arrive in India.
1809	Madras Army Officers 'rebellion' over tent contract.
1810	Valentine Blacker appointed QMG Madras Army.
1813	Valentine's marriage to Emma Johnson.
1814	Valentine promoted Major by Brevet.
1816	Pindaris emerge as serious military threat.
1817	4th Maratha & Pindari Wars.
1817	Valentine Blacker QMG Army of the Deccan.
1818	Valentine promoted to Major.
1818	Valentine Blacker appointed CB (Military).
1820	Appointed to Calcutta Prize Committee.
1821	Valentine Blacker on sick leave to Europe.
1821	A Memoir of the Operations of the British Army in India published.
1822	Extended sick leave in Europe.
1822	Appointed Surveyor General India whilst on sick leave.
1823	Valentine Blacker returns to Calcutta.
1823	Promoted to Lieutenant Colonel.
1826	Death of Lieutenant Colonel Valentine Blacker.

Surveying in India. (From *A Manual of Surveying in India*, 1855). (Courtesy of Author)

Blacker Memorial, South Park Road, Calcutta. (Courtesy Sanghani Kolkata)

Postscript

The British, after a considerable period of awe and wonder in 'the gorgeous east' during the 17th and early 18th century, later gravitated towards a separate existence; consoling themselves in voluntary exile with an often lavish life style imbued with a contradictory mixture of patrician affection and the arrogance of cultural superiority over the native inhabitants. In the late 18th century a former Governor General, Warren Hastings despite huge criticism over his former Governership of India had written in retirement to a successor that he knew 'native men of strong intellect, sound integrity and as honourable as any in India.'[1] He felt that the British should treat them with courtesy and allow them the same freedoms and rights as the British enjoyed. Such sentiment fell on stony ground. By 1835 Sir Charles Metcalfe the Governor General acknowledged that 'the British dominion over India was by conquest; it is naturally disgusting to the inhabitants and can only be maintained by force.'[2] Each Governor General together with their bureaucracies attempted to resolve the multiplicity of problems in different ways thereby creating what a recent author described as 'The Chaos of Empire.'[3] Additionally the conquering of India itself had created 'a fractured set of conflicting regimes,'[4] a cauldron of quarrelsome factions which all required frequent subjugation and reduction.[5] A soldier writing many years later of his experiences referred to the Government of India by the Honourable Company as a 'scroll of stupendous failures.'[6]

The catastrophe of the mutiny in 1857 further widened the social and cultural gap between British and Indian. All responsibilities for Government including the armed forces passed to the Crown in 1858.[7] The new regime was a basically conservative

---

1   J. Bowle, *The Imperial Achievement*. 1974, p. 108.
2   Ibid. *The Imperial Achievement*. 1974 p. 201.
3   J. Wilson, *India Conquered, The Chaos of Empire, 2016*.
4   Ibid *India Conquered. The Chaos of Empire,* 2016. p. 195.
5   R. Hallisey, *The Rajput Rebellion against Aurangzab. A Study of the Mughal Empire in 17th century India.* (Columbia & London: University of Missouri Press, 1977) pp. 90–96. Clearly dissent against Imperial rulers was not new. The Rajput rebellion was initially a succession dispute which threatened Mughal stability but never became a general uprising.
6   J.T. Nash, *Volunteering in India* (London: G. Phillip & Son, 1893) p. 120.
7   The Government of India Act 1858. Ed.

system of government headed by a Viceroy in Delhi, Governors in the various provinces and an India Council based in Whitehall.[8]

A great deal of the adverse criticism of British rule in India has often been led by the British themselves, 'the curious denigration of Imperial history' is how one historian described it.[9] That there were wrongs is undeniable but also, 'that there is much that was and remains fair and positive.'[10]

This is true to the extent that India is happy to acknowledge the British contribution to the Survey of India which commenced in the Bengal Presidency in 1802 and is still an effective department of the Government of India. Valentine Blacker's service was lauded at the time of his death and his legacy is remembered in India. A coloured image of Lieutenant Colonel Valentine Blacker, the third Surveyor General of all India is on the Government of India web site placed between his two Survey contemporaries, Major General John Hodgson and Colonel Sir George Everest. The provenace of the portrait of Valentine Blacker is uncertain. It is known that the artist George Chinnery[11] created a pastel portrait of Lieut. Colonel Valentine

Blacker, presumably in Calcutta, between 1823 and 1825 when Chinnery left Calcutta. The whereabouts of the original portrait has not been established. Certainly a black and white image of Blacker in uniform described as 'by an unknown artist' was published by the Survey of India and a copy of that, thought to be from a photogravure of 1913, is held at the National Portrait Gallery. Both the coloured image and the black and white images appear to be from the same portrait.

On his memorial in South Park Calutta the following words are inscribed "Beneath are deposited the remains of Lieut-Colonel Valentine Blacker, Companion of the Bath, of the Light Cavalry on the establishment of Fort Saint George. During ten years, Quarter Master General of the Madras Army, and subsequently Surveyor General of India. Obit.

Lt. Col V. Blacker.
(Courtesy Survey of India)

8   The Council was abolished in 1935. India was partitioned to create Pakistan upon Independence in 1947.
9   J. Bowle, *The Imperial Achievement.* 1974, p. x.
10   K. Lalvani, *The Making of India. The Untold Story of British Enterprise.* (London: Bloomsbury, 2016) p. vi.
11   Dictionary of Pastellists and Index of Sitters, George Chinnery, 1774–1852. Chinnery worked as an artist in Calcutta between 1802–25 when he left for reasons of heavy debts. <http://www.pastellists.com/> (accessed August 2017).

iv. February MDCCCXXVI. Aet. xl. Lieutenant-Colonel Blacker was an Officer distinguished alike for professional ability, for public zeal, for private worth, and for manliness of character. In testimony thereof his friends and comrades have caused this monument to be erected to his memory."[12]

12   <http//glosters.tripod.com/offzdiedb.htm> (accessed June 2017).

Bibliography

A Cadet's Guide to India. By A Lieutenant of the Bengal Establishment. (London: Black, Kingsbury, Parbury & Allen. 1820).

A Postscript to the Origin, Progress and Consequences of the Discontents of the Madras Army. (London: J. Ridgeway 1810).

Asiatic Annual Register, A View of the history of Hindustan, and of the politics, commerce and literature of Asia 1803.

Asiatic Journal and Monthly Register for 1800.

C.M. Augur, *The Church History of Travancore.* (Madras: E. Masillamani, 1902).

J. Baillie Fraser, *Military Memoirs of Lieutenant Colonel James Skinner, C.B.* (London: Smith Elder & Co. 1851 and Ambala: The Civil & Military Press. Reprint 1955).

S. Barden, *Elm Park 1626–1954.* (Belfast: Ulster Historical Foundation, 2004).

C. Barnett, *Britain and Her Army 1509–1970* (London: Allen Lane 1970).

T.H. Beaglehole, *Thomas Munro and the Development of Administrative Policy in Madras.* (Cambridge: The University Press 2010).

J.A. Bell, *A System of Geography* (Glasgow: A. Fullerton & Co. 1832).

A.S. Bennel, Editor. *The Maratha War Papers of Arthur Wellesley January to December 1803* (Stroud: Army Records Society 1998).

A. Bingham, *A Selection of the Letters and Despatches of the First Napoleon* Vol. I (London: Chapman and Hall 1884)

V. Blacker, *Memoir of the Operations of the British Army in India.* (London: Black, Kingsbury, Parbury & Allen 1821).

J. Blakiston, *Twelve Years Military Adventures.* (London: Henry Colburn, 1829).

J. Bowle, *The Imperial Achievement.* (London: Secker and Warburg, 1974).

British Library, Africa and Asia Collection, India Office Records.

C.E. Buckland, *Dictionary of Indian Biography,* (London: Swan Sonnenschein, 1906).

R.G. Burton, *A History of the Hyderabad Contingent* (Calcutta: Office of the Superintendent of Government Printing, 1905).

R.G. Burton, *The Maratha and Pindari War 1817. Compiled for The General Staff India 1910.* (Uckfield: Naval & Military Press reprint 2004).

I Butler, *The British in India – A Miscellany 1971.* No publisher details.

W.Y. Carman, *Indian Army Uniforms.* (London: L. Hill Books, 1962).

D. Chandler and I. Beckett, *The Oxford History of the British Army.* (Oxford: The University Press, 1996).

R.S. Chaurasia, *History of the Marathas*, (New Delhi: Atlantic Publishing, 2004).

Cobbets Political Register, May, 1806.

H. Compton, *Military Adventurers of Hindustan*, (London: T. Fisher Unwin, 1893).

J. Cotton, *List of Inscriptions on Tombs or Monuments in Madras.* (Madras: Government Press 1946).

Concise Oxford Dictionary, (Oxford: Clarendon Press, 1954).

B. Crosbie, *Irish Imperial Networks*, (Cambridge: The University Press 2012)

Daily Telegraph 17th January 2017, Obituary.

W. Dalrymple, *White Mughals*, (London: HarperCollins, 2002).

W. Dalrymple, *The City of Djinns.* (London: HarperCollins, 1993).

A. De Courcy, *The Fishing Fleet, Husband Hunting in the Raj.* (London: Weidenfield and Nicholson, 2012).

H. Dodwell, *The Nabobs of Madras* (London: Norgate and Williams, 1926).

E. Dodswell, and J. Miles, *An Alphabetical List of the Officers of the Madras Army 1760–1834 with their respective dates of Promotion, Retirement, Resignation or Death.* (London: Longmans, Green & Co. 1835).

W. Donigher, *The Hindus, An Alternative History.* (London: Oxford University Press, 2010).

C. D'oyley, *Tom Raw, The Griffin*, (London: R. Ackermann, 1824).

D. Dundas, *Principles of Military Movements* (London: T. Cadell, 1788).

J. Earle, *Commodore Squib, The Life, Times and Secretive Wars of Englands First Rocket Man Sir William Congreve 1772–1828.* (Newcastle on Tyne: Cambridge Scholars Publishing, 2010).

East India Military Calendar, being the Services of General and Field Officers of the Indian Army.1824 3 volumes. (Uckfield: Naval and Miltary Press Reprint 2007)

Edinburgh Annual Register July 1811.

H. Eyrl, *Diary of Private 3905 Henry Eyrl, 19th regiment of Foot, The Green Howards, 1855–62*, unpublished. (Leicestershire and Rutland Record Office. Ref. DE1633.)

J. Goldingham, *Madras Observatory Papers* (Madras: College Press, 1827).

R. Hallisey, *The Rajput Rebellion against Aurangzab. A Study of the Mughal Empire in 17th century India.* (Columbia & London: University of Missouri Press, 1977).

W. Hickey, *Memoirs of William Hickey.* (London: Hurst and Blackett, 1925).

His Majesty's Regiments of the British Army, (London: Metro-Provincial Publishing, 1949).

F. Hitchman, *Richard Francis Burton KCMG, His early Public and Private Life.* (London: Sampson Low, 1887).

William H. Hooker Collection, *Logbook of the Thetis.* (1984.)

B. Horrocks & D. Boyd, *Famous Regiments, The Royal Engineers*, (London: Leo Cooper, 1975).

J.H. Hutton, *Caste in India.* (London: Oxford University Press, 1961).

E. Ingram, Ed. *Two Views of British India, The Correspondence of Dundas and Wellesley.* (London: Adams and Dart, 1969).

L.K.A. Iyer, *The Mysore Castes and Tribes.* (Bangalore: Mysore University, 1935).

J. Keay, *The Honourable Company,* (London: HarperCollins, 1993).

E. Lake, *Journal of the Sieges of the Madras Army,* (London: Kingsbury, Parbury & Allen, 1825).

K. Lalvani, *The Making of India. The Untold Story of British Enterprise.* (London: Bloomsbury, 2016).

H.D. Love, *Vestiges of Old Madras.1640–1800* (London: John Murray, 1913).

P. McEldowney, *Pindari Society and the Establishment of British Paramountcy in India,* (University of Wisconsin, 1966).

A. Mackenzie, *History of the Munros of Fowlis.* (Inverness: Mackenzie, 1898).

A. Macleod, *On India,* (London: Longmans, 1872).

J. Malcolm, *Observations on the Disturbances in the Madras Army 1809.* (London: W. Miller & J. Murray, 1812).

G.B. Malleson, *The Native States of India.* (London: Longman Green, 1875).

C. Markham, *A Memoir of the Indian Surveys.* (London: W. Allen & Co. 1872).

P. Mason, *The Men who Ruled India.* (London: Jonathan Cape, 1987).

H. Maxwell, *The Life of Wellington.* (London: Sampson, Low & Co.1900).

E. Moor, *A Narrative of the Operations of Captain Little's Detachment Against Tippoo Sultan.* (London: George Woodfall, 1794).

F. Mount, *The Tears of the Rajahs, India 1805–1905.* (London: Simon & Schuster, 2016).

Museum of Wales/Articles 2014–01–31

J.T. Nash, *Volunteering in India,* (London: G. Phillip & Son, 1893).

National Archive of India, *Register of Meteorological Observations,* (Calcutta: Surveyor General's Office, 1825).

R. Orme, *A History of the Transactions of the British Nation in Indostan from the year 1745.* (Madras: Pharoah & Co. reprinted 1863).

J. Perkins, *The Most Honourable Order of the Bath.* (London: The Faith Press, 1920).

R.H. Phillimore, *Biographical Records of The Survey of India. 1815–1830* (Calcutta: The Surveyor General's Office, 1945).

K. Phythian-Adams, *The Madras Soldier,* (Madras: The Government Press, 1948).

R. Reynolds, *The White Sahibs in India,* (London: Secker and Warburg, 1937).

R.V. Russell, *The Tribes and Castes of the Central Provinces of India,* (London: Macmillan & Co. 1916).

J.A. Salmond, *A Review of the Origin, Progress, and Result of the Decisive War with the Late Tippoo Sultan.* (London: Cadell & Davis, London. 1800.)

P. Stanley, *White Mutiny, British Military Culture in India.* (New York: University Press.1998).

J.W. Stempel, Ed. *Autobiography of the British Soldier. Anonymous Officer,* (London: Headline Publishing Group, 2007).

H.T.B. St. John, *All is Well, Letters and Journals.* (London: J. Jackson, 1847).

A. & H. Tayler, (ed.) Letters of John Orrok. (Aberdeen: Milne and Hutchinson, 1927).

The Lady's Monthly Museum, Or Polite Repository of Amusement and Instruction, (London: Dean & Mundy, 1816)

E. Thornton, *A Gazetteer of the Territories under the Government of the East India Company*. 4 volumes. (London: W. Allen, 1854).

E. Thornton, *History of the British Empire in India*. (London: W. Allen, 1841).

E. Wald, *Vice in the Barracks 1780–1868*. (London: Palgrave, 2014).

J. Weller, *Wellington in India*, (London: Frontline Books, 2013 Reprint).

R. Wellesley, *Despatches, Minutes and Correspondence of the Marquess Wellesley*. (London: John Murray, 1836).

J. Welsh, *Military Reminiscences extracted from A Journal of nearly Forty Years Active Service in the East Indies*. (London: Smith Elder & Co. 1830).

M. Wilks, *Historical Sketches of Southern India in an attempt to trace The History of Mysoor 1810*. (Mysore: Govt. Printing Press, 1930).

J. Wilson, *India Conquered. The Chaos of Empire*. (London: Simon & Schuster, 2016).

W. Wilson, *History of The Madras Army*. (Madras: The Govt. Press, 1883).

H.C. Wylly, *Neills 'Blue Caps' The Madras European Regt. 1639–1826*. (Ballydehob, Cork: Schull Books, Reprint, 1996).

H. Yule & A.C. Burnell, *Hobson Jobson A Glossary of Anglo Indian Words and Phrases*. (London: John Murray, 1903).

Index

Index of people

Index of Places

Index of Military Formations & Units

Milton Keynes UK
Ingram Content Group UK Ltd.
UKHW020613111123
432387UK00008B/145

9 781912 390861